The 10 Lenses

Your Guide to Living & Working in a Multicultural World

By Mark A. Williams

CAPITAL
BOOKS, INC.
Sterling, Virginia

Copyright © 2001 by Mark A. Williams

Capital Books, Inc.
P.O. Box 605
Herndon, Virginia 20172-0605

This book is not legal advice. None of its contents, including the case studies and the Legal Concerns, are intended as or may be relied upon as legal advice. The various case studies identify one party or the other as the winner. As hypotheticals, these cases tend to be simpler than real cases to isolate the legal issue being demonstrated. In real cases, it would be more appropriate to say that the employee or the employer probably would win under the given facts.

ISBN 1-892123-59-2 (alk.paper)

Library of Congress Cataloging-in-Publication Data

Williams, Mark A., 1948–
   The 10 Lenses : Your Guide to Living & Working in a
  Multicultural World / Mark Williams.
     p. cm.
  Includes bibliographical references.
  ISBN 1-892123-59-2
   1. Diversity in the workplace. 2. Multiculturalism. 3. Communication in organizations.
  4. Interpersonal relations. I. Title: The 10 Lenses. II. Title.

  HF5549.5.M5 W55 2001
  658.3'008–dc21   2001037310

Printed in the United States of America on acid-free paper that meets the American National Standards Institute Z39-48 Standard.

First Edition

10 9 8 7 6 5 4 3 2 1

To Lauretta, Lukas, and Alexander.
Thank you for surrounding me with love.

Contents

The Lenses In Depth

Foreword

By my good fortune, I have come to know educator, author, and composer, Mark Williams. My associate, Paul Bryant, who introduced me to him, said, "If you are really interested in diversity and peace, here is a person and process you need to know about. This work can make a difference." Initially, I was somewhat skeptical, but I am now convinced that Paul was right.

My first opportunity to observe Mark was during a presentation at a community seminar of some 200 people in the spring of 2000. The participants were a representative sample of my own community in Lincoln, Nebraska. Lincoln Mayor Don Wesley, who was among them, said that the two-hour presentation led to "the most engaged dialoguing I have ever seen in this community." Feedback from other participants was equally supportive. I knew that Mark was onto something that would have significant, change-making impact when I witnessed first-hand the powerful effect his work had on my Midwest community.

During the summer of 2000, I had another convincing experience when Mark and his staff conducted a seminar for the Harvard Medical School, Boston, Mass. The audience was both diverse and sophisticated, and the result was as positive as it had been with my Midwest community. Attendees asked for more and recommended the program to other groups.

The next appropriate step was a presentation to a more rigorous and perhaps even skeptical group. The March Mid-Winter Conference of the Society of Psychologists in Management provided the right setting to collect comparative ratings. Mark and his staff presented a two-hour program on a spring Saturday afternoon in Alexandria, Virginia. The evaluations, as conducted and tallied by officials of the society, tell the story: *The 10 Lenses* received the highest ratings of any during the conference.

At this point, I was convinced that Mark had created an exciting and engaging program second to none. Not only could he compose songs; he could compose educational, life-changing programs and present them dramatically. I have seen many programs on diversity, and *The 10 Lenses* framework starts the dialogue toward inclusiveness better than any I have seen.

To facilitate the development of the program, The Gallup Organization agreed to create a lenses questionnaire to help individuals determine their dominant lens or the combination of lenses through which they filter individual perceptions.

Could the lenses withstand the rigors of statistical analysis? The first test was to discover whether the lenses were real or not: could they be objectively described? Could two or more persons correctly assign statements and behaviors to each of the lenses according to the definition given to each? Are the lenses actually modes of thought, feeling, and behavior that can be discerned in the general population? Do certain statements combine to describe a lens? Is each lens an internally consistent frame of reference for seeing people across different cultural backgrounds? While we knew that experts could classify the statements according to the description of the lens, would people in the general population see themselves as thinking and acting in alignment with these lenses?

Data were collected first from 318 Gallup Organization employees, then from 45 Harvard Medical School staff members, and finally from a national random sample that consisted of 1,001 participants. With each of the three sets of data, the lenses were tested through intercorrelation of the items/statements; through computation of the mean intercorrelation of each lens; and through factor analyses, regression analyses, and studies of reliability. The conclusion: *The lenses do exist as modes of thought, feeling, and behavior in the general population.* Other surveys are being planned, in particular, within groups that consist of larger minority populations and therefore lend themselves to greater analysis.

Mark is a consummate professional. First, it is evident that he has a mission and the vision and passion for bringing people together as one world—providing one song that expresses our commonality. Second, he has the talents and experiences gathered in seventeen years of leading diversity seminars. His articulation, presence, dramatizations, and content are close to perfect. He can respond to hard questions in a focused, clear, and specific way that satisfies both the questioner and the audience. His empathy exemplifies the understanding needed for this mission. Mark's presentation is critically important: the technology itself is amazing, and his inspiring compositions are brilliantly displayed.

The 10 Lenses makes sense to me. As a psychologist, I have long been familiar with the theories of perception. When we learn the different means by which people perceive others, we will have gone far in understanding the resulting behaviors. The underlying hypothesis is that *we can get along with people better when we learn to understand their modes for perceiving other people*. It appears that people can truly have different perceptions of the same events, objects, or people. The lenses framework will give us a means for seeing how a person perceives others with different backgrounds, especially different ethnic backgrounds. Instead of blaming others for being different, we can create an understanding that can lead us to acceptance and inclusion. As eminent psychologist Martin Seligman, Ph.D., has written, "Habitual thinking need not be forever. One of the most significant findings in psychology in the last 20 years is that individuals can choose the way they think." (Seligman, M.E.P. *What You Can Change and What You Can't.* 1993, New York: Knopf). I can envision that *The 10 Lenses* could eventually change the ways people think about each other.

There is much to be learned from the application of the lenses. We must determine whether current observations hold up in different cultures. We need to explore whether different cultures have different profiles with respect to the lenses. We need to learn whether individual profiles change as we learn about the lenses and which lenses change the most with learning. Perhaps we can follow children and observe the conditions that foster the growth of the different lenses. And so much more. . . .

With great interest, I will follow the contributions of Mark Williams and The Diversity Channel. I have huge expectations because I believe they can lead us toward peace on our planet. This book can change your life! Enjoy!

Donald O. Clifton, Ph.D., Chairman
The Gallup International Research and Education Center

Acknowledgments

The 10 Lenses was born of the unconditional love and support of many people in my web of life. I was blessed to be inspired, challenged, and supported by the wisdom and caring of many. I must thank a few publicly for their unwavering nurturing during the three years it took to complete this project.

First, Mark Gerzon—his insight and encouragement motivated me to undertake this project. I could not have proceeded without the trust and confidence of Mark Sanders, Dave Sampson, Richard Bell-Irving, and Pam Farr, present and former executives for Marriott, Inc., all of whom have been supportive of my work.

Ari Gerzon undertook hours of research to get us to a first draft. His wisdom and insight are interwoven throughout this book. Sara Schley's intellectual and spiritual grasp of the integration of people and the earth was invaluable as I began to shape the concepts underlying the Eleventh Lens. Doug Mishkin quickly grasped the Lenses concepts and skillfully translated them into the case studies and legal concerns contained in the book.

To my extended family of friends and colleagues who have been there from the beginning: Ray Whitfield, Howard Lamb, Gloria Fauth, Ethel Gabriel, Gary Zukav, Bill and Rita Cleary, Maureen Bunyan, Paul Bryant, Noerena Abookire, Marya Read, Octavia Seawall, and Rebecca Kirk—I say thanks many times from the bottom of my heart.

A special thanks to three very special people in my life, including my partner Laurie, for her always-cheerful reading and world-class editing and re-editing of numerous drafts; my life-long friend, Derek Jones, whose faith in me and my work motivates me to do the best that I can every day; and my friend, coach, and mentor, Tom Rautenberg, for constantly supporting my efforts to honor both the business agenda of *The 10 Lenses* as well as the possibilities the work holds for the realms of spirituality and deeper consciousness.

To the most capable executive assistant one could have, Robin Dougherty, who tirelessly fights the uphill battle to keep me focused and organized, to the most faithful program manager, Caroline Spinelli, who lovingly and skillfully coordinated and steered the manuscript through the rocky waters of research, graphics, and re-editing, and to Sue Lamb, who read and edited multiple drafts of the manuscript and shared her valuable insights—to these colleagues, my warmest and most respectful gratitude.

And finally, it is because of the dedication, support, and nurturing of my agent, Muriel Nellis, and her business partner, Jane Roberts, that this project has unfolded and is in your hands.

Mark Williams

Introduction

In the fall of 1992, I was conducting a workshop on diversity for a group of managers and employees in Los Angeles. At one point a young woman who recently had immigrated to the United States from India raised her hand and politely asked, "Why are American blacks still angry about slavery when they have been free for hundreds of years?" After a moment of silence, the room filled with the sounds of anger, confusion, agreement, and resentment.

Some of the African-American participants responded to her comments with emotional testimony that included first-hand accounts of injustices that they had suffered. Others responded to her with various historical analyses of the impact of oppression on the African-American community.

Still other participants expressed their concern that this kind of "negativity" was exactly what they feared was going to happen in the workshop. It was further evidence that by focusing on cultural differences we were "stirring up trouble." From their perspective, "If we could only focus on people as individuals, there would be no need for these kinds of sessions."

Several people argued that the emphasis on diversity and multiculturalism was taking the country in the wrong direction. They believed that our society should be focused on our national unity and that each person has a responsibility to give up his culture of origin to become an "American." The success of their great grandparents was proof for them that over time this strategy works. A few individuals spoke of diversity in terms of a mosaic that enriched all of our lives, while a few others timidly voiced fears that the company was about to lower standards in the name of diversity, spawning mediocrity and reverse discrimination.

As the conversation unfolded, I looked around the room and realized that the workshop comprised first-, second-, and third-generation immigrants from all over the world, as well as whites and African Americans of all ages.

1

Some people were from major cities and had quite a bit of exposure to, and understanding of, the urban multicultural dynamic. Others were from the Midwest or rural areas; Los Angeles was their first assignment to an urban area. There was also a wide range of class backgrounds and educational levels. These differences and life experiences created beliefs and attitudes that were in some instances subtly and in other instances dramatically different.

From that moment on, I knew that all of my old frameworks for cultural understanding were limited in their ability to interpret the wide range of values and beliefs that were on display during that workshop.

All of these reactions came from one person asking one question. People were passionate about their positions and perspectives. Most individuals were more concerned about advocating their own beliefs than about listening to the views of others.

I looked around that room at bright people who had good intentions struggling to find common ground. However, it was as if they were in a dark room trying to find a door or window to let in the light. Although it was my job to facilitate the process I must confess that, during much of the session, I was unable to offer the "right answer" to bring clarity and closure to the discussion. I was determined never to let that happen again. From that day on, I have dedicated a large portion of my professional life to decoding the perspectives in the room that day. I wanted to create a framework to both understand and communicate those differing perspectives about how racial, cultural, national, and ethnic differences were perceived and treated in this country. This is how the lenses concept was born.

Over time, I was able to recognize ten perspectives that I saw during workshops and classify them into ten patterns of thought and behavior. I saw these same patterns in books, conversations, movies, newspaper articles, political speeches, human resources policies, political opinion, and entertainment. I realized that these patterns—these lenses—were identifiable, predictable, and at the heart of a person's beliefs and actions with respect to race, ethnicity, nationality, and culture.

Once the ten lenses were defined, I field-tested them within client organizations. Their accuracy was validated in workshops, seminars, and other presentations with people at all levels in the workforce. Finally, The Gallup Organization provided research that enabled the development of a survey allowing individuals to self-test their preferences for the lenses.

Each of the lenses has inherent strengths and weaknesses. The challenge is that when we become locked into a particular lens or lenses, the door to understanding and cultural richness closes. My greatest hope is that the lenses concept will offer a key to open this door, so that individuals can reach out to one another across differences.

In this global society, advances in communications continue to connect us technologically with even greater numbers of diverse cultures and individuals. Our capabilities to connect in nontechnical ways need to advance as well. We need new tools to help us tune into, translate, and communicate.

Perhaps the central task of this century will be to create a world where we neither deny the richness of our cultural differences nor allow them to divide us. It is a daunting task, considering the many lenses through which we view our world. However, if each of us is willing to take on a small part of the task— to increase our self-awareness about our beliefs and behaviors about cultural differences—we can make a beginning. As you read *The 10 Lenses*, you will certainly see your colleagues, neighbors, family, and friends in it, but be sure to look for yourself as well.

What Are Lenses?

We all look at the world through our own set of "spectacles" or perceptual filters, comprising what we have been taught and what we have seen, heard, and experienced. These perceptual filters are the **lenses** through which we each look at differences such as race, culture, ethnicity, and nationality. I have identified and researched ten of these lenses. They are:

Assimilationist

Colorblind

Culturalcentrist

Elitist

Integrationist

Meritocratist

Multiculturalist

Seclusionist

Transcendent

Victim/Caretaker

These lenses influence our actions and reactions in a variety of arenas, whether selecting and managing employees, developing and maintaining customer bases, or communicating with and relating to community members.

The lenses are not mutually exclusive. You probably will not identify one lens you use above all others. More likely, you will have preferences for several lenses, and depending on the specific situation, you will select one or more of them. The concept of lenses is not designed to lock you into a category; nor is it designed to tell you if you or others are racist, prejudiced, biased, good or bad. Rather, its purpose is to help you to see the range of behavioral patterns that you and others exhibit and the impact of these behaviors on what you are trying to accomplish, communicate, encourage, or influence.

How Can Understanding Lenses Help?

In this book you will:

- Learn about your individual preferences for the ten lenses.
- Learn to recognize the lenses used by others at work and in your community.
- Learn to recognize how the lenses are embedded within institutional systems.
- Learn how to minimize the weaknesses and maximize the strengths of each lens.
- Learn about the physical and metaphysical indications of an emerging eleventh lens and what an inclusive organization operating from the eleventh lens perspective would be like
- Learn how you can contribute toward the emergence of an eleventh lens organization through the highest expression of your own preferred lenses in your behaviors as an individual employee and/or manager

When you are finished reading this book, you will be better prepared to build and maintain inclusive organizational cultures that nourish your diverse employees and serve your multicultural customers well.

On the Personal Level

The ten lenses provide a framework to understand what is at the heart of an individual's cultural belief system. As you begin to better understand your lenses and the lenses of others, you increase the possibility of building bridges, managing conflict, and finding common ground in everyday cross-cultural situations.

Recognition can help you to be prepared for, and respond to, the behavior of others and to communicate with greater confidence, clarity, and sensitivity. You will be better able to frame your needs and goals in a context that is respectful of other people's deeper values and beliefs.

Some questions that will help you explore the lenses concept on the personal level include:

- What lenses about race, culture, nationality, and ethnicity are operating within me?
- How did I develop my lenses?
- Am I using my lenses from their strengths or shadows?

- What do I need to do to move from intolerant toward inclusive behaviors in my interactions with coworkers, my boss, my customers, and members of the communities in which I do business?
- Which lenses are my employees, customers, neighbors, family members, or friends using to interpret my actions?
- How can I communicate and work more productively with coworkers who are using very different lenses from mine?
- How can I provide better leadership or manage more effectively in situations where people are operating out of conflicting lenses?

At the Organizational Level

The lenses that you and others in your organization use can influence business behavior in three critical areas:

- Your managers' abilities to recognize and develop strengths in employees across diverse populations
- Your leaders' abilities to create human resources systems that address the needs of diverse employee populations
- Your organization's ability to communicate with, and respond to, members of diverse populations who constitute the organization's customer base or the communities in which you do business

The lenses that managers use will influence how they recognize potential and talent among the employees within the work environment. Employees who mirror managers' own layers and legacies are apt to share their preferences for certain lenses and are likely to have an easier time gaining acceptance and opportunity in the organization. Alternately, employees who do not reflect their managers' layers, legacies, or lenses are more likely to experience barriers to inclusion and opportunity.

At the system level, lenses are usually embedded invisibly within key human resources systems, such as:

Recruitment

Hiring and job placement

Compensation and benefits

Performance management

Mentoring and development

Training

Succession planning

How the lenses operate affect the degree to which different members of your organization feel welcomed, valued, supported, and motivated to give the organization their best performance day after day. By understanding which lenses have the most influence on your key human resource systems, you will be better equipped to make decisions about how best to develop and implement policies that promote inclusiveness.

Lenses also affect how you view your customers and clients and how they view you. Some of the questions you may want to explore as you use the lenses as a tool to diagnose your organization's interactions with its external business environment include:

- What lenses are most influential in our strategic planning process?
- Which lenses are present in our niche markets?
- What strategies will our company use to penetrate these markets?
- What lenses are present in the communities where we operate?
- How can we develop a positive brand image in multicultural communities?
- How will our company relate to the lenses held by various advocacy groups?

How Do We Develop our Individual Lenses?

Legacies + Layers = Lenses

Legacies

Think of a legacy as a historic event, the nature of which was so powerful that its ripple effect continues to affect you today. The experiences that touched the lives of your ancestors, family members, and community of origin shape your perception of the world. Within the American society are many examples of such legacies, including:

- The discovery of land on this continent by early European groups and their settlement on lands previously inhabited by Native Americans
- The capture and transportation of Africans to become slaves in this country
- The processing of immigrants at Ellis Island, New York, and other ports of entry
- The redistribution of land as a result of the Spanish-American War
- The use of Chinese immigrants to build railroads across this continent
- The internment of Japanese citizens during World War II
- The civil rights march on Washington, DC, and Martin Luther King, Jr.'s speech, "I have a dream."

These examples have been stated in neutral language to the extent possible. However, depending on your race, ethnicity, and nationality, the mental pictures

8

that you form and the emotions that you experience in reaction to these examples are likely to be quite different.

The most profound awareness that the lenses concept reinforces is the notion that there is no single truth. Each lens has its own interpretation of and reaction to historical events that, in turn, shapes its perception of and reaction to contemporary events. It is very rare that we begin an interaction with others with a clean slate.

Layers

The other components that contribute to the development of your lenses are the layers of your experience in life, from the unchangeable to the elective. Some of the layers that influence your lenses are race, color, gender, ethnicity, sexual orientation, age, nationality, marital/parental status, family background, socioeconomic level, physical/mental ability, region of country, education level, religion or spiritual path, political affiliation, profession, and leisure activities.

You have a unique way of prioritizing the layers that are most important to you, and they become part of your core identity. For example, if your affiliation with a political party is one of your most important layers, you may have a tendency to view most events from that political perspective and "tune into" issues and situations that relate to how you and others who share your political perspective are treated. Perhaps you are focused on, and sensitive to, the layers relating to race, color, and ethnicity because those layers are of primary importance to your core identity. Alternately, you may be focused on other layers such as gender, religion, and socioeconomic status.

Once a layer becomes a part of your core identity and you have established a hierarchy of layers, then all of the legacies that correspond to that layer come into play. The recognition that layers and legacies are dynamically intertwined will help you to understand how two people who share certain layers in common may adopt very different lenses. For instance, the two well-known men, Colin Powell and Louis Farrakhan, share the layers of race and gender as African-American men. However, how the two men have experienced and prioritized additional layers such as education, religion, political affiliation, and profession causes them to interact with the world using very different lenses. Remembering that legacies and layers intertwine can help you better interpret the subtleties of culture in your world.

How to Use this Book

*T*he *10 Lenses* begins with a brief overview of each of the ten lenses and a quick "testing-the-waters" survey to help you identify your preferences. A more extensive lenses survey developed in conjunction with The Gallup Organization is available on our website at www.thediversitychannel.com.

After this overview, the lenses are discussed in more detail. Each chapter begins with an introduction to an archetypal character that reflects a particular lens. This is followed by a profile of that lens, its essence, and its strengths and shadows. Next is a brief historical perspective on the lens to provide a broader context and a better understanding.

The Lens at Work section begins with a focus on the individual:

- What motivates individuals who prefer particular lenses?
- How do they think about career advancement?
- What is important to understand in trying to relate effectively to them?
- What are some key points to keep in mind in coaching managers or supervisors who prefer particular lenses?

The Lens at Work section continues with important information about the impacts that each lens can have on the organization's human resources systems and its legal position when the lens is operating from a limited perspective. This is followed by a description of what this lens can contribute to your organization when it is functioning at its highest level of expression. Each chapter concludes with a set of quotations from historical and contemporary public figures that provide additional insights into that lens.

In the chapter on the Eleventh Lens, a case is made for an exciting visionary view of where we seem to be headed as an interconnected global community.

The core beliefs and values of the Eleventh Lens are described, as well as the obstacles to moving toward a living expression of this lens at the individual and organizational levels. A discussion of what it would be like to participate in a fully inclusive organization and some practical steps for beginning the journey to get there as individuals complete this chapter.

A Note to Our International Readers

Although the information presented in this introductory version of lenses is United States-centric, we believe that the concepts are universal. We are in the process of conducting comprehensive research to create a second volume of *The 10 Lenses* that will adapt the lenses concept to approximately twenty cultures around the world. In the meantime, as you read volume one you can begin the process of using your individual knowledge to translate the lenses concept to your own national culture or the cultures of countries with which you are most familiar. We are interested in hearing from you with respect to your insights and questions as you begin this translation process. We can be reached for this purpose at www.thediversitychannel.com.

A Note about Differences

I believe the lenses concepts offered in this book also apply to all difference issues—including race, color, nationality, ethnicity, gender, age, sexual orientation, physical/mental abilities, religion, socioeconomic class, educational level, marital status, parental status, or any other differences that contribute to the diversity of today's global workplaces.

The initial research used to develop the lenses concepts has focused on race, culture, nationality, and ethnicity. Future research will focus on additional areas of diversity—especially gender, age, sexual orientation, and physical/mental abilities—to continue to translate the lenses concepts directly to the full range of diversity-related differences.

A Note Regarding the Use of Gender

My aim is to present the lenses in a gender-neutral way. To do this, the chapters alternate between using "he" and "she." A lens described using the feminine pronoun does not mean it is a lens that applies to women only; similarly, the use of the masculine pronoun applies to both genders. All the lenses are perspectives that both men and women can have.

Testing the Waters

Following are ten introductions that briefly describe the ten lenses. These summaries should establish a context for you to explore your attitudes, views, and feelings about each perspective. When you have finished the book, you may want to test the waters again to see if your preferences have changed. If you wish to take the full lenses preference indicator created by Gallup Research Labs and The Diversity Channel and begin a more in-depth educational process related to your lens preferences, please visit our web site at www.the10lenses.com.

Assimilationist

Assimilation: Incorporate, Absorb, Fit In, Standardize

Summary Definition: Assimilationists want individuals to **submerge** their individual and cultural identities in favor of nationalistic and patriotic ideals. They believe that our primary allegiance should be to the welfare and unity of our nation.

Motto: "When in Rome, do as the Romans."

Quote: "It is one thing to offer guests a welcome; quite another to have them take over one's house, lock, stock and barrel. This is especially true when the guests have entirely different ideas about housekeeping. The thought in back of the original invitation was that the new races would become 'Americanized'—not that America would be made over in the image of the new races."

> Carleton Putnam, *Race and Reason: A Yankee View*.
> (Washington D.C.: Public Affairs Press, 1961), *104.*

Belief System: Immigrants and other subcultures should adopt the lifestyles, values, customs, and language of the dominant/majority culture.

Testing the Waters: Please read the following statements and indicate the degree to which you agree or disagree.

Statement	Strongly Disagree	Disagree	Neither /Nor	Mostly Agree	Agree Completely
America is a melting pot. Everyone gets thrown into the same pot, and in the end we are all Americans.	1	2	3	4	5
If racial and cultural minorities hope to gain acceptance, they need to relinquish aspects of their original culture, including language, dress, etc.	1	2	3	4	5
Our primary allegiance should be to the welfare of our nation, not our ethnic and cultural identities.	1	2	3	4	5

Score:

3–6: low preference for the Assimilationist Lens

7–10: medium preference for the Assimilationist Lens

11–15: high preference for the Assimilationist Lens

Colorblind

Blind: Sightless, Unseeing, Inattentive to color

Summary Definition: The Colorblind see people as individuals and ignore race, color, ethnicity, and other external cultural factors. They want to look at a person's individual qualities and character. They believe that **ignoring** race and color will have an equalizing effect.

Motto: "When I see you, I see a person, not your color."

Quote: "To ignore race and treat as an individual is the spring of justice and the river of hope."
> Leigh Van Valen, "On Discussing Human Races," *The Evolution of Racism.*
> (New York: Simon & Schuster, 1994) prologue.

Belief System: All men and women are created equal.

Testing the Waters: Please read the following statements and indicate the degree to which you agree or disagree.

Statement	Strongly Disagree	Disagree	Neither /Nor	Mostly Agree	Agree Completely
When I look at people, I see the person, not race or color.	1	2	3	4	5
Personality, character, and values are the most important aspects of who we are.	1	2	3	4	5
Cultural diversity programs raise divisive issues. We should focus on our commonalities.	1	2	3	4	5

Score:

3–6: low preference for the Colorblind Lens

7–10: medium preference for the Colorblind Lens

11–15: high preference for the Colorblind Lens

Culturalcentrist

Centric: Core, Heart, Focal, Central

Summary Definition: Culturalcentrists seek to improve the welfare of their cultural group by **accentuating** their history and identity. They argue that institutions that are detached from the mainstream are an important ingredient to the success of their culture because they encourage cultural pride and create a support network and a safe environment where intolerance and prejudice are not daily issues.

Motto: "My culture is central to my personal and public identity."

Quote: "Many people of color are isolated or have no sense of identity in the mainstream, for example, at work, at school, or in social settings. They need their ethnic community to develop a sense of self. Their communities may provide a better chance to learn about and develop a respect for their own race and culture. . . . for many the ethnic community makes a huge positive difference. At the very least, the availability of the option is vital."

> Bill Ong Hing, *To Be An American: Cultural Pluralism and the Rhetoric of Assimilation.* (New York University Press, 1997), 173.

Belief System: Racial minorities and ethnic groups should detach from the dominant culture to survive, rebuild, and/or maintain their cultural norms, customs, and traditions.

Testing the Waters: Please read the following statements and indicate the degree to which you agree or disagree.

Statement	Strongly Disagree	Disagree	Neither /Nor	Mostly Agree	Agree Completely
Ethnic and cultural minorities need their own schools, businesses, neighborhoods, and institutions to survive.	1	2	3	4	5
Assimilation into the dominant culture weakens the ability of ethnic and cultural minorities to control their destiny.	1	2	3	4	5
I want our children to understand history from the perspective of our group to foster pride and self esteem.	1	2	3	4	5

Score:

3–6: low preference for the Culturalcentrist Lens

7–10: medium preference for the Culturalcentrist Lens

11–15: high preference for the Culturalcentrist Lens

Elitist

Elite: Privileged, Select Few, Superior, Predetermined

Summary Definition: Elitists believe in the superiority of the upper class and embrace the importance of family roots, wealth, and social status. They believe it is their destiny to **perpetuate** their advantages through inheritance or social ties.

Motto: "Membership has its privileges."

Quote: "Elitism—meaning a disproportionate role in government and society by small groups—is inevitable. The question for any society is not whether elites shall rule, but which elites shall rule. The problem for any democracy is to achieve consent to rule by suitable elites."

George Will, *The Leveling Wind: Politics, the Culture and Other News.*
(New York: Penguin Books, 1994), 131.

Belief System: Lineage and innate qualities and abilities entitle some members of the culture to be advantaged within society.

Testing the Waters: Please read the following statements and indicate the degree to which you agree or disagree.

Statement	Strongly Disagree	Disagree	Neither /Nor	Mostly Agree	Agree Completely
Some people, because of their upper-class status, deserve special privileges.	1	2	3	4	5
My upper-class status requires me to be a philanthropic leader in society.	1	2	3	4	5
I believe we should recruit from the Ivy Leagues or other elite institutions to get the best talent in our organization.	1	2	3	4	5

Score:

3–6: low preference for the Elitist Lens

7–10: medium preference for the Elitist Lens

11–15: high preference for the Elitist Lens

Integrationist

Integrate: Mix, Incorporate, Combine.

Summary Definition: Integrationists support breaking down all barriers between racial groups by **merging** people of different cultures together in communities and in the workplace. They believe that we can replace our ignorance of each other's culture with a greater understanding and knowledge if we live and work together. Integrationists want our nation's laws to reinforce this idea.

Motto: "Ebony and ivory live together on my piano keys...shouldn't we?" "Ebony and Ivory," lyrics by Paul McCartney. MPL Communications, 1982.

Quote: "Men often hate each other because they fear each other; they fear each other because they do not know each other; they do not know each other because they cannot communicate; they can not communicate because they are separated."
> Martin Luther King Jr., "Stride Toward Freedom: The Montgomery Story."
> (New York: Harper & Brothers, 1958), 33.

Belief System: We can achieve greater racial and cultural equality, understanding, and harmony through working, living, and socializing side by side.

Testing the Waters: Please read the following statements and indicate the degree to which you agree or disagree.

Statement	Strongly Disagree	Disagree	Neither /Nor	Mostly Agree	Agree Completely
I believe that people of different races should be forced, if necessary, to live, work, and play side by side.	1	2	3	4	5
I am an advocate of strong civil and social laws, such as fair housing, to ensure an integrated society.	1	2	3	4	5
The integration of our society is a moral imperative.	1	2	3	4	5

Score:
3–6: low preference for the Integrationist Lens
7–10: medium preference for the Integrationist Lens
11–15: high preference for the Integrationist Lens

Meritocratist

Merit: Deserve, Worthy of, Earned, Accomplished

Summary Definition: Meritocratists believe in the individualist credo of America: If you have the abilities and work hard enough, you can **compete** with anyone to make your dreams come true. Meritocratists disapprove of programs that use race, culture, ethnicity, class, or any cultural attributes as criteria for opportunity, believing instead in personal merit.

Motto: "Cream rises to the top."

Quote: "I want it repeated because I hope it will give inspiration to young African Americans coming along, but beyond that, all young Americans coming along, that no matter where you began in this society, with hard work and with dedication and with the opportunities that are presented by this society, there are no limitations upon you."

Colin Powell, Secretary of State Acceptance Speech, January 2001

Belief System: Opportunity should be based only on an individual's initiative, competence, and accomplishments.

23

Testing the Waters: Please read the following statements and indicate the degree to which you agree or disagree.

Statement	Strongly Disagree	Disagree	Neither /Nor	Mostly Agree	Agree Completely
Merit should be the only criterion used to award opportunity.	1	2	3	4	5
Special programs, like affirmative action, lower standards and demotivate employees.	1	2	3	4	5
I believe that personal drive and self-sacrifice can overcome any obstacle.	1	2	3	4	5

Score:

3–6: low preference for the Meritocratist Lens

7–10: medium preference for the Meritocratist Lens

11–15: high preference for the Meritocratist Lens

Multiculturalist

Multi: Many, Varied, Mixed, Choices

Summary Definition: Multiculturalists **celebrate** the diversity of cultures in the United States and the contributions they make to our national character and history. The Multiculturalist wants to retain the customs, languages, and ideas of people originating in other cultures. The Multiculturalist believes these retained characteristics combine to create an appealing and colorful mixed salad, a metaphor often used to describe this perspective.

Motto: "The more cultural diversity, the better."

Quote: "... a real and vital multiculturalism requires a mutual commitment to the constant search for common ground in the midst of our diversity.... For without genuine and substantive respect for diversity, there can be only continuing oppression."

> Maulana Karenga, "Black and Latino Relations: Context, Challenge, and Possibilities," *Multi-America: Essays on Cultural Wars and Cultural Peace*, ed. Ishmael Reed. (New York: Viking, 1997), 196–197.

Belief System: We are enriched by the diversity of races and cultures in our country. Our future success is based on allowing each of our cultures to contribute to the mosaic.

Testing the Waters: Please read the following statements and indicate the degree to which you agree or disagree.

Statement	Strongly Disagree	Disagree	Neither /Nor	Mostly Agree	Agree Completely
I believe that all people should maintain their own cultural customs, languages, and beliefs.	1	2	3	4	5
I believe that history should be taught from the perspective of all cultures to be fair and accurate.	1	2	3	4	5
I believe that most systems and institutions need to change to reflect the styles, customs, and talents of multicultural employees and customers.	1	2	3	4	5

Score:
3–6: low preference for the Multiculturalist Lens
7–10: medium preference for the Multiculturalist Lens
11–15: high preference for the Multiculturalist Lens

Seclusionist

Seclusion: Isolate, Disconnect, Protect, Fragment, Partition

Summary Definition: Seclusionists feel strongly that they should **protect** themselves from racial, cultural, and/or ethnic groups that diminish the character and quality of their group's experiences within the society. They believe that the only viable solution to our societal challenges related to race and culture is for different groups to live and work apart.

Motto: "Birds of a feather flock together."

Quote: "…we're a nation of professional, religious, ethnic and racial tribes—the tribes of America—who maintain a fragile truce, easily and often broken. . . . We were never able to conquer our atavistic hatreds, to accept our widely diverse past, to transcend them, to live together as a single people."

Paul Cowen, *The Tribes of America*. (New York: Doubleday, 1979), 15.

Belief System: It is best for our race to remain separate from other racial groups to preserve our position and control.

Testing the Waters: Please read the following statements and indicate the degree to which you agree or disagree.

Statement	Strongly Disagree	Disagree	Neither /Nor	Mostly Agree	Agree Completely
I believe that different races, cultures, and ethnicities should live among their own kind.	1	2	3	4	5
Our culture's rights are violated when you force us to interact with other cultures.	1	2	3	4	5
I support initiatives to limit the influence of different racial and cultural groups within my community and society.	1	2	3	4	5

Score:

3–6: low preference for the Seclusionist Lens

7–10: medium preference for the Seclusionist Lens

11–15: high preference for the Seclusionist Lens

Transcendent

Transcend: Rise Above, Sacred, Inspire

Summary Definition: The Transcendent Lens focuses on the human spirit, our universal connection, and our shared humanity. The Transcendent **elevates** our belief in each soul in relation to the divine and to one another. Race, ethnicity, and nationality are a part of God/the Universe's plan and contribute to the richness of humanity.

Motto: "There's really only one race—the human race."

Quote: "Who can separate his faith from his actions, or his belief from his occupations? Who can spread his hours before him, saying, 'This for God and this for myself; This is my soul, and this other for my body?'"
Kahlil Gibran, *The Prophet*. (New York: Alfred A. Knopf, 1951), 77.

Belief System: Our common divine origin transcends racial, national, ethnic, or cultural identity.

Testing the Waters: Please read the following statements and indicate the degree to which you agree or disagree.

Statement	Strongly Disagree	Disagree	Neither /Nor	Mostly Agree	Agree Completely
I believe that love is more powerful than our racial or cultural differences.	1	2	3	4	5
When I look at people, I see only the divine.	1	2	3	4	5
I believe we are born at a time and into a race/culture for a higher purpose.	1	2	3	4	5

Score:

3–6: low preference for the Transcendent Lens

7–10: medium preference for the Transcendent Lens

11–15: high preference for the Transcendent Lens

Victim/Caretaker

Victim: Injured, Persecuted, Abused, Exploited

Caretaker: Custodian, Guardian

Summary Definition: People who see through the Victim/Caretaker Lens see their **liberation** as a crucial goal. Victim/Caretakers feel that they are still suffering from the generational impact of previous oppression. Therefore, they continue to deserve compensation from society and the dominant culture. Victims/Caretakers see oppression as not only historical, but also contemporary, still producing overwhelming odds for their group's survival and prosperity.

Victim Quote: "It is unnecessary in 20th-century America to have individual Negroes demonstrate that they have been victims of racial discrimination; the racism of our society has been so pervasive that none, regardless of wealth or position, has managed to escape its impact."

Justice Thurgood Marshall, in Kimberle Crenshaw, *Critical Race Theory*. (New York: The New Press, 1995), 263.

Caretaker Quote: "Until the great mass of people shall be filled with the sense of responsibility for each other's welfare, social justice can never be attained."

Helen Keller, *Treasury of Women's Quotations*, ed. Carolyn Warner. (New Jersey: Prentice Hall, 1992). www.motivationalquotes.com/People/Keller

Motto: "We shall overcome."

Belief System: People of color and ethnic minorities are systematically victimized by the dominant culture and exploited in ways that have crippled their ability and opportunity to be successful.

Testing the Waters: Please read the following statements and indicate the degree to which you agree or disagree.

Statement	Strongly Disagree	Disagree	Neither /Nor	Mostly Agree	Agree Completely
The dominant culture continues to systematically oppress minorities and people of color.	1	2	3	4	5
I cannot overcome discrimination easily because the force is too powerful.	1	2	3	4	5
We have a responsibility to help people who are less fortunate than ourselves.	1	2	3	4	5

Score:

3–6: low preference for the Victim/Caretaker Lens

7–10: medium preference for the Victim/Caretaker Lens

11–15: high preference for the Victim/Caretaker Lens

Assimilationist

Assimilationist Archetype

Meet Joe Buhler

Joe is a thirty-year-old manager from Ohio who has an associate's degree with a concentration in hotel management. He is employed as the director of food and beverage for a global hotel chain, where he manages all restaurant operations, including room service, kitchen, nightclub, coffee bar, and two full-service restaurants.

Joe has been with the company since he graduated and is enthusiastic about his job. He has been a dedicated and conscientious worker from the start, and his management, which has promoted him fairly quickly, has recognized his loyalty and hard work. He is viewed by most of his colleagues as knowledgeable about the business and a solid team player who is proud of the organization and cares deeply about its success. Joe has never been able to understand why many of the people who work for him do not share his sense of loyalty and willingness to do whatever it takes to get ahead in the company.

Lately, Joe has been having some difficulties with some of his employees, many of whom are first-generation immigrants from Central America, Asia, and the Caribbean. These employees speak mostly in their native languages and have very heavy accents. Joe is frustrated with them because, from his perspective, they do not appear to be particularly motivated to improve their English. Joe is amazed that they complain that they are unable to move up in the food and beverage area.

With the support of other hotel executives, the human resources director has developed a variety of strategies to deal with this issue, including multilingual training that requires managers to acquire a limited vocabulary in the native languages of their employees to communicate more directly. The company is considering recruiting new managers who are bilingual. Joe is opposed to these strategies. He believes that the employees should learn to speak better English and that their advancement should be contingent upon good English communication skills.

Some of Joe's African-American employees have become upset with him over this issue. He told all of his African-American employees from the inner city that they need to speak English well enough to effectively communicate with the staff, managers, and customers. He has also discussed with them the inappropriateness and unprofessional nature of their hairstyles and dress. He has made it clear to these employees that their career progress will be limited unless they speak proper English and dress, groom, and act appropriately.

Joe has been counseled that his performance feedback to the African-American employees was inappropriate and that his lack of support for the company's English-as-a-Second-Language program and new bilingual management competency requirement could hurt his career. He has been reprimanded for being insensitive to the scheduling requests related to various cultural holidays. He is growing increasingly concerned that his staff members do not seem to appreciate that the hotel's success depends upon providing good, reliable customer service to a mainstream clientele that prefers a professional environment.

Joe demonstrates a strong preference for the Assimilationist Lens.

Assimilationist Profile

The Assimilationist thinks of himself as a patriot, a real American, and argues that our primary allegiance should be to the welfare of our nation. He has strong national pride and believes that people of all races and cultures who come to this country should become true Americans by speaking English well and accepting the values, behaviors, and lifestyles that historically have defined the American tradition. He believes that this is true not only for immigrants but also for minority and ethnic cultures that have long been a part of American society. The Assimilationist lens reminds us of the very first promise all of America's children made as they began a new day of school: "*I pledge allegiance to the flag of the United Sates of America . . . One nation under God, indivisible.*" These ideas evolve from the melting pot theory: everyone who wants to become a part of the American culture gets cooked down to one type of "American soup."

The Assimilationist's vision of the perfect America features close-knit neighborhoods, strong community institutions like churches and civic clubs, and traditional community pastimes such as high-school dances, baseball on Sunday afternoons, patriotic parades on national holidays, and Thanksgiving Day celebrations. This is the way of life that Americans should strive to honor and preserve. The Assimilationist rejects the influences and changes that immigrant cultures or minority groups bring to this way of life. He sincerely believes that it is more advantageous for these groups to give up aspects of their cultural traditions and behaviors to reap the benefits of membership in our American society.

This lens does not agree with the idea of externally imposed multiculturalism. On the contrary, the Assimilationist thinks that an overemphasis on cultural diversity will tear this country apart, with every group pledging allegiance to the cultural group first and the United States second. It is a simple, uncomplicated philosophy: change whatever you need to change to fit in or you risk second-class citizenship. If you live in America, then become an American.

The strong desire of the Assimilationist to create a unified national culture usually translates into a need to create and maintain a strong and consistent organizational culture. One of the Assimilationist's strengths is that he recognizes and supports the organization's traditional values and ways of doing business, becoming the guardian of formal and informal organizational norms and business practices, such as established policies, work procedures, dress codes, celebrated holidays, and traditional social activities.

The Assimilationist's belief in the need to have everyone fit in is challenged by people who are different from him in a highly multicultural business environment. Like Joe Buhler, the Assimilationist may have the tendency to counsel employees on how to act more American and how to submerge ethnic and cultural behaviors, such as style of language and dress, to blend in more easily. The fact that some employees would be offended by this tendency would shock an Assimilationist, since he has seen how fitting in has benefited so many careers in the past—including his own.

The Assimilationist has a hard time with the emerging global economy and the demands that it places on historically American businesses to seek markets overseas, move production plants abroad, create global alliances, and build a global and culturally diverse workforce. These actions are viewed as betrayals to the national interest. Consequently, if an Assimilationist is present during the plotting of a global strategy or involved in the execution of such a strategy, he could negatively influence transactions with global customers and alliance partners by demonstrating an attitude that could be construed as western cultural arrogance.

As a customer, the Assimilationist wants to "buy American" and spends his money on an American company that produces its products and services in America, using an American workforce and demonstrating sensitivity to the issues in American communities. Assimilationist customers and clients expect and are most comfortable with communication in well-spoken English during service transactions.

Of all the issues that bother the Assimilationist, the use of the English language is paramount. As of April 2001, twenty-six states had passed referenda or laws that declare English the sole official language of the state. The Assimilationist continues to be in the forefront of movements to pass similar laws in the remaining states, claiming that to preserve America as a nation, we must keep English as our single language of business, education, and social interaction. The Assimilationist is vocal about any societal or community issues related to bilingual education.

Another educational issue of concern to the Assimilationist is that of the introduction of ethnocentric curricula in schools. He insists that the way for all children to succeed in our society is to be exposed to traditional American history and culture.

A third concern for the Assimilationist in the area of education is the belief that the work habits of Asian students are changing the cultural norms in our educational systems. Because of the success that Asian students achieve with their study habits, competition is forcing more and more students to spend longer hours studying. The Assimilationist believes that "Americans" should not have to compete with Asian study standards in "our own country."

The Assimilationist is in the lead of the argument to curb immigration. He believes it is necessary to set limits as a way to maintain the integrity of American customs and traditions. The Assimilationist grieves every time he is greeted in airports by bilingual signs, every time he sits down at a restaurant table and cannot find recognizable American cuisine on the menu, every time he has to respond to a prompt to "choose English" when he is using interactive technology. What is happening, he asks, to the American way of life?

Assimilationist Strengths and Shadows

Each of the lenses has its Strengths and Shadows that are operational in all aspects of the lens' life. The primary Strengths and Shadows of the Assimilationist Lens include the following:

Strengths

Assimilationists:

- Act out of a primary desire for the country to be unified and enjoy stability
- Remind us that the welfare of the nation depends on our ability to respect and promote our common national identity
- Are not afraid to challenge us to honor our responsibility to serve our nation
- Are loyal and dedicated to the organizations and institutions to which they belong
- Understand and support the organization's mission, vision, and values
- Help establish a common set of organization norms and business practices and want to see everyone adhere to them
- Are eager to mentor others in the organization and help them adapt to "our way of doing things"
- Are often the "glue" that holds many of our community institutions together, serving in leadership positions or on all kinds of committees to support traditional activities and events

Shadows

Assimilationists:

- Minimize or overlook the powerful legacies that stripped some cultures of their ethnic identities through oppression

- Minimize or misunderstand the impacts that race and culture have within the American society because they tend to view events from a national identity perspective only

- Use the example of the successful immigration and assimilation of European immigrants from the late 1800s to support the melting-pot theory, while ignoring the different experiences of immigrants from the rest of the world that have been far less positive

- Tend to believe that everyone wants to fit in and have a hard time understanding that some groups want to bring different values, beliefs, and practices into the workplace or community

- Are unwilling or unable to move beyond "the way we've always done things/ the *right* way to do things" and consider the ideas of others, especially when those others are new to the organization or represent other cultural groups

Historical Perspective

As America's leading politicians of the eighteenth century, the founding fathers established the roots of Assimilationist policies because they expected that the immigrants coming to America would be of European origin with white skin. The rhetoric of politicians from John Adams to Theodore Roosevelt to Patrick Buchanan makes clear that new immigrants have been expected to take on the values and traditions of America rather than to maintain their old cultures. These politicians believed that "American" must be the most essential aspect of each individual's identity.

Clearly, the arrival of the Europeans and their adjustment were different from those of recent immigrants from Mexico, Africa, the Caribbean, or Latin America. The European immigrants expected that the willingness to assume Assimilationist-type loyalty to their new country and to refashion their cultural identity was the price they had to pay for more opportunity.

Groups of Americans of color who could not trace their origins to Europe discovered that their ability to assimilate was limited because of institutional racism and societal prejudice. Race and color were impenetrable barriers to full-citizen status. One reason that these ethnic and cultural groups clung to many aspects of their cultures was that they were only marginally accepted by, or fully welcomed into, the European-descended American culture. Cultural pride became a source of strength for these groups.

During the twentieth century, more diverse nationalities arrived in America and expected to maintain their own cultures. This is evident in the well-established separate ethnic communities of New York, Miami, and Los Angeles. The influx of nonwhite immigrants during this century has changed the face of this country dramatically. Many of these new immigrants came with the desire to find political freedom or seek economic opportunity, while still being able to maintain pieces, if not all, of their old culture.

With the advent of the global economy and a more competitive business environment, these immigrants became highly desirable as customers. Businesses targeted them to provide culturally specific products and services. The result is that advertising, marketing, public relations, product design, and the delivery of services today are conducted with a great deal of study, sensitivity, and respect for cultural differences. Every attempt is made to appeal to consumers based on cultural preferences, even to the extent of conducting targeted advertising campaigns in multiple languages. Numerous newspapers, magazines, and television and radio stations reflect the values and philosophies of various cultural groups. Once a culture has become a market, it reduces the need for anyone within that group to totally give up aspects of their culture to "fit in." Cultural niche marketing reinforces the maintenance of unique cultural perspectives.

The advent of improved travel and communications technologies means that today's immigrants are not permanently isolated from their cultures and ties to their homelands. In certain industries, like the service industry, immigrants serve as a pipeline to the employee base. Businesses in these industries do not have time to wait for immigrants to fully acculturate or learn the language and social norms before they must be put to work to fill jobs in a very tight labor market. Businesses, therefore, accommodate cultural differences by providing training in multiple languages. As a result, some industries no longer require a new employee to speak English as a prerequisite to employment.

The convergence of trends such as these reduces the pull toward assimilation that the European immigrants felt at the turn of the prior century. It is highly unlikely that Joe Buhler will ever again see the kind of national cultural cohesion for which he longs.

The Assimilationist Lens at Work

Motivation and Career Advancement from the Assimilationist's Perspective

The Assimilationist cares deeply about the organization and work group to which he belongs. He is motivated by the desire to protect the organization's and unit's welfare and contribute to their successes. As long as the Assimilationist believes that the organization's way of doing business is supportive of the American economy and "way of life," he gives his all. It is important to the Assimilationist to feel like he can look up to and identify with company management as "my kind of people."

It comes naturally to the Assimilationist to do whatever is needed to fit in with and support the organization's vision, mission, values, business strategies, and cultural norms. From his perspective, this is the foundation for any kind of career advancement strategy, along with working hard, showing loyalty to the company, and making sure not to rock the boat. The Assimilationist is respectful in conversations with higher-ups and peers and courteous in conversations with those at lower levels of the organization, but he still wants to be firm and clear about consequences when individuals are not toeing the line as they should be.

Impacts of This Strategy on the Individual's Advancement Potential

During times of steady state operations, this advancement strategy can serve the Assimilationist well. Members of the dominant group in the organization feel comfortable with the Assimilationist, who shares their history, values, and outlook on life. They know they can trust him to do as they would do in responding to the demands and requirements of an executive position. However, during turbulent times when the organization is facing competitive, economic, or legal challenges or engaged in major growth and expansion efforts, it is less certain that the strategy will have positive results. In some cases, members of the dominant group want to hold on all the harder to that which is familiar and, therefore, trustworthy. In other cases, they may recognize that "new times call for new thinking" and look to those who are willing to bring up the hard questions and think out of the box to fill executive roles.

Impacts of This Strategy on the Organization's Human Resources

When employees think that they need to conform or risk exclusion, they become unwilling to ask questions, acknowledge and learn from their mistakes, suggest innovative approaches, or take other risks. The loss of creative thinking results in the loss of competitive and economic edges for the organization. The threat of exclusion hits people of difference particularly hard, making it difficult for them to want to continue to work in such an organization. If there is an obvious lack of diversity in management and senior ranks, the organization leaves itself open for legal and public-relations challenges related to charges of bias and discrimination.

Working with the Assimilationist

If you are working with or managing a person who has a strong preference for the Assimilationist lens, it is important for you to understand the legacies and layers that have shaped that lens.

Listen carefully when the Assimilationist speaks. Most likely, you will realize that the layers on which he seems to focus include:

> *Nationality*—The individual is interested in where you were born, where your loyalties lie, and the strength of your patriotism.
>
> *Ethnicity*—He wants to make it clear that you are talking to a "tried and true American" and that he hopes you are one, too.
>
> *Religion*—While he does not come right out and ask about this, he is interested in knowing if you support and practice Judeo-Christian values.
>
> *Race/Culture*—Your national identity takes priority over your racial or cultural identity.

Each of us may have been shaped by entirely different legacies and layers. If you are feeling defensive or confused during a conversation, this may be because you have prioritized your layers differently or other lenses may be operating unconsciously. It may help to keep the following guidelines in mind when you are having a disagreement with an Assimilationist:

- Remind yourself that the Assimilationist's concern for the country's and organization's welfare is his core motivation.

- Understand that in today's world the Assimilationist often feels attacked and/or goes underground; he may be reticent to share his views with you directly.

- Listen to his feelings of disappointment and frustration and find ways to empathize with how hard these changes are for him. Help him keep the conversation focused on business objectives and workplace needs.

Coaching the Assimilationist Manager or Supervisor

A person with a strong preference for the Assimilationist lens has difficulty understanding that the organization and the community must change to respond to new business imperatives related to global markets, cultural niche markets, shifting demographics, a global workforce, and multicultural employees and customers. He has trouble recognizing that different racial, ethnic, and cultural groups bring different values and beliefs to the workplace that need to be respected. The Assimilationist may not appreciate the need to use multiple languages to orient various employee groups and may not have the skills to mentor, coach, counsel, and give feedback to members of a multicultural workforce.

Unmonitored and underdeveloped, the Assimilationist stance could lead to charges of bias, high turnover, low morale, and poor use of human resources because employees are not being developed. Your job as a manager or a leader is to coach the Assimilationist so he is competent, confident, and willing to use or modify the organization's systems on behalf of all employees.

Specifically, you can require the Assimilationist manager or supervisor to use the organization's systems in ways that:

- Enable employees to hold on to appropriate aspects of their cultural or ethnic traditions in the workplace
- Train employees in languages and styles that are sensitive to their cultural backgrounds
- Provide support to affinity groups and mentoring programs to ensure full utilization of your employees across differences
- Adapt U.S. business norms appropriately, given global norms and standards
- Provide non-biased performance feedback based on multicultural standards
- Develop and nurture multicultural talent based on multicultural and global standards

The Assimilationist and Organizational Systems

The Assimilationist brings a strong desire to reinforce and maintain the organization's traditional ways of doing business. Most diversity initiatives try to balance the need for employees to change in order to fit into the existing organizational culture with the need for the organization to change to accommodate diverse employees. This balancing act recognizes that social and business trends are converging to require more openness, respect, and utilization of cultural diversity. The Assimilationist stance could have the effect of fostering an environment that feels exclusive and, at times, intolerant to some members of different cultural or ethnic groups.

Each of the lenses influences the organization's human resources systems in different ways. The essence of the ways in which the Assimilationist Lens influences these systems is presented in each of the statements below. As you review these statements, think of the impact of the Assimilationist stance on these same types of programs and activities in your work environment.

> **Assimilationist Stance:** "I will ensure that my organization's systems, policies, and practices help maintain our traditional management culture and our current way of doing business so that we can continue to be as successful as we have been in the past."
>
> **Recruiting:** "I will go to the schools from which we have traditionally recruited because they produce candidates who we know can adapt quickly and effectively to our organization's culture."
>
> **Hiring:** "I will hire people who 'fit' and can hit the ground running."
>
> **Compensation and Benefits:** "I will enhance existing policies, but I am opposed to programs that create special benefits for subsections of our workforce."

Job Placement and Assignments: "I will place people in jobs where they will most likely succeed because the 'fit' is right."

Building Effective Teams: "I will help people adjust to the formal and informal norms of team membership."

Performance Management: "I will give people honest feedback about how they need to change to be more effective in our organization."

Mentoring: "I will help the people I mentor understand how they have to change their attitudes, politics, personal attire, and whom they associate with so they are seen as having potential."

Training: "I will create training that reinforces our ways of doing business. It would be better if people can speak English and read and write proficiently before they attend."

Succession Planning: "I will recommend that people who assume leadership roles should be well acculturated to our organization."

The Assimilationist and the Law

The Assimilationist Lens could affect your business' bottom line in several ways. As you read the following hypothetical case, consider whether your organization may be manifesting the Assimilationist Lens in similar ways.

The Case

The manager of a bank in a small town recently interviewed several candidates for a teller position. Of the group, one man was especially well qualified and had prior experience as a teller in a different town. However, the candidate's physical appearance prompted the following exchange toward the end of the interview:

Manager: You obviously have some good experience and credentials. But I must tell you that we have a dress code that mandates that all employees be "neat and well-groomed." Would you be willing to abide by our code?

Candidate: Sure—I've held jobs before where I had to wear a business suit. I don't see any problems.

Manager: Well, under our code, you would not be able to wear your dreadlocks.

Candidate: Why not?

Manager: Our customers need to be able to feel comfortable around our tellers, so that they are willing to hand over their money and know that they are being taken care of. There are not a whole

	lot of people in this community who have dreadlocks. I think it will make our customers uncomfortable.
Candidate:	I am a Nazarite, and I wear dreadlocks as a religious practice and to take pride in my African-American culture. You are asking me to sacrifice my religious and cultural values because the customers may not be able to deal with my hair?
Manager:	As a bank, we have a corporate image that we have to consider. If that was a Mohawk on your head, or your hair was dyed bright pink, we wouldn't allow it, either.

Based on this exchange, the manager does not hire this candidate. The candidate sues, alleging religious discrimination. Who wins?

Result

The candidate wins. Title VII requires that employers make "reasonable accommodations" to the religious practices of employees. An employer may establish dress and grooming standards for employees, but those standards must yield to the religious practices of an employee, absent a health or safety consideration. Mere speculation about the probable response of customers is not sufficient to establish undue hardship. If, in fact, the candidate-employee's performance did not measure up to the bank's standards, then the bank could terminate the person's employment, because the "reasonable-accommodations" requirement does not require an employer to tolerate subpar performance from an employee.

Legal Concerns for the Assimilationist Lens

The Assimilationist strongly supports what he would identify as the ideals of American patriotism and mainstream traditional values. If you think you may use the Assimilationist Lens, be aware of the following:

1. Some religious practices are entitled to an accommodation under Title VII or comparable state law. Where an employee's religious practice conflicts with a policy or norm of an organization, the law may well require deferring to the employee's religious practice. For example:
   • Having a dress code does not negate a person's right to wear religious garments, absent a health or safety concern.
   • Assuming your customers have certain preferences ("I think our customers would be more comfortable interacting with someone who does not wear a turban") does not allow you to dictate an employee's dress or language.

2. Employees can be restricted from speaking a language other than English in the workplace if there is a business justification for the restriction.
   - An English-only policy must be supported by a business justification. For example, assembly-line workers can be required to speak only English while working on the assembly line, if there is a clear link to productivity, health, and safety. They cannot be required to speak only English on a break.
3. Making jokes about people's ethnic backgrounds, on the assumption that America is one big melting pot, may give rise to complaints of a hostile work environment.

No one, including an Assimilationist, should assume:

- That he knows how the listener really is responding to a joke
- That the listener will not repeat the joke to another employee
- That no one else overheard the joke

Ethnically offensive jokes may give rise to liability under Title VII for a work environment that is hostile on the basis of national origin.

Assimilationist Highest Expression

What the Best of the **Assimilationist Lens** Contributes to the Organization and Community

Shared Vision

The Assimilationist wants to achieve unity by demonstrating allegiance to national or organizational ideals. From a limited perspective, the Assimilationist thinks that this requires individuals to submerge, deny, or devalue aspects of their identity and culture to a larger societal or organizational identity. From a higher and more holistic level of expression, the Assimilationist continues to seek unity, but he moves from submerging aspects of self and culture to creating a shared vision for all.

Every organization and community needs commonly held values and norms that guide the behavior. Organizational norms about dress, vocabulary, style, use of vacation time, interactions with superiors and subordinates, and lunch and break activities are all part of a system that, when mastered, can lead to greater acceptance and opportunity within the organization. The challenge for the Assimilationist is to reassess who is in the workforce today and to make sure the fundamental norms that serve as currency within the organization reflect the shared vision and values of all of today's employees. Forcing conformity to outdated norms and values has a detrimental effect on various populations within the workforce because many of the norms were created when the workforce did not include them. Having said this, throwing out all of the old norms is irresponsible and, in most cases, impossible. A new vision of how the organization will work, based on input from all employees, is the key.

The process of recreating norms may, at first, seem alien to the Assimilationist. Appropriately blending the past and the present to create a future that inspires allegiance and faith to a higher ideal requires specific beliefs and skills that the Assimilationist needs to develop and nurture. These beliefs and skills include:

- The willingness to engage in ongoing dialogue to find common ground
- The capacity to experience cross-cultural empathy
- The ability to bring to the surface and manage interpersonal conflict in healthy ways
- The desire and ability to collaborate with others

In a society as multicultural as the United States, finding ways to create and support shared vision is essential to our future. In its highest expression, the Assimilationist Lens can lead the way, helping organizations balance the needs for stability, cohesiveness, and change.

Assimilationist Quotes

"Let us agree that ethnic and racial affiliation should be as voluntary as religious affiliation, and of as little concern to the state and public authority. Let us understand that more and more Americans want to be Americans simply, and nothing more, and let us celebrate that choice, and agree it would be better for America if more of us accepted that identity as our central one, as against ethnic and racial identities."

Nathan Glazer, *We Are All Multiculturalists Now.*
(Cambridge: Harvard University Press, 1997), 159.

"I am proposing immigration reform to make it possible to fully assimilate the 30 million immigrants who have arrived in the last 30 years.... Without these reforms, America will begin a rapid drift into uncharted waters. We shall become a country with a dying culture and deepening divisions along the lines of race, class, income and language. We shall lose for our children and for the children of the 30 million who have come here since 1970 the last best hope of Earth."

Patrick Buchanan, "On the Issues," *USA Today*, February 21, 2000.

"You cannot become thorough Americans if you think of yourselves in groups. America does not consist of groups. A man who thinks of himself as belonging to a particular national group in America has not yet become an American."

Woodrow Wilson, "Americanism and the Foreign-Born," May 10, 1915.
Speech given in Philadelphia before an audience of naturalized Americans.
www.geocities.com/Athens/Styx/1070/1901/amrchism.htm.

"Moreover, he must not bring in his Old World religious, race, and national antipathies, but must merge them into love for our common country, and must take pride in the things which we can all take pride in.... Above all, the immigrant must learn to talk and think and be United States."

Theodore Roosevelt, "True Americanism," *Forum* Magazine, 1894.
Online source: http://www.theodore-roosevelt.com.

Colorblind

Colorblind Archetype

Meet Casey Dunn

Casey is a forty-five-year-old woman with a recent master's degree in human resources management. She has worked in retail for the last ten years and has enjoyed the variety of people with whom she interacts as colleagues and customers. Casey is the regional manager of employment for an upscale retail chain that sells men's and women's apparel. Casey's responsibilities include screening, interviewing, and referring potential employees to department managers at the twelve stores in her region. Her job brings her into contact with a wide range of people from different cultural and socioeconomic backgrounds. Casey is almost oblivious to the color of an applicant's skin. On the other hand, she can remember exactly how well every applicant she has interviewed in the last week handled himself or herself in the role-play that Casey did with them in which she takes the part of an impatient and dissatisfied customer.

Recently, she received unsatisfactory feedback from two of her client managers in the field. From their perspectives, the applicants she has sent them are not appropriate for the environments in which they must work. Some of these same applicants expressed feelings of discomfort after they returned from their interviews with the department managers. When Casey probed more with the two managers, she found that they wanted candidates who more closely mirror the cultural demographics of their customer base. For example, some of the stores in urban areas serve a very multicultural customer base, while stores in affluent suburban locations tend to serve less culturally diverse customers.

Casey insists that a person's race or cultural background should not be used as a criterion for qualifying applicants or assigning them to specific stores. Casey is concerned only about whether applicants have the necessary business and interpersonal skills to be successful sales people and provide good customer service. She judges people based on their character, personality, and individual attributes. She is offended that we still separate out people based on "superficial" criteria such as dress, language, or cultural attributes. Furthermore, she is concerned that consideration of cultural characteristics in the employment process opens the door for discrimination. Casey believes that most people honestly do not care who serves them in the stores, as long as they receive courteous and responsive service. Unless she is forced to change, she plans to continue referring potential employees to her stores based on how they conduct themselves in their interviews with her and their experience and qualifications for the job.

Casey demonstrates a strong preference for the Colorblind Lens.

Colorblind Profile

The words of Dr. Martin Luther King, Jr.—"People should be judged based on the content of their character and not the color of their skin"—ring particularly true for the Colorblind, who believes that if everyone saw the world in this way and behaved accordingly, race would not be a problem in this country. By ignoring racial differences among people, the Colorblind hopes to create a more level playing field on which people can be seen for who they really are and what they are capable of doing in our workplaces and communities.

Considered a strong individualist, the Colorblind Lens asserts that all people should be treated as individuals, assessed and valued based on their unique talents, characters, values, and personality traits. Those who prefer this lens argue that as we come together to accomplish common goals, qualities such as individual effort, talent, and teamwork quickly take precedence over racial and cultural differences.

The Colorblind Lens is similar to the Assimilationist Lens in the sense that both lenses de-emphasize the importance of the layers of race and color and are uncomfortable with those layers being the defining measurement of a person's identity. However, the two lenses differ in their choice of which layer should be predominant in an individual. The Assimilationist emphasizes the layer of nationality, while the Colorblind focuses on the layers of personality and character.

Because she looks at everyone as individuals, the Colorblind is unlikely to recognize patterns of discrimination. Her tendency is to look for individual rather than systemic explanations for such phenomena. At work, when issues or tensions arise based on the perceptions of different identity groups within the organization, the Colorblind wants to resolve such differences at the individual rather than group level: "Oh, this whole thing got started over nothing more than the different ways that Joe and Akia think the sampling should be done" rather than "We've got some major tensions between the African Americans and Latinos in this work group." As a result of this tendency, other lenses that are more focused on identity issues often experience the Colorblind team member or supervisor as glossing over conflicts that need to be surfaced and resolved among organizational members who belong to different identity groups.

The Colorblind Lens is not likely to focus directly on trying to create an inclusive culture in the organization because any efforts devoted to forcing harmony would end up drawing attention to race, which is what she is trying to avoid. However, inclusiveness is often a natural by-product of the Colorblind approach, since she engages in friendships and social activities with the people she likes, regardless of their race, color, or ethnicity.

The Colorblind individual does not recognize the discrepancies between her own idealistic world view and the realities of discrimination experienced by many others in our society and organizations. She is usually oblivious to the ways in which the organization's systems, policies, and culture may be subtly biased against those who do not share enough of the cultural attributes of the organization's preferred style. Discrimination and conflict based on race, color, nationality, and ethnicity do exist in organizations. When the Colorblind denies or minimizes this, she can make it more difficult for those who are experiencing it.

Because the Colorblind Lens is optimistic and idealistic about people being treated as individuals, she expects that everyone has a fair chance at being hired, being promoted, or winning a contract. She believes that quotas and affirmative action programs or any other types of programs that benefit or discriminate against particular racial or cultural groups do more harm than good by resulting in divisiveness and reverse discrimination, and she adamantly opposes the assignment of opportunities based on a person's race or color. The Colorblind does not support racial affinity groups or diversity training; from her perspective, calling attention to issues of race or color only risks making matters worse.

For the Colorblind customer, the formula is simple: "I will spend my money in an organization that treats employees and customers fairly and delivers products and services that are good." The Colorblind customer does not bring identity politics to the consumer process. She is not likely to monitor societal issues but reacts to issues focused on in the news. For example, she is not aware of which groups are having trouble seeking employment, but she is upset when a large company is identified as discriminating in its employment practices. True to the type, her response to the discriminating company is likely to focus on the need to identify the guilty individuals and hold them accountable, rather than to question what the company is doing at a systemic level to promote discrimination. At the same time, however, she recognizes that the company now has a public-relations problem and that maybe this may be a motivating force for the company to institute needed reforms.

While the Colorblind can appreciate the advantages of multiculturalism when it relates to food, art, and music, she draws the line at inserting race and culture into community dialogue in other ways. For example, the Colorblind in the community is in favor of outlawing the census classification of Americans based on race, believing that racial identifications such as Asian American, African American, Latin American, and Native American perpetuate an unhealthy focus on race and culture. From this viewpoint, the government has been complicit in fostering divisiveness by continuing this practice and deepening the problem by expanding the census to create more racial categories.

The Colorblind has difficulty acknowledging the direct impact of race. She rationalizes racial profiling by the police in traffic pullovers as something that could happen to anyone at some point. Further, the Colorblind contends, if the person has done nothing wrong, he has nothing to fear. In the face of more convincing data about the unequal treatment of certain groups who are pulled over more often, the Colorblind talks about individual officers being too aggressive and needing more training or discipline. It is very difficult for the Colorblind to see patterns of discrimination based on race, color, or culture in any situation because this is so foreign to her own way of being in the world.

Colorblind Strengths and Shadows

Among the many attributes of the Colorblind Lens are these key Strengths and Shadows.

Strengths

The Colorblind:

- Recognize and value each person's individuality
- Are more interested in a person's character and personality traits than in skin color, dress, appearance, or other surface attributes
- See each new interaction as an opportunity to begin a positive relationship, based on the merits of the interaction
- Make up their own minds about a person rather than rely on stereotypes from the society at large
- Offer relief to people of color, allowing them to feel like they can step out of the "prison" of racial or ethnic identity and be treated as themselves rather than one of "them"
- Encourage all people to come together, discover their similarities, and let go of divisive factors
- Help build inclusive organizations

Shadows

The Colorblind:

- Deny what is often a central part of an individual's identity
- Often miss the evidence of systemic discrimination, as well as its many impacts

- Are uncomfortable focusing on the positive aspects of difference, such as unique cultural traditions and experiences that make interaction among people more exciting

- May overlook, ignore, or be unaware of just how much race, color, ethnicity, and nationality determine where people live and go to school; whom they vote for, date, and marry; with whom they do business and how much they pay; with whom they socialize; the community organizations and activities in which they participate; and other aspects of their lives

Historical Perspective

A well-known statue that could serve as the icon for the Colorblind Lens is the statue of the blind justice used to represent the American judiciary system. The symbolic message that justice is blind supports the viewpoint of the Colorblind Lens that people should be judged by their personal characteristics and actions rather than by their race, ethnicity, or culture.

Another symbolic representation of this lens is the Statue of Liberty, given to the United States by France in 1886. The French intended the statue to serve as a symbol of the international friendship between the two countries. However, it soon came to represent much more to the millions of immigrants who have come to America since the late 1800s—a symbol of freedom and the opportunity to fullfill one's dreams, regardless of skin color, religious beliefs, or cultural practices.

In 1896, Supreme Court Justice John Marshall Harlan put words to these symbols when he declared: "Our constitution is colorblind and neither knows nor tolerates classes among citizens."

The civil rights movement of the 1950s and 1960s attempted to make our educational, political, and social institutions reflect in reality the ideals that these historic symbols and words represented. The notion that we are all the same under the skin was used as a rallying point to integrate our schools, work-places, and neighborhoods. While it created formal structures for integration, the Colorblind perspective also had an unintended negative impact: it enabled people from different races who were now sitting next to each other in schools, working side by side on assembly lines, or living down the block from each other to live their parallel lives without having any discussion about race or what their differences might mean to them.

In 1996, Louisiana governor Mike Foster signed a state order banning affir-mative action; on the same day, he declared Martin Luther King, Jr.'s, birthday a state holiday. He saw the two actions as consistent: "This just says we've got to be colorblind. I do not believe I have any prejudice—never had, in my opinion.

I don't look at color.... Dr. King dedicated his life to the pursuit of quality and opportunity for all Americans." Governor Foster's actions provide a good example of how disparate the actions arising from a Colorblind Lens can be. Conversely, recent decisions to downplay or eliminate certain federal and state affirmative action programs demonstrate how the *same* action can result from the Colorblind Lens, depending on the motivational frameworks involved.

Three different motivational frameworks can be identified among those who prefer the Colorblind Lens. First, there are the somewhat naïve Colorblind who truly believe that we can achieve harmony with each other and eliminate all forms of discrimination if each of us just acts out of good intentions. They know that they themselves do not treat people differently based on their race, color, ethnicity, or nationality and do not believe that we can legislate morality. In fact, they believe, affirmative action programs or any other type of legislated programs that benefit one group over another cause more dissension. They rely on interracial marriage, global connectedness, spirituality, and other forms of economic, technical, and social progress to help us with the necessary evolution. They are content to live out their lives on a personal level, satisfied that they are behaving consistently with their stated value of colorblindness.

Then there are the politically shrewd Colorblind who use the ideology to further an agenda of subtle discrimination. They gloss over the point that race, color, ethnicity, and nationality must first be acknowledged and respected before they can be dismissed as unimportant. While they are ignoring these layers, they are also ignoring the important implications of these layers on educational, political, economic, and social conditions for many Americans. They are unwilling to address the forces of discrimination, inequality, and unequal opportunity that foster these conditions.

Finally, there are the hopeful but practical Colorblind, who want to recognize race, color, ethnicity, and nationality for all of the "right" reasons—celebrating diversity, acknowledging discrimination and unequal opportunity as major problems in our society—but who recognize how complicated and difficult it is to arrive at systemic solutions that make sense and can be supported by all.

The Colorblind Lens at Work

Motivation and Career Advancement from the Colorblind's Perspective

The Colorblind is motivated by humanitarian ideals. She cares deeply about people being treated with dignity, respect, and fairness, and she wants them to be seen as the individuals they are with unique talents, values, characters, and personalities. The Colorblind wants to address any situation in which a friend or coworker complains of unfair treatment, but she wants to "fix" the situation from the perspective of how to help the individuals involved work out their problem and get along better. It is important to the Colorblind to have company management express her values. The Colorblind Lens appreciates hearing about how "our human resources are our greatest asset"—whether the organization acts on that—because this is such a core belief for her.

When seeking career advancement, the Colorblind actively campaigns for higher level positions emphasizing how she met all of the objective requirements, including knowledge of the industry, in-depth experience with functional areas, understanding of financial and legal issues facing the organization, and proven ability to work effectively with all organizational levels as well as external stakeholders. It does not even occur to the Colorblind to consider whether her membership identity (race, color, ethnicity, nationality, gender) is similar to, or radically different from, those with whom she would be working. From the Colorblind's perspective, this should be totally irrelevant to those making the decision about promotion.

Impacts of This Strategy on the Individual's Advancement Potential

The Colorblind's advancement strategy works well for her as long as the individual's membership identity is in line with that of the dominant group in the organization and there is a strong fit between her style and the organization's culture. In these cases, the Colorblind assumes that the organization is promoting based on individual qualifications for the job. If the fit is not there, however, the individual is disappointed not to get the position. Given her idealistic world view, the Colorblind assumes that she was not really as well qualified as she thought, that some personality-based issue stood in her way, that it was bad timing, or that there is some other reason unrelated to organizational fit.

Impacts of This Strategy on the Organization's Human Resources

When well-qualified individuals are promoted, most employees tend to have a positive response. Employees share a sense of equity and fairness about the organization's practices and trust that opportunities are truly open to all—at least, to all who share the same identity characteristics as the dominant group in the organization. Those who do not share these identity characteristics may feel more cynical about the accessibility of advancement for them, no matter how qualified they are. When well-qualified individuals are promoted, regardless of their membership identity, all employees can feel certain that the organization's promotion policies are truly equitable and that the organization understands the value of diversity.

Working with the Colorblind

As you work with or manage a person who has a strong preference for the Colorblind Lens, you are likely to discover that she has prioritized legacies and layers that emphasize personal values and individuality. In particular, as you listen to the Colorblind, you may hear strong interest expressed about:

> *Family background*—How were you raised? What values did your parents impart? How did your childhood shape who you are as a person?
>
> *Personal Style/Characteristics*—What kind of a person are you? What do we have in common? Can I trust you?
>
> *Personal abilities*—What are your special talents and capabilities? Are you qualified to do the job?
>
> *Religion*—What does your religion teach you about how we should treat one another? About how we should manage our differences?

Your interest in, and responses to, questions such as these will create bridges between you and a Colorblind. If, on the other hand, you feel defensive or confused during conversations with this individual, you may have prioritized your layers differently and are operating from a conflicting lens.

When you are having problems communicating with those who emphasize the Colorblind Lens, it may help to remember that:

- The Colorblind need to feel that everyone is being treated as individuals rather than as group members.

- They do not realize that at times an employee or customer may be more comfortable talking with someone from the same racial or cultural group, especially when there is a problem.

- Many Colorblind do not recognize discrepancies between their own idealistic worldview/experience and the realities of discrimination experienced by others in our society and organizations.

- Some Colorblind are not naïve but are strongly principled individuals who rarely change their minds, even when they are concerned about discrimination or some inequity that someone they know is experiencing.

Coaching the Colorblind Manager or Supervisor

A person with a strong preference for the Colorblind Lens has difficulty acknowledging that people of color and different cultural groups have identity group experiences and circumstances that have contributed significantly to their development, both positively and negatively. Because of her idealistic expectation that everyone will be treated equitably, the Colorblind may be oblivious to the existence of discriminatory circumstances and events in the organization that need to be addressed and resolved. She has trouble recognizing that demographic and cultural markets do exist and that companies need to appeal to different identity groups when offering different products and services.

Unmonitored and underdeveloped, the Colorblind stance could lead to resentment on the part of some employees who believe that important parts of their identity are being ignored, eruptions from time to time of suppressed racial or ethnic tensions and conflicts, charges of bias, and the loss of certain demographic or cultural markets. Your job as a manager and a leader in your organization is to coach the Colorblind so she is competent, confident, and willing to use or modify the organization's systems on behalf of the full range of employees in your organization today.

Specifically, you must require the Colorblind to use the organization's systems in ways that:

- Recognize and respond to the reality of multicultural employees' concerns, such as targeted recruitment, underrepresentation in various departments or levels of the organization, and other inequities or barriers

- Acknowledge and respect the diversity of every individual, while still treating him or her as an individual

- Incorporate the realities of today's cultural niche markets in developing products or considering ways to improve customer relations

- Leverage the diversity of your workforce to better serve your diverse customer base

The Colorblind and Organizational Systems

The Colorblind Lens believes strongly that the organization's systems should focus on developing and rewarding individual competence, knowledge, and character. She objects to any policy, program or initiative that uses race, color, ethnicity, or nationality as criteria for selection, development, promotion, termination, or any other organizational action. She expects organizational systems to be neutral with respect to these differences and does not agree that they should be discussed openly as part of the work process. By assuming that the organization's systems are fair and neutral, the Colorblind Lens can unintentionally sanction racial and cultural bias. When things go awry, the Colorblind individual believes that it is the result of a few bad people in the organization, rather than of bias embedded in the systems.

The essence of the ways in which the Colorblind Lens influences the organization's human resources systems is presented in each of the statements below. As you review these statements, think of the impact of the Colorblind stance on these same types of programs and activities in your work environment.

Colorblind Stance: "I will use our human resources systems in such a way as to provide equal opportunity to all employees who are motivated to succeed in our organization."

Recruiting: "I will recruit from any place that has people who fulfill our requirements."

Hiring: "I will hire the individuals who have the experience, abilities, and personal characteristics to get the job done."

Compensation and Benefits: "I will create benefits that, on average, everyone would want."

Job Placement: "I will place people in the jobs that match their qualifications and experience."

Building Effective Teams: "I will build teams that have the right mix of personal and professional talents and characteristics."

Performance Management: "I will give people feedback when they are not pulling their weight or when they are exhibiting personal or professional deficits."

Mentoring: "I will mentor anyone who has demonstrated the required motivation and ability."

Training: "I will endorse training that gives employees what they need to get the job done."

Succession Planning: "I will ensure that the right people with the right skills and characteristics needed to get the job done are in the mix."

The Colorblind and the Law

The Colorblind Lens could affect your business' bottom line in several ways. As you read the following hypothetical case, consider whether your organization may be manifesting the Colorblind Lens in similar ways.

The Case

Jessica was hired as the supervisor of the company's office services division. She was told to "turn around" the division, whose employees were notorious for showing up late, dressing out of uniform, and submitting sloppy time sheets. At her first meeting of the division, she announced a new no-tolerance policy. Two days later, Jessica terminated Jose for being 15 minutes late to work. Manuel, another employee in the division, met with Jessica to discuss the situation.

Manuel: Jose asked me to talk to you. He speaks very little English and he does not understand why he was suddenly fired for something that is common around here.

Jessica:	As I said at the meeting several times, "no-tolerance" means we are not going to put up with the old stuff any more. People have to show up for work on time, in uniform, ready for their shift. If you do not, you are gone.
Manuel:	Look, you know that many people in this division are not native English speakers. A guy like Jose just would not understand what you are talking about. You have to recognize: people are different.
Jessica:	When it comes to things like showing up on time for work, I do not see people's differences. What I see is people who are late. And if you're late, you are gone.

Jose sues, claiming national origin discrimination. Who wins?

Result

The company. Sometimes, a supervisor's blindness to differences can impair the supervisor's ability to make the most out of people's talents. However, in this case, the supervisor had a legitimate business objective (getting people to show up on time) and took an appropriate action. In fact, had she applied the policy differently to Hispanic and non-Hispanic employees, she might have become vulnerable to a claim of discrimination by non-Hispanic employees. None of this would preclude the supervisor from taking steps to ensure that non–native English speakers do in fact understand what she is saying.

Legal Concerns for the Colorblind Lens

The Colorblind has a strong need to see people as individuals without focus on their race, color, ethnicity, or culture. If you think you may use the Colorblind Lens, be aware that:

1. People from different cultures might respond differently to the same stimulus. For example, not looking someone in the eye might be a sign of evasiveness in some cultures, but it might be a sign of respect for a supervising employee in others. Being aware of this distinction is important when a human resources professional or other agent of management is charged with investigating an allegation of misconduct in the workplace and must make assessments of credibility of the people interviewed in the investigation.

2. Certain differences in behaviors that are culturally driven do not necessarily lead to differences in quality of performance. Assuming that people with accents derived from non-American national origins cannot

communicate adequately with customers or vendors may lead to hiring or job assignment decisions about candidates or employees of different national origins that are not based on merit.

Colorblind Highest Expression

What the Best of the **Colorblind Lens** Contributes to the Organization

Individuality

The Colorblind Lens seeks to achieve harmony by demonstrating allegiance to the notion that inner qualities and characteristics should be the primary criteria for judging individuals. From a limited perspective, the Colorblind insists that we ignore race and culture and look only at personal attributes. From a higher and more holistic level of expression, the Colorblind Lens continues to seek harmony by focusing on individual attributes, but it also includes racial and cultural identity as important components of a person's individuality.

The Colorblind Lens reminds us that to cultivate an identity is one of the greatest gifts of a lifetime. We are the artists and life is our canvas. It is up to each of us to paint the picture of who we are, what we stand for, and what our legacy will be. To the Colorblind, the paints we use are our values, beliefs, and philosophies as expressed in the personal choices we make. The character and personality that emerge in each of these individual portraits is multifaceted and unique. The Colorblind wants all of us to recognize that narrow cultural or racial definitions of people fail to capture the dynamic and complex richness of what these individual portraits are really about. These definitions do not allow us to know and wholly embrace each other's individual essences.

At the highest level of expression, the Colorblind Lens is able to combine this idealistic valuing of individuality with the realistic recognition that culture and race are key factors in shaping who we are; for each individual, the extent to which these factors influence our lives is different. For some, such as those who prefer the Culturalcentrist Lens, racial and cultural identity are absolutely central to this portrait, and personal and public identities are inextricably linked. For others, the experiences they have had based on their racial or cultural differences have had significant impacts on their values, beliefs, and character, but they also have been influenced substantively by other legacies and layers.

The highest expression the Colorblind Lens offers us is the opportunity to see the whole person, to acknowledge cultural identity, to negate the negative impact of judging people based solely on their group membership, and to appropriately leverage cultural differences. This dual focus on, and acknowledgement of, both the cultural identity and the intrinsic attributes of each individual can help organizations to create the kind of valuing environments in which employees are motivated to do their best work.

Colorblind Quotes

"This melting pot credo lies at the heart of our nation's ethos, but we now must choose how this pot will look in the new century. We can continue to make progress in stirring the pot or . . . dogmatically separate each racial and ethnic group, pitting one against the other. The choice is between a diversity rooted in colorblind public policy that makes us stronger and one based on tribalism that tears us apart."

Edward Blum and Marc Levin, "Kudos to HISD Board for Moving Beyond Tribalism," *The Houston Chronicle*, January 4, 2000.

"America has been called 'the melting pot,' with good reason. But few people realized that America did not melt men into gray conformity of a collective: she united them by means of protecting their right to individuality."

Ayn Rand, *The Virtue of Selfishness*. (New York: New American Library, 1964).

"Does Americans' embrace of the slogan "be like Mike" mean white people want to be black? No, and it probably never will. But by saying they don't see Jordan as black, whites may really mean they see him as *human*—and that is still an unalloyed good."

Leon Wynter, "The Jordan Effect: What's Race Got to Do with It?" Online Magazine: Salon.com, January 29, 1999.

Culturalcentrist

Culturalcentrist Archetype

Meet Jamal Edmunds

Jamal is a thirty-nine-year-old African-American man who works in the health-care industry and supervises a staff of twenty lab technicians, most of whom are African American, Latino, and Asian. He is generally regarded as a very good manager. Production is consistently high in Jamal's department, and he is known for his problem-solving and crisis-management skills. He is seen as a straight shooter, loyal to the company and his staff. He is sensitive to people's personal needs, encouraging individuals to take time off when they need it to avoid burnout.

He is an enthusiastic and outspoken member of the company's diversity committee and takes great pride in representing the concerns of black employees. Some of his employees from other cultures have complained quietly to his superiors that he does not mentor Asians, Hispanics, and whites to the same degree that he mentors African Americans.

Jamal has been in the same position for five years and is frustrated because he cannot seem to break out of first-line supervisory ranks into management. He gets performance feedback that he needs to broaden his experience and take classes in communication and diversity to better understand the needs of everyone in the workforce.

He recently met with his mentor to discuss his situation. His mentor is also African American and has been with the company for fifteen years. Jamal's mentor told him that he is seen as an advocate and supporter of positions, programs, concerns, and needs of black employees first and foremost. Furthermore, the mentor told Jamal that at times he has been perceived as overly assertive and insensitive in the display of his Afrocentric perspective.

For example, the mentor said, Jamal had gone through a list of potential vendors and criticized management because none on the list were small black-owned businesses that would return money to the black community. In the same communication to management, Jamal opposed recruitment policies that give only superficial consideration to graduates of traditionally black colleges and universities. He filled out a complaint form several weeks ago about the Eurocentric menu in the cafeteria and suggested that the magazines in the waiting area should include black periodicals and publications.

Jamal and his mentor discussed the need for him to tone down his critical stance and to attend to the interests and needs of all employee groups if he is interested in moving into management.

Jamal demonstrates a strong preference for the Culturalcentrist Lens.

Culturalcentrist Profile

The Culturalcentrist thinks of himself as having a mission in life to preserve and protect his own culture and community by making sure that everyone shows the proper respect for his race, culture, nationality, and ethnicity. He does not separate his personal identity from his ethnicity, racial customs, or language, and he is most comfortable living, working, and socializing with people who are in the same cultural identity group. The Culturalcentrist waves the flag or sings the anthem of his own ethnic background with pride. He demonstrates as much, if not more, loyalty to his race or ethnicity as he shows to his nationality as an American. He is dedicated to connecting with the rituals and traditions of ancestors as a source of strength and pride to anchor his day-to-day life. By living and, when possible, working with a supportive group of people who share the same ethnic and racial backgrounds, the Culturalcentrist tries to reduce the impact of racism and restore the self-esteem and well being that he believes have been eroded by oppressive or integrative forces. He thinks that even the most liberal-minded outsiders cannot be trusted to fully understand and nurture his cultural needs.

As with other lenses, the Culturalcentrist style varies in depth and intensity within the larger group. Some may wish to insist militantly on recognition and rights, dressing, speaking, and carrying themselves with a style and purpose that is distinctly ethnic and would not be perceived as mainstream. Others may take a softer approach to preserving their personal and cultural dignity. Still other Culturalcentrists see the value of conformity at the public level but privately adhere to specific cultural practices in terms of their cuisine, dress, family traditions, religious or spiritual practices, and other aspects of their lives.

It is not unusual to find that this is the preferred lens of people who seek out employment in work environments where there are already many people of the same race or ethnic background. As a result of this choice, he does not have to deal with racism as part of the day-to-day pressure among coworkers. It also makes it easier to pursue his interest in recognizing and celebrating the holidays, traditions, and practices of his group within the organization. If the organizational environment is inclusive and the Culturalcentrist is open without being abrasive, he can foster a sensitivity and responsiveness to the cultural concerns and needs of his group among organization members. This understanding and appreciation can be incorporated into the organization's strategic thinking related to customers, clients, and constituencies, as well as to its human resources management systems.

Since much of the Culturalcentrist's motivation is to honor his own culture, he often spends his breaks and lunch times with coworkers from his cultural group, seeks out mentors who share his cultural identity, and makes extra efforts to support and promote his "kindred" coworkers. He may have trouble recognizing or supporting the need for all members of the organization to subscribe to a set of commonly held values, norms, and business practices for the organization to be successful. The Culturalcentrist resists participating in the traditional social rituals of the organization, such as company picnics, annual recognition events, or holiday dinners, and he is reluctant to attend social functions outside of work that take him too far from his community or comfort level.

The Culturalcentrist manager unintentionally or intentionally may focus on mentoring and supporting members of his own group as he tries to move upward in the organization. While this can relieve the isolation often felt by some ethnic and cultural minorities, it can be demoralizing for others in a multicultural workforce.

The Culturalcentrist is sensitive to how the organization responds to and interacts with members of their community and wants the organization to support community efforts in which the Culturalcentrist can volunteer and participate. He will monitor everything in the organization for parity and fairness, down to how much money is spent on minority vendors and the type of food served in the cafeteria to ensure representation.

The Culturalcentrist customer spends money in an organization that regularly demonstrates its respect for his racial or ethnic group and is located preferably in his community. He wants products and services that meet his specific cultural needs and are advertised in the media he watches, reads, or listens to. He prefers to have people from his culture serve him and is most comfortable in an environment where he knows he is not being measured by standards outside of his group. When he purchases items for his children, he searches for the doll or action hero/heroine that is culturally specific as a method of reinforcing self-esteem.

Businesses that "give back to the community" are high on the Culturalcentrist's list of places to patronize. He avoids organizations that have a history of negative treatment toward members of his group and passes the word on, either formally or informally, within his community when he perceives that an injustice or unfair treatment has occurred. He notices and reports being followed in stores, profiled by police, or treated with suspicion. In many cases, he speaks up and confronts situations, participating in boycotts or otherwise sending messages about the treatment his group has experienced. Another community-minded value associated with Culturalcentrism is the notion that giving time back to community-based programs, celebrations, and initiatives serves to empower or uplift members of the group.

The Culturalcentrist argues that separate institutions encourage cultural pride, create a support network, and establish a safe, nonthreatening environment free of racism and other forms of discrimination. People of color and members of different religious and ethnic groups have not always been able to choose where they live. Even though antidiscrimination housing laws have been enacted, some Culturalcentrists prefer to live in separate communities with established places of worship and study that ensure survival of their cultural traditions.

The Culturalcentrist wants, in a positive way, to establish what historian J. Harvie Wilkinson calls "pride separatism." By transforming anger and victimization into power, the Culturalcentrist can function peacefully and productively in an autonomous environment, thereby increasing cultural pride and stabilizing supportive resources. He can support ethnic businesses, see beauty in his own race and ethnicity, worship a God created in his own image, learn his history, marry his "own kind," and vote for politicians from his racial or ethnic group.

Culturalcentrist Strengths and Shadows

The attributes of the Culturalcentrist Lens include the following Strengths and Shadows:

Strengths

Culturalcentrists:

- Inspire people to become self-reliant by stressing self-determination and the need to rise above oppressive forces
- Are sensitive and respond to the important need for ethnic cultures to feel safe and secure
- Help maintain cultural traditions and gifts that could disappear through assimilation or integration
- Have a keen interest in recognizing and celebrating the traditions and practices of their cultural group
- Establish bonds with and support those of their own group, creating a sense of community and solidarity within the larger organizational setting
- Make organizations more aware of the ways in which they may unintentionally discriminate against minority groups
- Contribute significantly to their own communities

Shadows

Culturalcentrists:

- Have difficulty seeing beyond the needs of their group to the needs of the entire community or organization
- Want us to believe that one of the most important and central facets of our identity is our racial or ethnic heritage; for many, this is simply not the case
- Often are unwilling to recognize or are insensitive to the importance some individuals from their racial or ethnic group place on other layers such as age, marital or parental status, or physical ability
- Can be unable to find or have limited faith in finding common ground with other racial or ethnic groups, thereby isolating themselves from the advantages of diversity
- Can believe that they have no personal work to do in the area of diversity because of their minority status

Historical Perspective

Culturalcentric groups are not new in this country. Early immigrants to the United States found that their survival depended on having a network of people who spoke their same language, sold their native foods, and worshipped in the same way. Thus, Jewish, Irish, Asian, Hispanic, Polish, and other ethnic groups established communities of familiarity, usually around places of worship and commerce.

Today, the same kind of culturalcentric tendencies still exist in many regions of America, as well as in most of our urban areas. For example, Andrew Buchanan points out the culturalcentric tendencies of Chicago: "While there are pockets of diversity in the city, these newcomers seem to be following the path that led Irish, Polish, and Italian immigrants to establish their own communities."

From the Culturalcentrist Lens, assimilation—exemplified by conformity to language, standards, and style imposed by the majority culture—is perceived as a strategy that would undermine one's own culture. An underlying premise of this lens is that there can never be equal relations among the races or different ethnic and cultural groups without economic parity. Accordingly, it is important to Culturalcentrists that they maintain their own centers of commerce. Cultural niche marketing further serves to reinforce cultural identity and boundaries by effectively catering to different cultural impulses in the consumer market.

Another reason for maintaining separate identities, in addition to pride and economic concerns, is that many Culturalcentrists have become increasingly frustrated by the ongoing racial and ethnic conflicts in this country. They choose to live in their own communities where they will not have to confront these issues so frequently or extensively. "New America is rapidly becoming a self-segregated nation," J. Harvie Wilkinson reports in *One Nation Indivisible*. He points out that "self-segregation is becoming the guiding maxim of a multi-ethnic nation." This push toward separate communities perpetuates a single cultural experience instead of a multicultural one.

As segregation becomes the way of life for multiple American minorities, the goal of "One Nation Indivisible" will gradually disappear. Indeed, this is already happening. The desire of the races to be left alone is growing.

A report issued in April 2001 by the Civil Rights Project at Harvard University states that intense racial separation continues in metropolitan areas despite the removal of legal and socioeconomic barriers that prohibited integration. This analysis is based on census 2000 data which reflects little if any change in segregation levels from 1990.

The Culturalcentrist Lens at Work

Motivation and Career Advancement from the Culturalcentrist's Perspective

The Culturalcentrist is motivated by the drive to see his racial or ethnic group get the respect and appreciation it deserves from the organization or the community at large. This lens does all within its power to ensure that its "group" receives equitable and respectful treatment from the powers that be in the organization. The Culturalcentrist expects all those of the same racial or ethnic group within the organization to identify as closely and strongly as he does with other members of that group. He cannot understand how others of the same racial or ethnic identity can define themselves primarily as anything but members of the group, and he is likely to feel betrayed or resentful when this happens.

The Culturalcentrist's approach to career advancement is to help the organization recognize that it needs more representation of his racial or ethnic type at the top and that these representatives should be allowed to advance without giving up who they are. His focus is on meeting the competency criteria for a senior position without worrying about "fit" with the organizational culture in terms of such things as personal appearance, dress, language, and socializing. Often, he is prepared to leave if the organization is not willing to value his cultural attributes or allow him to behave as he wants, independent of the behavior patterns of the dominant group in the organization, as long as his appearance, language, and behavior do not negatively impact on job performance. In today's business world, he believes some other company will have a more enlightened view about the Culturalcentrist's value to the organization.

Impacts of This Strategy on the Individual's Advancement Potential

If an organization recognizes its need for more diversity in management and executive ranks and has created an inclusive work culture, the Culturalcentrist will find himself at the right time and the right place with this advancement strategy. If the organization does not recognize a need for more diversity, this strategy may well keep the Culturalcentrist from moving up in the ranks. Members of the dominant group in the organization may feel uncomfortable with, or even threatened by, the obvious differences demonstrated by the Culturalcentrist and may be unwilling to accommodate his obvious "lack of fit" with the organization's culture.

Impacts of This Strategy on the Organization's Human Resources

All people of difference in the organization will have the experience of feeling more valued and included when this strategy is successfully implemented by Culturalcentrists. Members of the dominant group or people of color who are less cultural centric may believe that standards have been lowered to satisfy legal or public-relations requirements for more diversity in management and executive ranks. In most cases, however, there will be increased support for acknowledging and valuing differences and a fuller utilization of all the organization's human resources assets.

Working with the Culturalcentrist

If you are working with or managing a person who has a strong preference for the Culturalcentrist Lens, it is important to understand the specific stances and priorities that he has established with respect to key legacies and layers. If you listen carefully in conversations with the Culturalcentrist, you are likely to hear the following emphases:

> *Race/Culture*—My race is central to my identity, and I will not submerge it to gain acceptance.

> *Ethnicity*—The customs, traditions, and beliefs of my ethnic group are part of my community and me.

Religion—Our faith and all of its customs and practices are interwoven into our culture. They cannot be separated.

Nationality—My national identity is central to my identity. I can continue to honor the traditions of my country of origin and still be a good American.

Class/Socioeconomics—Our people must unite and develop our community through economic empowerment.

When you are experiencing tension or conflict in interactions with Cultural-centrists, it may help to follow these guidelines:

- Remind yourself that the Culturalcentrist's desire to preserve his group's heritage and self-esteem is his core motivation; he typically is not motivated by hostility toward or contempt for others.

- Listen empathetically to his feelings about why he believes he must challenge the system to be more tolerant of his cultural group's attributes.

- Take the time to understand his perspective on issues facing your organization or community.

- Do not shy away from giving needed performance feedback to him because of fear of reprisal or being perceived as "biased."

Coaching the Culturalcentrist Manager or Supervisor

A person with a strong preference for the Culturalcentrist Lens has difficulty understanding that the need of the organization is to successfully manage a multicultural workforce. The concerns of this multicultural workforce go far beyond the issues of any one racial or ethnic group's relationship to the dominant group in American society. This requires that a broad band of attention, concern, and support be given to all groups in the organization. As part of this broader focus, managers and supervisors need to know how to build bridges between their groups and other groups in the organization; they need to learn to see people based on their individual differences as well as their group identities; and they need to accept members of their own group whom they believe have "sold out." Culturalcentrist managers and supervisors have to be willing to pay more attention to the potential for cultural niche markets other than those of their identity group.

Unmonitored and underdeveloped, the Culturalcentrist stance could lead to charges of bias, high turnover among employees of other identity groups, low morale, and poor use of human resources. Your job as a manager or leader in the organization is to coach the Culturalcentrist so that he is competent, confident, and willing to use or modify the organizational systems on behalf of the full range of employees in your organization and not just members of his own group.

Specifically, you can require the Culturalcentrist to use the organization's systems in ways that:

- Recognize and support the need for all members of the organization to subscribe to a set of commonly held values, beliefs, and business practices
- Balance the need to recognize and celebrate the traditions and practices of different cultures within the organization with the need to establish and support a common organizational culture that reinforces teamwork and performance
- Foster increased understanding and appreciation among members of their own and other identity groups through dialogue sessions, social events, and other informal contacts
- Understand and act on preferences related to product development, sales, services, and customer interactions of other identity groups as well as their own racial, cultural, and ethnic groups

The Culturalcentrist and Organizational Systems

The Culturalcentrist is acutely aware of how the current systems either create or minimize barriers that affect issues such as inclusiveness, advancement, and success in the organization. He tends to challenge and attempt to reform the systems to support opportunities for his racial, ethnic, or cultural group. The Culturalcentrist supports diversity training and other sensitivity initiatives if they are focused on the important issues his group faces in the workplace and in the community. He is less supportive of broad diversity initiatives that move beyond race or ethnicity.

The Culturalcentrist can lose focus on the needs of the entire organization and the rest of the workforce because of his special emphasis on the needs of his group. The Culturalcentrist stance could cause multiple groups such as African Americans, Asian Americans, Latin Americans, Native Americans, and others to be primarily concerned about their membership group's issues and concerns to the exclusion of others. As a result, these groups could compete and work at cross-purposes on the same issues.

The following statements reflect the ways in which the Culturalcentrist Lens can influence the human resources systems in an organization. As you review these statements, consider the impact of the Culturalcentrist stance on these same types of programs and activities in your work environment.

The Culturalcentrist Stance: "I will use my organization's systems, policies, and practices to increase parity, inclusiveness, upward mobility, and freedom of expression for my cultural group."

Recruiting: "I will go to schools that have a good reputation within my cultural community."

Hiring: "I will hire people who come from my community to increase our representation in the organization."

Compensation and Benefits: "I will try to change the systems so that they are sensitive to our cultural needs for things like flexible holidays, time to volunteer in community efforts, and broad definitions of family so that more people are covered under various policies."

Job Placement and Assignments: "I will use the system to get members of my group into areas within the organization where they will be supported."

Building Effective Teams: "I will challenge the cultural norms that we are not comfortable with and that are biased toward the dominant cultural group. I will look for ways to strengthen bonds among members of my group so that we are not isolated from one another."

Performance Management: "I will change the system so that it is not biased toward the strengths and characteristics of the dominant group."

Mentoring: "I will help members of my group succeed in the organization and look for members of my group who have been successful to mentor me."

Training: "I will change the training programs so that they are more sensitive to the unique preferences and needs of my group."

Succession Planning: "I will use the systems to make sure our people are included in the future plans of the organization, and I will keep close watch to see how many people from our group make it to senior positions."

The Culturalcentrist and the Law

The Culturalcentrist Lens can affect your business' bottom line in several ways. As you read the following hypothetical case, consider whether your organization may be manifesting the Culturalcentrist Lens in similar ways.

The Case

Michael Chiluba, a naturalized U.S. citizen originally from Zambia, is a junior software engineer at Zencon Incorporated. His supervisor, Todd Smith, is an African American. In a recent performance evaluation, supervisor Smith criticized Mr. Chiluba for not being a team player. This criticism led to denying

Mr. Chiluba a promotion. Mr. Chiluba went to Mr. Smith to protest:

Mr. Chiluba: What do you mean by saying that I am not a team player?

Mr. Smith: Michael, I've noticed you don't interact well with other black employees. You don't greet them, you don't sit with them during lunch, and you don't attend social functions outside the office or belong to any black professional organizations.

Mr. Chiluba: I don't understand what that has to do with the quality of my work.

Mr. Smith: I think it's important for someone to understand his obligations to the community. We need people on top who will help other blacks. It seems like you Africans refuse to acknowledge that you are black.

Mr. Chiluba sues for the denial of his promotion. Who wins?

Result

Mr. Chiluba. Title VII prohibits making employment decisions based on race. In this case, Mr. Smith imposed a requirement upon Mr. Chiluba that Mr. Smith did not impose upon nonblacks: to be active within the black community and behave like other black employees. Therefore, Mr. Chiluba would have a strong claim for race discrimination under Title VII.

Legal Concerns for the Culturalcentrist Lens

The Culturalcentrist has a strong desire to support the needs of his group within the organization. If you think you may use the Culturalcentrist Lens, be aware of the following:

1. Taking into account a person's race or ethnicity in making decisions about terms or conditions of employment may violate Title VII or comparable state laws.

    "It's about time we had [an African American/Hispanic/Native American] in this job."

    "I don't think we should fill that job with another white male; I'd rather wait for [an African American/Hispanic/Native American] candidate."

2. Identifying or characterizing people in the workplace by their race or ethnicity may violate Title VII or comparable state laws.

    "Joe is a white guy, and, well, you know, those white guys just don't know how to manage a Hispanic employee."

"Jose is Hispanic, and, well, you know those Hispanics really wouldn't know how to manage someone like Joe."

Culturalcentrist Highest Expression

What the Best of the **Culturalcentrist Lens** Contributes to the Organization and Community

Building Alliances

The Culturalcentrist seeks cultural empowerment by demonstrating allegiance to his culture and race. From a limited perspective, the Culturalcentrist thinks this requires individuals to withdraw from the dominant culture to restore and preserve the essence of their own culture. From a more holistic level of expression, the Culturalcentrist continues to seek cultural empowerment, but he moves from doing this in isolation for his own group to building cooperative alliances with others who seek the same goals for all racial, cultural, and ethnic groups.

One organizational example of how the Culturalcentrist plays out his preference for this lens is through affinity and/or advocacy groups. These groups usually work independently, but their goal of increasing the level of inclusion and opportunity is the same. The only difference is that these advocacy/affinity groups are focused on the level of inclusion for their group, not for other groups. While there may be subtle differences in the specific needs and concerns of each group, typically the underlying desire to ensure fairness, opportunity, and respect remains consistent across all of the groups. In its highest expression, the Culturalcentrist Lens recognizes this and moves to form alliances with other groups to accelerate institutional reform. Identifying systemic patterns of behavior that create barriers for some groups would lead to equity and opportunity for all groups. In collaborating with others, the Culturalcentrist can operate from a more powerful position and champion the higher value of inclusion for all.

In alliance with other groups, the Culturalcentrist can dramatically influence the degree to which members of cultural groups feel forced to choose between honoring the style attributes of their birth culture or rejecting fundamental aspects of who they are to "fit" in the organization. The leveraged actions of the Culturalcentrist help organizations and society resist the temptation to "overhomogenize" that reduces creativity and diminishes the emergence of new ideas from different perspectives.

In the highest level of expression, the Culturalcentrist is not only motivated by the needs of his own group but also by the needs of other groups. He is able to benefit from intellectual and spiritual capital from outside of his group and be replenished by the energy and resources of like-minded partners. He understands the interconnectivity of his group and others and actively works to protect the precious cultural strands of diversity. In this way, the Culturalcentrist strengthens the entire organization and the larger society.

Culturalcentrist Quotes

"...there was a greater consensus in the past on what it meant to be an American, a yearning for a common language and culture, and a desire...to assimilate. Today...there is more emphasis on preserving one's ethnic identity, of finding ways to highlight and defend one's cultural roots."

William Booth, "The Myth of the Melting Pot,"
The Washington Post, February 22, 1998, A1.

"The American black man should be focusing his every effort toward building his own businesses and decent homes for himself. As other ethnic groups have done, let the black people wherever possible, however possible, patronize their own kind, hire their own kind, and start in those ways to build up the black race's ability to do for itself. That's the only way the American black man is ever going to get respect. One thing the white man never can give the black man is self-respect! The black man never can become independent and recognized as a human being who is truly equal with other human beings until he has what they have, and until he is doing for himself what others are doing for themselves. "

Malcolm X, Autobiography of Malcolm X.
(New York: Grove Press, 1965), 278–279.

"Pride separatism, in contrast to power separatism, involves ethnic or racial affiliation with an emphasis on cultural identity."

J. Harvie Wilkinson, III, *One Nation Indivisible: How Ethnic Separatism Threatens America*. (New York: Addison-Wesley, 1997), 79.

"We need to foster, I believe, a sense of identity that maintains the integrity of (our) culture in all its complexity and uniqueness but expands our psychological and, ultimately, our political capacity to reach out and connect with other communities."

Itabari Njeri, *The Last Plantation: Color, Conflict, and Identity*. (New York: Houghton Mifflin, 1997), 8.

Elitist

Elitist Archetype

Meet Bradley Grayson

Bradley is the son of one of the most venerated board members of a prestigious northeastern university. Three generations of Grayson men have attended the university, and a distinguished chair and building in the school of business were named for his grandfather.

Bradley is about to become the dean of the school of communications, the youngest dean in the history of the university. He completed his doctorate six years earlier and taught a mix of graduate and undergraduate courses prior to this appointment. He served on several key university committees, where the depth of his knowledge about the institution's inner workings impressed his colleagues.

While Bradley was an undergraduate, his father arranged an internship for him in the Chancellor's office. Bradley sat in on meetings with key administrators and officers of the university and every once in a while gave the "students' point of view." He volunteered for every committee possible and even donated some of his trust fund to various fundraising campaigns. When he was in graduate school, he was asked to serve as co-chair of the university's fundraising campaign, which brought in more money than had ever been raised before in one year.

His family hosts the annual university holiday party attended by board members, federal cabinet members, celebrities, corporate leaders, faculty, distinguished alumni, and student leaders. Since Bradley was twenty-one years of age, his father has required him to assume the responsibility of officially welcoming the guests at these parties, and everyone has always been delighted with his wit, composure, and style.

It came as no surprise that, when the dean's position opened up, Bradley was at the top of the list. Although his academic record is not particularly distinguished, his work record is good and he is well liked by his peers and the administration of the communications school.

The search committee selected Bradley over another candidate, a woman of color who had a very distinguished career at another prestigious northeastern school and had served as a network executive of a major news organization. Some people on the committee thought that her real-world experience would bring an important perspective to the communications school's program and would demonstrate the school's commitment to diversity. While the majority of committee members agreed with these points, they preferred Bradley for the position of dean. Several coalition groups representing students of color supported the woman's candidacy because of the university's dismal record on diversity at the higher levels. These groups plan to protest Bradley's selection by staging a demonstration at the chancellor's office and demanding a meeting to voice their anger at the "rigged process." They are considering legal action.

Bradley is dismayed at this reaction and does not want to be at the center of a controversy. Nonetheless, he believes that he is claiming what is his—the job for which he has been groomed since he was eighteen years old.

Bradley demonstrates a strong preference for the Elitist Lens.

Elitist Profile

The Elitist builds his life around his privileged membership in the upper social class. He comes from a distinguished and well-connected family background where there is a strong emphasis on family lineage, elite education, and high social standing in the community or society at large. An air of entitlement underlies this lens. The Elitist sincerely believes that those with the most advantaged backgrounds are best equipped to assume leadership roles, since they have the appropriate social preparation, the best education, and the widest exposure to the ways of the world, including the arts, politics, travel, high society, and social etiquette.

Money, although attractive, is not a necessary requirement to being an Elitist. When money is involved, the "age" of the money is key. "New money" is not nearly as esteemed as "old money." The implication is that old money has been around for a long time in a family that is well established, rooted in tradition, with historical ties to the community. New money is associated only with current cash and assets and indicates nothing about background and breeding.

The Elitist believes he is prepared to make distinguished contributions and that, with a brief but appropriate orientation and a little seasoning, he can take charge of most situations. He understands politics and networking, and he realizes that "a deal" can be made on the golf course, over drinks, during dinner, or on any other private social occasion where you have access to the "right" people. He knows that a significant portion of the business world works based on whom you know and to whom you have access informally. When there is an opening in the organization, the Elitist is able to reach into his personal network to identify a person of choice, thus creating an organizational culture that minimizes the input from those who do not have the same background as the Elitist. As an employee, the Elitist may resent having to "work his way up the ladder." He believes that the intangible assets of his prestigious background are of great value to any enterprise he chooses to support.

The Elitist generally knows how to entertain graciously and hosts events naturally and effortlessly. The Elitist also excels at fund-raising, recruiting, co-chairing special events, serving on boards, and similar duties that make good use of his knowledge of social mores and networking abilities. Tapping into networks to get the inside information on policy, politics, strategy, or scuttle is easy for the Elitist because he almost always has contacts in high places.

Not all Elitists are part of the top corporate group. The Elitist can be a coworker who feels and acts superior based on his family's history with the organization or his educational background. Because of this sense of importance, the Elitist often feels empowered to speak up and challenge the system in ways that other lenses do not. Many Elitists are not income dependent, have strong sponsors within the organization, care deeply about the mission of the organization, and see themselves as its guardians. As a result of these circumstances, they can become the champions of various organizational initiatives and take on pet projects that otherwise might receive little attention or consideration.

Because of his background and lifestyle, the Elitist often is out of touch with the everyday concerns of the "average worker." The executive team of a very large Fortune 100 company was baffled because various groups of employees were not using the company's savings plan benefit until it was pointed out to them that an average salary of $375 per week did not leave much to save once housing, transportation, food, and other essentials were deducted. They were genuinely surprised to realize that there would be no money left for savings, and, as a result of this experience, became committed to reshaping their benefits program to meet the real needs of their workforce.

As customers, the Elitist wants to deal with established, world-class organizations that produce superior products and services. He assumes that such companies will have the best minds and talent available and will be capable of meeting and exceeding industry standards in any area. When purchasing something, he is more comfortable with and responds better to senior, experienced salespeople. He tends to regard his purchases as an indication of his endorsement of a company and its goods and services.

The Elitist often believes it is his moral obligation to stand up for those who are less advantaged and to protect the rights of others. He can be a strong social activist and tends to support causes that make the world a better place for the disadvantaged or for victims of inequality. From time to time, he may choose to lend his name and financial support to organizations and events that focus on justice, freedom, equality, and the arts.

In public situations, the Elitist may be very upset that others not of his background or breeding have penetrated his class. The Elitist expects to be treated differently, in accordance with the standards he deserves.

In the community, the Elitist Lens often takes the form of the benevolent philanthropist who is the catalyst, sponsor, or endorser of appropriate causes—the one who funds the Special Olympics, the restoration of an honored museum, or the creation and endowment of a chair at a prestigious university or school. Another manifestation of this lens is the Elitist who believes that the lowered, more relaxed standards of behavior and decorum of contemporary society are disheartening. He wants to see a renaissance of sorts that will take America back to traditional or "classic" standards of refinement and civility. In whatever form, Elitists expect to be heard, to lead, and to use their resources to serve.

The Elitist is sought after to support and participate in community and society events. His name spices up invitation lists and appears in newspaper gossip columns. People are interested in the lives of Elitists because their family names elevate them to near-celebrity status. Some Elitists seek the limelight, reveling in their anointed status, while others are more private and sometimes even embarrassed by their family's worth and status. This latter brand of Elitist can become almost reclusive over time.

Elitist Strengths and Shadows

As with the other lenses, the Elitist Lens has many attributes. Among the primary Strengths and Shadows of the lens are the following:

Strengths

Elitists:

- Are deeply imbued with the sense of "noblesse oblige" and carry a sense of responsibility about taking care of those "less fortunate" than they are
- Are interested in bringing socially conscious programs to their organizations and communities
- Dedicate much of their time, energy, and financial resources to causes in which they believe
- Have a strong desire to establish and maintain high standards and will challenge the system and its leaders to do so
- Can bring prominence and positive public-relations benefits to the organizations with which they work or are affiliated

Shadows

Elitists:

- Are often insensitive to the financial, educational, or social difficulties experienced by those who were not born to the privileged class

- Can have a tendency to ignore or belittle the contributions made by those who do not belong to the Elitist's "club"
- May be oblivious to how others are unwilling to take them seriously because they are perceived as not having earned what they have acquired in terms of organizational positions or recognition
- May have difficulty interacting on an informal basis with coworkers or subordinates who do not come from the same background

Historical Perspective

Elitism in America was transported from England with its rigid class designations based on lineage. From our beginnings, a segment of American society has remained attached to the English custom of primogeniture, the practice of the oldest male child inheriting the family assets. This system, rooted in England, has served to keep estates intact and to perpetuate the aristocracy.

Aristocracy is not solely a British or American phenomenon, nor is it connected solely to wealth or economic strata. There have been overt or implied ruling or superior classes in every civilization from ancient Greece to African and Mongolian tribes. In some cultures, occupation, appearance, or unusual abilities have served as the basis for elevated status rather than wealth or social class. In this country, elitism is mainly a class issue. However, since the ruling class in America traditionally has been of European descent, elitism has become an issue of race and culture as well.

In the early 1800s, America's economy blossomed. According to historian Edward Pessen,

... the nation's richest men were almost invariably born to families of wealth and renown. The great majority of Americans, though by no means poverty-stricken, nevertheless owned few worldly goods and enjoyed little improvement in their condition during what used to be called "the era of the common man" ... But the well to do, whether in the urban Northeast or the rural West, not only survived but also thrived.

Since this era, there has been a very small but well-established upper class. According to a recent study, the top 1 percent of the population is in control of 38.1 percent of the nation's wealth, demonstrating that a very prominent economic ruling class remains.

The emergence of wealth from means other than primogeniture or an inherited sense of privilege is gradually blurring our economic and social picture, as perhaps the Founding Fathers intended. Yankee ingenuity and good luck flourish alongside inherited wealth, so that entrepreneurs, rap and rock musicians, athletes, and lottery winners can become millionaires without being born to it. However, our democratic process is not ideal; it is slow, and the Elitist still knows how to use his influence in the highest levels of government and business.

The Elitist at Work

Motivation and Career Advancement from the Elitist's Perspective

The Elitist cares deeply about the prestige and status of the institutions with which he is associated. He does all within his power to protect and elevate the image of the organizations with which he works and to ensure that the "right kind of people" serve in positions of power. He enjoys planning and hosting social events that will benefit the organization, and he does not hesitate to call on his social or political networks to contribute time and resources on behalf of the organization's success.

His career advancement strategy revolves around being known by those who matter when it comes to this kind of decisionmaking in the organization. The Elitist believes that he can count on other Elitists in the organization—or those outside the organization who have influence in it—to lobby for him, since this would help ensure that the right kind of people are at the helm. In some cases, the Elitist will exhibit a sense of entitlement about the position, similar to that of Bradley Grayson's at the beginning of this chapter.

Impacts of This Strategy on the Individual's Advancement Potential

Relying primarily on background and connections for advancement may work for the Elitist in certain situations, particularly when the Elitist point of view is firmly entrenched in the organization's culture and the organization is enjoying a period of steady state operations. However, these situations are becoming increasingly rare in today's globalized and ever-changing marketplace. It is more likely that this strategy will not suffice to ensure the Elitist's advancement in the organization, especially if the Elitist is perceived as invested in preserving the status quo.

Impacts of This Strategy on the Organization's Human Resources

The subtle or not-so-subtle message communicated when the Elitist implements this advancement strategy successfully is that everyone who does not belong to this one group is somehow inferior and not entitled to the same opportunities and privileges. The Elitist's tendency to ignore or minimize contributions made by those from other backgrounds further compounds this unwarranted sense of inferiority. Membership identity is critical from the Elitist's perspective, and because it is based on the accident of birth, it is extremely difficult for anyone outside of the tightly drawn circle ever to be accepted for membership in it. This narrow definition of "fit" with an organizational culture will not survive the pressures of current socioeconomic, political, legal, and cultural trends with respect to diversity in the workplace.

A different set of circumstances exists when an entire organization has positioned itself as Elitist, with the assumption that all organization members are superior performers. In this case, the Elitist perspective takes on a different meaning and can serve as a positive motivational force.

Working with the Elitist

If you are working with or managing a person who has a strong preference for the Elitist Lens, you are likely to hear the following emphases with respect to the legacies and layers that matter most to them:

> *Family Background*—Where is your family from? What kind of standing do they have in the community or society?
>
> *Socioeconomic Class*—What kinds of financial, intellectual, or social capital do you have? How much do you have? How old is it?
>
> *Personal Style/Characteristics*—Are you well educated and well grounded in the appropriate social graces?
>
> *Education*—Where did you attend school? How prestigious an institution is it?

While the legacies and layers that have had the most influence on you may be quite different, you still can attempt to connect with the Elitist by recognizing how important family background and class have been for him and demonstrating interest in what he has to say about them.

When you are experiencing problems or tensions working with the Elitist, the following guidelines may help:

- Remember that the Elitist is often unaware of the privileges and opportunities extended to him because of his lineage, connections, and exceptional abilities, and sometimes assumes that others experience the same kinds of treatment.
- Appeal to the Elitist's interest in maintaining the highest of standards for the organization.
- Recognize that the Elitist's concerns about the prestige, status, and image of the organization are important to the organization's brand image and public relations.

- Keep in mind that some Elitists are actually embarrassed by their privileged status and connections and want to have these downplayed or ignored.

Coaching the Elitist Manager or Supervisor

A manager or supervisor with a strong preference for the Elitist Lens may assume that coming from the right family and background is a better predictor of success in the organization than other data—such as previous experience and demonstrated knowledge, skills, and interests. Accordingly, he may have a tendency to ignore the organization's established recruitment, development, and promotion policies in considering all potential candidates for openings in favor of using personal connections to find the "right" person for the job. Another concern for the Elitist manager or supervisor is that he might not recognize that the circumstances faced by others as they try to advance in the organization may be very different from those he experienced. There may be very real biases or injustices that need to be addressed, including those that he himself may be perpetuating.

A third major problem may be the difficulty that an Elitist manager or supervisor has in valuing the importance of cultural niche markets that may be comprised of identity groups very different from those who have been historically defined as the "right" people.

Unmonitored and underdeveloped, the Elitist stance could result in legal problems for the organization and poor use of its human resources. Your job as a manager and leader in your organization is to coach the Elitist so that he is competent, confident, and willing to use or modify the organization's systems on behalf of the full range of employees in your organization, and not just on behalf of those who are entering at the highest levels from special backgrounds.

Specifically, you can require the Elitist to use the organization's systems in ways that:

- Establish and maintain employee development and training programs that help **all** employees make the fullest possible use of their potential to support organization and individual goals.

- Identify and address real or perceived inequities in the ways in which human resources systems are administered or the ways in which individual employees are treated by managers.

- Recognize that merit—relevant experience, knowledge, skills, and abilities—must be a central part of the employment equation.

- Identify, develop, and remain responsive to cultural niche markets in line with the organization's strategic goals and business plan.

The Elitist and Organizational Systems

The Elitist has a strong desire to use the organization's systems, policies, and programs to recruit and reward those who he thinks have the right background and education to contribute the most to bringing "world-class standards" to the organization. The Elitist sees himself as an important stakeholder, and in his concern to ensure that the organization's reputation and image are constantly on the rise, he may be unaware of how he causes advantage or disadvantage for others. In situations where the Elitist advances further and faster than colleagues with similar credentials, experience, and accomplishments, the organization risks charges of bias and fosters low morale.

Each of the lenses influences the organization's human resources systems in different ways. The essence of the ways in which the Elitist Lens influences these systems is presented in each of the statements below. As you review these statements, think of the impact of the Elitist stance on these same types of programs and activities in your work environment.

The Elitist Stance: "I will use the human resources systems to ensure that we have the world-class employees we need to maintain our position as a world-class organization."

Recruiting: "I will use my personal network to recruit prospective job applicants from the right backgrounds."

Hiring: "I will hire the best available people—those who graduated at the top of their class from the most prestigious universities."

Compensation and Benefits: "I will use the systems to create benefits and compensation that will attract the right people."

Job Placement and Assignments: "I will get the right person in the right job at the right level."

Building Effective Teams: "I will select people to be members of the team who understand our standards and can maintain them—people who fit in with how we work and play."

Performance Management: "I will give people the feedback they need to perform at a high level."

Mentoring: "I will identify people who have the right background, knowledge, and exposure to become executive leaders and informally prepare them for senior leadership."

Training: "I will develop training programs that will help us educate our people to world-class standards."

Succession Planning: "I will make sure that the right people are placed in jobs that prepare them for senior leadership positions."

The Elitist and the Law

The Elitist Lens could affect your business' bottom line in several ways. As you read the following hypothetical case, consider whether your organization may be manifesting the Elitist Lens in similar ways.

The Case

Michael Sumner is the owner of a 300-person public-relations firm in Chicago. Heads Up, a summer-internship program at the firm, hires college juniors interested in public relations. To be hired for a permanent entry-level position at the firm, an applicant needs to have participated in the Heads Up program. Mr. Sumner insists that all summer interns at the firm must be graduates of his alma mater, Woodsworth Preparatory School, a prestigious private boarding school in Vermont. Recently, a qualified Vietnamese-American applicant was denied a summer internship at the firm and a less qualified Woodsworth graduate was chosen. Ms. Miller, the Human Resources manager, is worried that all entry-level hires for the past five years have been white. She decides to have a conversation with Mr. Sumner.

Ms. Miller: I am concerned that qualified minority applicants are being turned down for summer positions because they are not Woodsworth graduates. All of our recent entry-level hires are white.

Mr. Sumner: That's unfortunate. I am not against hiring minorities. I just feel it is my duty to assist graduates from my old high school. I would hire any minority applicant who is a graduate of Woodsworth.

The Vietnamese-American applicant sues Heads Up, claiming that the company's hiring policies have a disparate impact on minorities. You are the judge. Who wins?

Result

The Vietnamese-American applicant probably would win. Title VII prohibits employment practices that have a disparate impact on minorities unless the employer can point to a business justification for the practice. The results of Mr. Sumner's Woodsworth policy are that minorities have not been hired for entry-level positions in the last five years. Mr. Sumner's policy is equivalent to saying, "Nonwhites need not apply." Moreover, Mr. Sumner's desire to assist Woodsworth graduates is not an adequate business justification for a policy that has a disparate impact upon nonwhite candidates. Thus, the Vietnamese-American applicant would have a strong claim under Title VII.

Legal Concerns for the Elitist Lens

The Elitist is accustomed to working and playing with those blessed by advantage, whether educational, financial, or social. If you think you may use the Elitist Lens, be aware of the following:

1. Hiring people in one's own image (graduates of a particular university hiring only graduates of that university; members of the ABC Club hiring members of the ABC Club) may tend to exclude members of protected categories that are underreprsented in a company's workforce, creating potential liability under Title VII of the Civil Rights Act of 1964 and comparable state laws.

   "We Ivy Leaguers [read: mostly white and Anglo] know that an Ivy League degree is a mark of the kind of person who is likely to succeed in this organization."

2. Thinking that "the rules don't apply to me" may lull a person into engaging in conduct in the workplace without due regard for applicable employment laws.

   "I've heard about those lawsuits where an employee claims to have been offended by conduct in the workplace, but I don't need to worry about that because that stuff really doesn't apply to me. The people here know me and like me, and they know I wouldn't do anything to harm or offend them."

Elitist Highest Expression

What the Best of the **Elitist Lens** Contributes to the Organization

Universal Standards of Excellence

The Elitist Lens wants to promote standards of excellence in all endeavors of the organization. From a limited perspective, the Elitist Lens defines excellence in conjunction with ancestral roots embedded in wealth; Ivy-League education; high social standing; and the wielding of power in venerable institutions of education, commerce, or government. He believes that this special legacy and upbringing prepares and entitles him to excel in whatever arena he may choose.

This definition of excellence minimizes or excludes the achievements and contributions of others who cannot claim the same family lineage and social status. From this limited perspective, the Elitist believes distinction cannot be earned through merit or hard work; one must be born into the upper class to be the "right kind."

In its highest and more holistic mode of expression, the Elitist Lens moves from defining excellence in ways that exclude the contributions of others to acknowledging, respecting, and cultivating multiple standards of excellence. At the individual level, this higher perspective acknowledges that all human beings are created equal and that the true origin of perfection is divine or universal, not ancestral or royal. From this perspective, the Elitist recognizes that we may look different across cultures, family backgrounds, or socioeconomic classes, but our ultimate bloodline and ancestry is universally derived and shared. At the cultural level, this higher perspective recognizes that each race and culture has something special and unique to contribute to this world. There can be no rank ordering of groups; each has its own special role to play.

From its highest expression, the Elitist Lens is less concerned with perpetuating personal status and entitlement and more deeply concerned with changing society and its institutions so that everyone has the opportunity to self-actualize unrestricted by the conditions of their birth.

Elitist Quotes

Duncan Kennedy writes, "My attitude toward meritocracy grows from my experience as a white male ruling-class child who got good grades, gained admission to one elite institution after another, and then landed a job and eventually tenure at Harvard Law School. I belong to a group (only partly generationally defined) that, since some point in childhood, has felt alienated within this lived experience of working for success according to criteria of merit which these elite institutions administer. . . . we just don't believe that it is real 'merit' that institutions measure, anywhere in the system; success is a function of particular knacks, some socially desirable (being 'smart') and some not (sucking up)."

Kimberle Crenshaw, *Critical Race Theory*. (New York: The New Press, 1995), 159.

"It turns out that what the Bushes dislike about being called a dynasty is the implication of power being passed along rather than individuals earning it on their own. . . . Still, the Bushes fit the accepted definition of a dynasty. They do pass down power."

Calvin Trillin, "The Dynasticks," *Time*. January 29, 2001, 20.

"American society has lost the confidence and common ground to believe in standards and hierarchies. We have taken the legal notion that all men are created equal to its illogical extreme. Every corner of the human race may have something to contribute. That does not mean that all contributions are equal."

William Henry, *In Defense of Elitism*. (New York: Anchor, 1994), 13.

Integrationist

Integrationist Archetype

Meet Sue Mocha

Sue Mocha is a forty-six-year-old African-American woman who works as the assistant news director for a local television station. She is a community activist who serves on the local board of a community civil rights group. Sue believes that if we are not careful, the societal gains we have made in civil rights over the last twenty years will be nullified by a disinterested populace, resulting in setbacks for women and minorities.

Sue uses her influence at work to keep her viewing public focused on civil rights issues. Whenever there are stories concerning the end of court-ordered busing or a violation of any civil rights laws, Sue lobbies hard to have her station cover these stories. While she does not always succeed in getting the go-ahead for coverage, she is respected as an honest and competent advocate. She also encourages her station to highlight more positive stories about black and white people working together to overcome bigotry and intolerance. She covers the Martin Luther King, Jr., holiday celebrations every year, including events where high-school students recite his famous "I have a dream" speech in competition. In the past, she has volunteered her time to serve as a judge for these competitions.

Sue believes the only way to promote racial harmony in America is through integration. She is a member of several media organizations that promote the advancement of minorities in the communications industry. She mentors several communications students of color. When she speaks to students majoring in communications, she discourages them passionately from choosing to live in cultural-specific dorms, which she likens to "de facto segregation." She does not understand or agree with young people who seem eager to live isolated lives, apart from one another along racial lines, sharing music and entertainment but little else across cultures. In fact, some of the younger people at her workplace see her as a throwback to the 1950s and 1960s and out of touch with today's world.

She has been challenged by upper management about her tendency to report the news predominantly from a black/white perspective. Several of her Latino colleagues have complained that she treats them as though they are "just lighter black people." During a meeting about diversity at the station, she gave a very eloquent defense of minority hiring goals but was pulled aside after the meeting and told that her focus was too narrow, since she only spoke on behalf of African Americans. To her credit, once confronted she acknowledged that she knew everything about the black/white ratio numbers but little about any other minority group's employment statistics. Sue admits that she does not understand the issues facing Latino or Asian communities, but she thinks that once we solve the black/white problem, life will be better for all minorities. She sincerely believes that the problems for black Americans are worse than for any other minority group.

Despite her single-minded focus on African-American concerns, she is highly regarded by management as a reasonable voice and is viewed as someone who knows how to work skillfully within the system. The general manager depends on Sue to be her "eyes and ears" in the black community and relies on Sue's presence on her news teams to build goodwill and trust between the station and that community. Sue is perceived as an ally for many important human resources initiatives because of her strong desire to know people better across the black/white racial divide and her support of programs like affirmative action, mentoring, and targeted recruitment.

Sue demonstrates a strong preference for the Integrationist Lens.

Integrationist Profile

The Integrationist thinks that integrating the boardroom, classroom, workplace, and neighborhood, and placing people of color and whites side by side will increase tolerance and reduce prejudice. An integrated society, she believes, will ensure that resources are more fairly and equitably distributed across the black/white racial divide. She tends to hold forth from an intense moral high ground, believing strongly that integration is the "right thing to do" and that the ongoing struggle for civil rights is a fight for justice and equality for all people in our society.

The Integrationist distinguishes her vision of America from that of the Assimilationist because integration does not require anyone to leave their culture behind. While Assimilationists hope to eliminate racial differences, the Integrationist wants to eliminate the distance between races so that a new common culture is forged. As Clarence Page puts it, "True integration, unlike assimilation, is a two-way street. It involves *cultural sharing*, a genuine respect and interest in difference, not cultural submergence by one party to please another."

The Integrationist tends to see the world through a bipolar lens that emphasizes the black-and-white axes. If the Integrationist is a person of color, she will sometimes find herself subtly at odds with Culturalcentrist members of her own racial group who advocate separation to build pride and empowerment. She also can be at odds with the Multiculturalist Lens, which does not want to integrate every culture into every other culture but rather to let all people maintain and celebrate different aspects of their specific race, culture, and ethnicity.

The Integrationist attempts to change society in ways that invite cross-cultural sharing and interaction. Her hope is that integration can be achieved peacefully through dismantling legal barriers that separate ethnicities and through building coalitions that emphasize common goals and sharing of cultures. She was an early supporter of school busing and approves of affirmative action initiatives and college scholarships designated to increase the educational opportunities of minorities.

At work, the Integrationist advocates for programs, policies, and initiatives that promote understanding, acceptance, and fairness across racial groups as well as redress of past wrongs. Some of her preferred strategies include: mentoring programs to help minorities gain greater understanding of the cultural norms of the organization; hiring goals and targets to ensure that management takes seriously the organization's commitment to equal opportunity; special development programs to fast-track minority group members; and sponsorship of special celebrations and education fairs. She is an advocate for the organization's involvement in community organizations that foster these aims. Participating in school-based mentoring programs, donating equipment to "disadvantaged" community groups, and volunteering to aid community-service organizations are high on the Integrationist's agenda for her organization.

The Integrationist is acutely aware of the civil rights laws and her organization's compliance with them. She is likely to have ties outside of the organization, either through direct membership or association with advocacy groups whose mission is to advance the rights of its members. She tracks the positions of every employee who is a member of her cultural group, knowing who is in the most senior positions and where they have hit glass ceilings. Once inequities are discovered, the Integrationist proposes the use of the organization's internal systems to address the problem, expecting that the organization can be self-correcting. She believes people of difference need to be at all levels of the organization to inspire organization members, serve as mentors and leaders, and ensure that the organization "walks its talk." The Integrationist thinks that when a member of her group does succeed, that member has a responsibility to help others. Since she tends to frame the success of one individual in terms of the group, as though everyone contributed to the individual's success, she may miss the important role the systems and culture of the organization play in reinforcing old behavior.

Although the Integrationist does not feel that people need to conform to fit in, she will be inclined not to work in a militant, isolated fashion. She enjoys and wants to hold on to the benefits she has reaped from integration and is perplexed by those who do not want to take advantage of these advances. The Integrationist prefers to work within the system, correct it when necessary, and hold it accountable for fairness. From her perspective, working within the system is always more advantageous.

As a customer, the Integrationist spends money in an organization that demonstrates its commitment to integrating its workforce, markets and sells products directed to blacks and whites alike, uses its economic capacity to reach out to minority suppliers and vendors, and is an active player in communities to promote economic empowerment for traditionally excluded or disadvantaged groups. In a service transaction, being treated with respect and dignity is crucial to the Integrationist, who is likely to lodge a complaint or protest to management if there is the slightest suspicion of discriminatory treatment.

The Integrationist customer is well informed of the business practices of the companies with which she does business. She knows what kind of people make up the workforce, who is on the board, and whether the organization is committed to equal opportunity. She monitors how much of the organization's resources are being used within her communities. She is likely to support boycotts and pass on negative information about a company to her family, friends, and professional networks. Because the African-American/black church is so much a part of the civil rights movement in the United States, the Integrationist always has a grassroots organizational base from which she can spread the word through communities quickly, powerfully, and informally.

The Integrationist has taken her sociopolitical agenda from the community into the greater world. Many Integrationist advocacy groups have access to the highest levels of corporate America and have become political forces within the society. When some of these advocacy groups organize, corporations have quite a challenge on their hands until the situation is, in the eyes of the wronged group, fairly resolved.

The Integrationist is an activist within her community to promote the ideals of integration. She joins civil rights organizations, volunteers to serve on committees that promote her ideals, and donates money to causes that promote her agenda. Organizations that promote and support the ideals of integration will challenge business, government, and social institutions and typically use the courts, the legislative process, or the media as a way to spur change.

Integrationist Strengths and Shadows

Among the many attributes of the Integrationist Lens, the primary Strengths and Shadows include the following:

Strengths

Integrationists:

- Remind us of the importance of cross-cultural interaction and dialogue

- Demonstrate that vocal and active support of integration can help to break down stereotypes and improve the quality of interactions among people of different races
- Show their dedication to a just democracy through legal battles, legislation, and local responsibility
- Challenge us to go beyond our comfort zones and use social strategies to turn our caution and skepticism into tolerance
- Want to change the system by working within it
- Help create an organizational culture that recognizes and values diversity within a united whole

Shadows

Integrationists:

- Are focused primarily on black/white issues and may be unable or unwilling to encompass the concerns of a more multicultural global society in which different strategies are needed from those employed in the past
- May be impatient with, or insensitive to, the needs of others to move more slowly toward the goal of full integration
- May be intolerant of expressions and choices related to racial or cultural pride, especially when these are associated with the beliefs of the Culturalcentrist Lens
- May miss some of the subtleties related to their roles and responsibilities to become advocates for members of other racial, ethnic, and cultural groups as well as their own

Historical Perspective

Historian Manning Marable notes that the roots of integration can be found in the free black communities of the North before the Civil War. In a sense, Abolitionists also could be said to be early Integrationists. Although in the mid-nineteenth century the simple idea of freeing blacks from slavery was seen as radical, the idea of living next to them or dining at the same lunch counter was far more radical. Once emancipation had been achieved, the struggle moved to integration of the races. The work of organizations like the National Association for the Advancement of Colored People (NAACP), founded in 1908, has provided foundational support toward achieving this goal. Throughout the twentieth century, civil rights advocates have sought to remove legal barriers and establish the rights, opportunities, and civic responsibilities of blacks to provide them with full access to civil society.

The legal trail for integration starts with *Plessy v. Ferguson* in 1896, when the Supreme Court ruled that state laws enforcing segregation by race were constitutional, as long as accommodations were equal. It took fifty-eight years before the Supreme Court overturned the separate-but-equal doctrine in *Brown v. Board of Education* and directed Little Rock, Arkansas, to integrate its schools.

Desegregation became the official U.S. civil rights policy in 1964, when Lyndon Johnson signed the Civil Rights Act, which prohibited discrimination in voting, education, and use of public facilities. This was the first time that the government had the power to enforce desegregation because Title VII of the act barred the use of federal funds for segregated programs and schools. Because of this stipulation, 6 percent of the black students in the South were placed in integrated schools by the next year. In 1967, 22 percent of black students in seventeen southern and border states were in integrated schools.

Many Integrationists believe that integration received a setback in 1970, when President Richard Nixon placed the responsibility of desegregation of schools on the courts, saying that his administration would de-emphasize strong desegregation procedures. However, despite this change in emphasis on the part of the executive branch of government, by 1972, 44 percent of black students in the South were in integrated schools.

In the 1970s, another very controversial method of integration was introduced—that of busing students to different schools. The Supreme Court supported this method until *Miliken v. Bradley* in 1974, when a more conservative court allowed a predominantly white Detroit suburb to be excluded from the desegregation plan. Busing remains a controversial method today, with both black and white families strongly opposed to having their children involved.

Affirmative action, a major initiative in the history of integration, was introduced in the 1960s to overcome the effects of past discrimination and segregation. Various programs were developed to provide opportunities for blacks and other minorities in education, government, and business. In the late 1960s and early 1970s, affirmative action programs slowly lost steam. In the late 1970s, the practice brought about charges of reverse discrimination by people who felt they were losing jobs to their minority counterparts. Perhaps as a reaction to this, the federal government reduced its role in affirmative action in the 1980s, although the Civil Rights Act of 1991 began by restating the government's commitment to affirmative action. In the late 1990s, fears of reverse discrimination and questions about the efficacy and legality of affirmative action caused some states, like California, to ban the use of race- and sex-based preferences in admissions to state-run institutions of higher education and in any programs or businesses receiving state funding.

The Integrationist Lens at Work

Motivation and Career Advancement from the Integrationist's Perspective

The Integrationist cares deeply about the need for blacks and whites to work together in harmony—understanding, respecting, and valuing each other's cultures. Employees who prefer the Integrationist Lens seek out informal opportunities to befriend those from the other race, ignoring the teasing or threats of coworkers. There may be times when their impassioned attempts to integrate work groups on an informal basis backfire on them, because members of their own or another race are not ready to move in this direction. In these cases, the Integrationist truly cannot understand why people feel the way they do. The Integrationist is at the forefront of advocacy groups focused on equal treatment for blacks and whites within the organization. She may feel so passionately about a perceived inequity that she is willing to stake her job on the outcome.

As an example, the Integrationist's approach to career advancement might be expressed as follows:

"If we're serious about diversity in this organization, then we should be developing and implementing some kind of cohort system. Each of us interested in being considered for a senior management position should identify one qualified individual who belongs to the other race. Then the two of us should work for a while as a team, learning each other's job, getting familiar with each other's style, and helping each other understand how we experience our interactions with the organization in terms of this issue of 'fit.' When senior positions open up, we should be considered as a team for one position, with each of us serving in the position on a rotating basis—maybe for six months or a year at a time—while the other one continues to serve in one of the positions that we held before advancing."

Impact of This Strategy on the Individual's Advancement Potential

This type of innovative thinking could have a wide range of possible consequences on an individual's career advancement—from extremely positive to extremely negative. In cases where an organization was sincerely committed to increasing diversity at all levels and where the leadership liked to see itself as cutting edge in its human resources practices, this strategy might result in the Integrationist and her cohort being welcomed to executive ranks sooner rather than later. In other cases, the strategy might be perceived as yet another indication of the Integrationist's harebrained, unrealistic thinking.

Impacts of This Strategy on the Organization's Human Resources

The implementation of this strategy would send a strong message to all members of the organization about the organization's values and its authentic commitment to increasing diversity. Some employees might think that the teaming approach was one more example of management putting excessive resources into its ranks while ignoring more important resource requirements at the functional and work group levels. Other employees might feel proud of the organization's innovative approach to diversity. All employees would recognize that the organization was serious about establishing equitable promotion policies that fostered both competency and diversity.

Working with the Integrationist

If you are working with or managing a person who has a strong preference for Integrationist views, "read between the lines" when you are having a conversation and you are likely to hear some of the following questions about prioritized layers:

> *Race/Color*—What is your position on racial integration? How comfortable are you about interacting with me when we are from different races? Where do you draw the line around people from different races living together, having children, living in the same neighborhoods, and working together.

> *Education*—I want my kids/your kids to have the same educational opportunities and advantages as anyone else since these are the keys to advancement for minority groups and harmony within the American society. How can we make this happen?

> *Politics*—How can we use the societal laws and organizational policies to increase opportunity and representation in the organization? How can we ensure that intended and unintended barriers are broken down so that our differences are no longer organizational liabilities?

If the two of you have prioritized your legacies and layers differently, you may feel somewhat defensive or confused during discussions, or you may experience some conflict. In these cases, it may be helpful to remember the following guidelines:

- Understand that the Integrationist's strong support for integration is grounded in the belief that we would all give up our stereotypes and prejudices if we could just get to know one another as individuals.

- Acknowledge that she brings a passionate concern for social justice to her worldview that comes either from personal experience with segregation and discrimination or from knowledge of how systems, laws, and customs have been used historically to promote segregation.

- Recognize that she is not "out of touch" but rather *in touch* with one of the important aspects of the current cultural dynamic within American society.

- Help her to realize that the self-righteousness that sometimes accompanies her stance is a turnoff to others and may blind the Integrationist from seeing the rationale and appropriateness of aspects of other lenses in given situations.

Coaching the Integrationist Manager or Supervisor

A person with a strong preference for the Integrationist Lens has difficulty recognizing that people from other minority groups may not have the same needs as the black/white Integrationist, or that racial dynamics are different in the U.S. from the way they play out on the global level. As a result, she may have trouble including perspectives beyond black/white concerns when she is trying to think broadly about cultural diversity or speak "on behalf of all cultural groups." She also may have difficulty learning to present her perspectives in terms of business needs as opposed to moral imperatives for society at large.

Unmonitored and underdeveloped, the Integrationist stance could lead to charges of bias and reverse discrimination, increased divisiveness in the workforce, and high turnover of whites and cultural groups other than African Americans/blacks. Your job as a manager and leader in your organization is to coach the Integrationist so that she is competent, confident, and willing to use or modify the organization's systems on behalf of the full range of employees in your organization today.

Specifically, you can require the Integrationist to use the organization's systems in ways that:

- Respond to the complexities of identifying and serving the needs of a multicultural global workforce and customer base.

- Develop and promote cultural niche markets that address the needs of many different identity groups, not just African Americans/blacks.

- Ensure that business needs and sound management practices serve as the foundation for any actions that address contemporary societal needs with respect to integration and the elimination of discrimination against various cultural groups.

The Integrationist and Organizational Systems

The Integrationist has a strong desire to integrate work groups and use the organization's systems to increase minority representation and break glass ceilings for all people of color. With her primary focus on black/white dynamics, the Integrationist may miss the discriminatory impacts of certain policies and practices on other racial and ethnic groups. An unintended result could be distrust and divisiveness among the different minority groups in the organization and a weakening of her power to effect organizational change.

Each of the lenses influences the organization's human resources systems in different ways. The essence of the ways in which the Integrationist Lens influences these systems is presented in each of the statements below. As you review these statements, think of the impact of the Integrationist stance on these same types of programs and activities in your work environment.

> **Integrationist Stance:** "I will use the organization's systems to support my vision of a just and integrated society and workplace."
>
> **Recruiting:** "I will go to well-integrated schools and institutions that turn out good people who can fit into our organization if given a fair chance and opportunity to succeed."
>
> **Hiring:** "I will ensure that there is a good mix of minority and nonminority candidates and that minorities are given the advantage, if all else is even."
>
> **Compensation and Benefits:** "I will advocate that managers be rewarded and/or punished based on their success in building and managing diverse teams."
>
> **Job Placement and Assignments:** "I will use the system to make sure that key areas of our organization are integrated and that glass ceilings are broken."
>
> **Building Effective Teams:** "I will integrate work groups and give blacks and whites the opportunity to come to know each other as individuals."
>
> **Performance Management:** "I will ensure that all managers and supervisors are evaluated on how effectively they have recruited and promoted minority candidates."
>
> **Mentoring:** "I will use the mentoring system to identify and support candidates who have the potential to break glass ceilings."
>
> **Training:** "I will make sure that classes are integrated so that people receive both cultural perspectives."
>
> **Succession Planning:** "I will identify candidates who are qualified and who will advocate that managers advance a certain number of minority candidates."

The Integrationist and the Law

As is the case with the other lenses, the Integrationist Lens could affect your business' bottom line in several ways. As you read the following hypothetical case, consider whether your organization may be manifesting the Integrationist Lens in similar ways.

The Case

Employees at a midsized factory eat meals in a large lunchroom. To accommodate everyone, the employer staggers employee lunch breaks in thirty-minute intervals. For the sake of convenience, lunch groups are determined according to production lines, so that all employees in a single production line are sent to lunch at the same time.

Gary, a line supervisor, decided to reassign several African-American employees to other production lines. James, one of the reassigned employees, was upset by the change and met with Gary in his office, where they had the following conversation:

James: Why have I been reassigned to a different production line? I haven't had any complaints, and I get along well with the people on my line. We're like a family.

Gary: Don't take it personally. I reassigned you because I think our production lines are just too one-dimensional. Have you seen the lunchroom lately? I walked through it the other day, and the 12:00 group was all white guys, while the 12:30 group was entirely African American.

James: Maybe, but that's only because we get put on lines with people we work well with. And it's not completely the same—we have some Asian employees and some Latino employees on our team, too.

Gary: Just try it out. We need to mix things up here—this way, you'll get a chance to get to know other people on your shift better. Who knows, maybe you'll get along with them just as well. Either way I can't have people visiting this factory and seeing groups of employees separated by race. It's bad for business.

After encountering difficulty on his new production line, James quits and sues, alleging race discrimination. Who wins?

Result

Probably James. Title VII prohibits employers from taking race into account in making any employment decision. Here, the integrationist supervisor may have been well intentioned, but he violated Title VII by making an employment decision based on James's race.

Legal Concerns for the Integrationist Lens

In promoting integration, the Integrationist is likely to be conscious of a person's race, national origin, or membership in other categories protected under Title VII of the Civil Rights Act of 1964 or comparable state statutes. If you think you may use the Integrationist Lens, be aware of the following:

- Making decisions based on race, national origin, or any of the other protected categories is impermissible, even if the motivation for the decision seems noble. Employees may feel they are missing out on work opportunities if they are moved or given different job assignments for reasons unrelated to the merits of their performance. In rare instances, the law recognizes that a person's gender, national origin, or religion is a "bona fide occupational qualification" for a job (for example, you must be a woman to be an attendant in a woman's locker room).

Integrationist Highest Expression

What the Best of the **Integrationist Lens** Contributes to the Organization and Community

Fostering Cross-Cultural Mutuality

The Integrationist Lens seeks equity and understanding across cultures with emphasis on improving the historic disparity in the relationship between blacks and whites. The principal strategy of the Integrationist is to use the legal system to eliminate segregation in schools, neighborhoods, workplaces, and social institutions. The Integrationist hopes that increased cross-cultural contact will translate into increased understanding and a more equitable allocation of societal resources.

From a higher and more holistic perspective, the Integrationist continues to seek equity and understanding, but she evolves from focusing on eliminating segregation to fostering a sense of cross-cultural mutuality and relationship. She recognizes that being in proximity with each other is a key requirement for increasing understanding and equity, but it is not the goal. The reality is that we can live side by side and know little of who the other is; we can be colocated in schools and still choose to avoid mixing in social situations; we can be employed by the same organization and still migrate toward cultural ghettoes within the organization. Certainly, the laws and principles that foster integration are an essential starting point. However, we must add to these laws and principles the attitudes and skills that it takes to leverage integration into increased understanding and a more harmonious society.

The Integrationist recognizes that the dynamics of today's multicultural society require all of us to broaden the scope of our discussion to include the relationships among other cultural groups. In most major cities and institutions, the cross-cultural relationships between components of the Latin-American community and the African-American community and between the Latin-American community and Asian-American community also are strained by lack of understanding and inequities.

In its highest expression, the Integrationist acknowledges that we have no other sane choice but to be in relationship with one another and together. She knows that it takes a conscious decision to move beyond proximity and colocation toward a cross-cultural relationship based on mutuality in which we engage cooperatively with people from different cultures, each striving to understand the other's cultural perspectives, needs, and goals. The Integrationist recognizes that our interdependence requires us to invest in and act responsibly toward the relationship, without either party becoming submerged in it.

She believes that we can make this essential leap forward into cross-cultural mutuality if we all will reach out proactively to each other, have open and honest dialogue, identify win-win resolutions to conflicts, and are willing to engage in ongoing cross-cultural give and take based on respect and mutual valuing.

Integrationist Quotes

"Integration, no matter how painstakingly slow to achieve, is far preferable to voluntary segregation, 'an idea that the very worst racists would be all too happy to live with.' With integration, we take our chances on an unpredictable admixture of racial conflict and harmony. But without integration, there will be no possibility of interracial dialogue, no prospect for interracial friendship, and no potential for interracial understanding. Without racial integration, Americans will be left to sulk in a long Seclusionist silence."

J. Harvie Wilkinson, III. *One Nation Indivisible: How Ethnic Separatism Threatens America*. (New York: Addison-Wesley, 1997), 40.

"Men often hate each other because they fear each other; they fear each other because they do not know each other; they do not know each other because they cannot communicate; they cannot communicate because they are separated."

Dr. Martin Luther King, Jr., Online Source: Center for Healing Racism page. (Houston, Texas, March 7, 2001, http://www.centerhealingracism.org).

"Basically if you were to ask me what's the most important thing we could do, I think the more people work and learn and worship, if they have faith and serve together, the more likely you are to strike the right balance between celebrating our differences, instead of being afraid of them, and still identifying common values."

Bill Clinton. "Presidential Dialogue on Race," WETA-TV, PBS studio, Washington, DC. July 8, 1998.

"The imagination is integrative. That's how you make the new—by putting something else with what you've got. And I'm unashamedly an American integrationist."

Ralph Ellison, Online Source: Be More Creative Quotes, http://www.bemorecreative.com/one/441.htm.

Meritocratist

Meritocratist Archetype

Meet Jody Yamada

Jody is a thirty-seven-year-old second-generation Japanese American. She has an advanced engineering degree and leads a staff of 200 engineers who serve as senior project managers overseeing a variety of major construction projects for a large engineering and construction firm. Jody's work has been viewed as outstanding ever since she started with the company as an intern while she was still in college. Her rise through the ranks from associate to senior engineer to manager has been meteoric, and she is viewed as having the potential to join the ranks of executive management very soon.

Jody enjoys her role as a manager and believes that she does a good job of supervising her staff. She meets every two weeks with lead staff members to get an update on the status of key projects and discuss any problems they are encountering. She has made it clear that she is available to discuss professional development and career advancement with them whenever they are interested in doing so. She sees herself as a positive advocate for people who are dedicated, hardworking, and competent.

Recently, Jody was surprised to discover that three members of her staff—two blacks and a Hispanic—had sought career advice and guidance from another manager. They complained to the other manager that she mentors ineffectively and lacks sensitivity about the organization's bias against them. They believe the organization has a history of holding back qualified, non-Asian minorities.

Jody was flabbergasted to hear this. In her opinion, if these three employees would just "step up to the next level" in their work ethic, they would be just as successful as she has been. Jody contends her success is the result of a good education, her organizational skills, and her ability to present and defend ideas confidently in a highly competitive and demanding environment.

Since she started school, she and her family made her education and achievement the primary focus of their lives. From her perspective, she worked hard, made sacrifices, and reaped the rewards of all of her and her family's efforts.

She believes that she cannot help those on her staff who do not want to help themselves but rather blame "the system" for their lack of progress and success within the company.

Jody demonstrates a strong preference for the Meritocratist Lens.

Meritocratist Profile

The Meritocratist believes that the ladder to success is available to anyone who works hard enough to meet or exceed the predetermined standards at each rung along the way. The Meritocratist places a lot of weight on personal drive, self-sacrifice, and competent work. From her perspective, the individual gains respect and honor for her competitive spirit, mastery of the domain, and proven results. As with other lenses, the Meritocratist viewpoint varies in degrees and details among those who prefer this lens. However, Meritocratists all share the belief that what matters most is individual ability and achievement. They avoid identifying with a group and put their faith in self-reliance and individualism.

A central tenet of the Meritocratist belief system is that no one fails unless she has failed to work hard enough. When provided with examples of discrimination or societal barriers, she will begrudgingly admit that these obstacles do exist for some people. However, she will quickly add, "Everyone has obstacles to overcome. What separates successful people from those who are not is the individual's ability to overcome these obstacles." She will point to successful people across all groups and ask directly, "If they made it, why can't others?"

When the Meritocratist is a member of a minority group and has achieved more than other members of that group, she is likely to believe that it is her hard work that paid off. She is happy to help others whom she believes have the work ethic, skills, and determination to succeed, but she is disdainful of those of her racial or ethnic group who do not demonstrate the same drive.

The Meritocratist differs from the Elitist in her strong opposition to status being determined by anything other than personal achievement and competence. Whether the criteria used to bestow status are based on family lineage, social connections, and politics, or based on economic disadvantage and racial or ethnic group membership, the Meritocratist is equally opposed.

The strict Meritocratist has little sympathy for the legacies of past discrimination and the negative impact this may have had on some members of the organization. The Meritocratist starts the game with the here and now and looks curiously at those who use terms like "level the playing field." Nothing can be gained by correcting past legacies, she believes, except more unfairness and disadvantage for others. There cannot be a coherent workplace culture if it is riddled with special privileges based on race, gender, and other social criteria. That the system may be biased toward one or two groups in the organization, or that the inner workings and informal aspects of the organization may be mysterious and inaccessible to some, are not relevant from her perspective. She greets the suggestion that a diverse employee base will bring fresh perspectives to the organization with skepticism.

In keeping with their viewpoint, the Meritocratist says that quotas and affirmative action are not necessary. They tend to think that people who are the beneficiaries of affirmative action have been hired or promoted regardless of their professional qualifications. This lens wants to omit race and ethnic identity entirely as factors in any decision-making processes focused on organizational job or advancement opportunities. She prefers a simple question: If you were to fly on an airplane or have brain surgery, would you want the services of the best qualified pilot or doctor or the one who the organization had to hire to meet targets and goals?

The Meritocratist assumes that hiring and promotion decisions are based solely on stated objective criteria. She misses the subtle interpersonal implications of how an individual's style and cultural background influence the decision-maker's comfort level with a candidate. This intangible factor usually operates unconsciously and often is referred to as an individual's "fit" with the organization. For example, if a Meritocratist were assessing two candidates who were equally qualified and came from different races or cultures, the Meritocratist would never be able to believe that her unconscious bias in favor of one candidate's race or culture might skew the selection process. Instead, the Meritocratist would argue that two people cannot be equally qualified, and that if she continued to investigate, she would eventually find that one candidate had more experience or proven success than the other.

As a customer, the Meritocratist spends money in an organization that has a reputation for competent leadership; industrious, well-trained, and experienced staff; and excellent products and services. It is unlikely that the Meritocratist brings social agendas or cultural identity-group politics to the consumer process. The Meritocratist simply cannot tolerate incompetence of any sort and is likely to complain and give suggestions about how to improve less-than-perfect products or service transactions. In the process of focusing on whatever happened in a transaction, she is likely to be oblivious to cross-cultural dynamics and may offend those with whom she is interacting.

The Meritocratist typically supports the ban on the use of race as a factor in college admissions or the awarding of government contracts and the like. She argues for merit and high standards in our educational system, but she is uncomfortable when the dialogue turns to culturally biased tests. Overall, however, she thinks it is more detrimental to provide advantages of any kind when people have not really earned them. She favors initiatives like back-to-work programs so that people can pull themselves up by their own bootstraps and be proud of their accomplishments.

If the Meritocratist is a member of a group that is eligible for affirmative action, she may make no connection between her advancement and society's use of these programs. The Meritocratist points to distinguished people across all races and cultures who broke barriers in sports, the arts, business, government, and the military. She says that while laws and programs were attempting to eliminate unfair obstacles, these individuals forged their way ahead on the strength of their own merit. As a result, team members, coworkers, or society at large do not view these people as having attained their goals illegitimately because the standards were not lowered for them to succeed. Their courage and determination made it possible for others to follow on the same path and proved that merit alone is what counts.

Strengths and Shadows of the Meritocratist Lens

Strengths

Meritocratists:

- Are self-reliant and strong individualists
- Believe fervently in the American credo: if you have the ability and work hard enough, you can make your dreams come true, regardless of your race, gender, national origin, or other differences
- Insist that hard work, individual initiative, and self-sacrifice to meet or exceed given standards should be the only criteria used to determine opportunity in society and organizations
- Advocate for high standards of excellence in our institutions of education, commerce, and government
- Serve as guardians of fairness to ensure that organizational systems are applied fairly and evenly
- Believe every person counts
- Acknowledge and show support for the individual initiatives, competencies, and accomplishments demonstrated by others

Shadows

Meritocratists:

- May be insensitive to and/or unaware of the ways in which the organizational culture and infrastructure create barriers for certain groups based on their lack of "fit" with the predominant organization culture
- Focus on the need for the individual to find a way to overcome barriers, rather than acknowledging the existence of system inequities and seeking systematic change

- May demonstrate a subtle form of bigotry arising from unconscious biases—for example, certain groups may conjure up unconscious stereotypes and negative impressions for the Meritocrat, and if these are not challenged, she may respond to people with masked bias

Historical Perspective

The stories of American writer Horatio Alger capture the essence of the Meritocratist philosophy that one can rise from rags to riches through hard work and virtue. Prominent Meritocratists throughout our history have been of all colors and races. Examples include Benjamin Franklin, Frederick Douglass, Booker T. Washington, and Harry S Truman.

Douglass, a former slave, once called by President Lincoln "the most meritorious man in the United States," was driven by his own belief that "the true basis of rights is the capacity of individuals." In the late nineteenth and early twentieth centuries, Booker T. Washington headed Tuskegee Institute, a college for blacks in Alabama. He believed that we should be valued for our knowledge and skills and that these abilities would always take primacy over race, gender, or social origin. He wrote that:

... there is something in human nature which we cannot blot out, which makes one man, in the end, recognize and reward merit in another, regardless of color or race.

Anne Wortham, The Other Side of Racism: A Philosophical Study of Black Race Consciousness (Ohio State University Press, 1981) 287.

From Abraham Lincoln to Bill Clinton, the highest position of leadership in America has been occupied by people who have had to struggle against economic, social, and political odds on the way to becoming president. Harry Truman was a humble farmer who failed as a shopkeeper. His quick intelligence, work ethic, and courage were admired by all, however, and paved the way for his ascendancy in politics.

General Colin Powell, the first black American ever to hold the positions of National Security Advisor to Ronald Reagan and Secretary of State under George W. Bush, is an exemplary Meritocratist with deep roots in the black community and his Jamaican heritage. Of his career, he says:

My career should serve as a model to fellow blacks, in or out of the military, in demonstrating the possibilities of American life. I hoped then and now that my rise might cause prejudiced whites to question their prejudices and help purge the poison of racism from their systems, so that the next qualified African American who came along would be judged on merit alone.

The Meritocratist Lens at Work

Motivation and Career Advancement from the Meritocratist's Perspective

The Meritocratist is motivated by the belief that she can achieve whatever she wants to achieve as long as she acquires the necessary education and skills, works hard, and is willing to pay the required "dues." Evidence that top management appreciates and rewards the kind of dedication and commitment that the Meritocratist is eager to demonstrate fuels her readiness to give the organization the best she is capable of giving—which is a lot. She is demotivated by any efforts on the part of the organization to initiate affirmative action programs, even if such programs are meant to support members of her own racial or ethnic group.

In line with her straightforward belief system that merit is recognized and rewarded, the Meritocratist's career advancement strategy is equally simple and direct: demonstrate the experience, business knowledge, technical competencies, interpersonal relationships, and loyalty required to assume a senior position in the organization. She will also remind those in decision-making positions of times when she has taken the initiative and substantially contributed to the organization's success. Once the Meritocratist has done her best to make her case, she sits back and trusts that the company will select the best person for promotion into the job.

Impacts of This Strategy on the Individual's Advancement Potential

If the Meritocratist holds the same identity characteristics as the dominant group in the organization and there is a good fit between her style and the organization's culture, the Meritocratist is soon seated on "Executive Row." In these cases the Meritocratist remains oblivious to the importance of membership identity and style in gaining access to senior positions. However, if the fit is not there, the Meritocratist finds herself nonplussed as to why someone else was selected for the position when the Meritocratist clearly had the greater experience and business knowledge for the job. In some cases, she asks questions and perhaps is mentored by someone with more understanding and political savvy. In other cases, the Meritocratist may simply become demoralized and unwilling to work as hard in the future, since she is not getting what she thinks she deserves from the company.

Impacts of This Strategy on the Organization's Human Resources

When those who believe in promotion based on merit do get promoted, this strategy can serve as a source of motivation for everyone who is willing to work hard to get ahead in the organization. When the hidden criteria of membership identity, style, or connections are used to decide who should get promoted into senior ranks, employees may become demoralized when they see people who they do not think are as well qualified advance ahead of those who they think are—including themselves.

Working with the Meritocratist

If you are working with or managing a person who has a strong preference for the Meritocratist Lens, the likelihood is that she has been influenced by legacies and layers that emphasize personal initiative and abilities and wants to relate along the following dimensions:

- Having the self confidence, determination, and discipline to go after what you want
- Being able and willing to take on whatever obstacles are in the way
- Having gained the right experience, credentials, track record, and respect to earn the job you are in

In those cases when you are experiencing confusion or tension during discussions with this employee, it may be because you have prioritized your layers differently or other lenses may be operating unconsciously. The following guidelines may help in these situations:

- Understand that the belief in personal responsibility for one's successes and failures is at the core of the Meritocratist's approach to organizational life; rejection of special programs like affirmative action does not stem from a desire to keep others down but rather from this core belief.
- With this in mind, do not jump to the conclusion that someone who is opposed to special programs and initiatives is biased, racist, or prejudiced. Also, keep in mind that the Meritocratist usually is oblivious to cultural biases or discriminatory practices within the organization.
- Acknowledge that when a Meritocratist is made aware of a discriminatory practice within the organization, she usually is upset and ready to take action to try to eliminate the practice.

Coaching the Meritocratist Manager or Supervisor

A person with a strong preference for the Meritocratist Lens believes that individual initiative can overcome any obstacle. She may not recognize that people who overcome significant obstacles are the exception rather than the rule. The Meritocratist has a difficult time understanding that different groups have different ways of defining competency and merit. Because she is so focused on individual abilities and work habits, the Meritocratist manager or supervisor is unlikely to pay attention to cultural biases in the organization that may be creating inequalities among employees on the basis of racial or cultural stereotypes.

Unmonitored and undeveloped, the Meritocratist stance could lead to charges of bias from a variety of cultural groups and create a perception that your organization is perpetuating a "good-old-boy" network. Your job as a manager and a leader in your organization is to coach the Meritocratist so she is competent, confident, and willing to use or modify the organization's systems on behalf of all employees.

Specifically, you can require the Meritocratist to use the organization's systems in ways that:

- Respond with sensitivity and flexibility to the multiple differences your employees are bringing to the workforce. In today's business world, "one size" does not fit all; different demographic groups within your workforce need and expect customized benefits and policies just as customers do.

- Ensure organizational support for those individuals who want to compensate for the lack of educational opportunities and skill development earlier in their lives by furthering their education and training now.

- Broaden the accepted criteria for work styles to reflect the style attributes of today's multicultural workforce.

The Meritocratist and Organizational Systems

The Meritocratist is focused on the consistent, objective application of the organization's human resources management systems. She wants each person to compete for hiring and advancement under the same rules and to have agreed-upon standards and measurements before the competition for opportunity begins. The Meritocratist stance could have the impact of delegitimizing programs that your organization has created to provide support for the needs of various groups in the workforce. When this stance is predominant in the organization, the beneficiaries of such programs often are perceived as having achieved their positions in an illegitimate manner.

Each of the lenses influences the organization's human resources systems in different ways. The essence of the ways in which the Meritocratist Lens influences these systems is presented in each of the statements below. As you review these statements, think of the impact of the Meritocratist stance on these same types of programs and activities in your work environment.

Meritocratist Stance: "I will use the organization's human resources systems to establish objectively based criteria for hiring, development, and promotion, and to hold each person to these criteria. I do not want the organization to make exceptions based on cultural group membership, social status, or politics."

Recruiting: "I want to recruit from schools that have a record of producing competent graduates who excel in their field of study."

Hiring: "I will hire people who are qualified based on our standards."

Compensation and benefits: "I will reward people based on performance and dedication. Everyone should have the same opportunity to reap the benefits of what they have helped accomplish."

Job placement: "I will place people in positions that match their experience, education, and abilities."

Building Effective teams: "I will create the best team possible, drawing from those who have demonstrated their capabilities, loyalties, and willingness to work hard."

Performance Management: "I will give people honest and specific feedback about the deficiencies I perceive in their job performance so that they have the opportunity to make the improvements necessary within a reasonable time period."

Mentoring: "I will identify and select people to mentor who have demonstrated the raw talent and potential to succeed in this organization."

Training: "I want training programs to focus on important core competencies that our employees need to perform at the highest possible level."

Succession Planning: "I will use our succession planning program to identify people with demonstrated track records and high potential and place them in positions where they will acquire the necessary experience to assume higher management positions in the future."

The Meritocratist and the Law

The Meritocratist Lens could affect your business' bottom line in several ways. As you read the hypothetical following case, consider whether your organization may be manifesting the Meritocratist Lens in some of these same ways.

The Case

Money Movers, a prestigious investment firm in New York City, is in the midst of its recruiting season. John Moore, the human resources manager, recently read a newspaper article stating that Latinos and African Americans sometimes get admitted to Ivy League business institutions with lower than average Graduate Management Admission Test (GMAT) scores. Mr. Moore sends a memo to firm interviewers requesting that they ask all Latino and African-American applicants for their GMAT scores. Mr. Moore's memo explains that the new policy is to ensure that the firm maintains its reputation as the number one employer of top-notch investment bankers. Pedro Martinez, John Case, and Bill Wilkinson are enrolled in the Masters in Business Administration program at Harvard and have interviewed at Money Movers. Mr. Martinez is Cuban American. Mr. Case and Mr. Wilkinson are both white. After their interviews, they meet outside to discuss the interview process.

Mr. Martinez: Hey, did you guys think it was strange that they asked about GMAT scores?

Mr. Case: I was not asked about my GMAT score. Are you serious?

Mr. Wilkinson: I wasn't asked about my scores either. The interviewer asked me how I did in Corporate Finance but not about my scores.

Mr. Martinez: That's funny. At the last Latino Business Students Association meeting, I remember a bunch of people said that they were asked their GMAT scores during their interview at Money Movers. I was so worried about my scores that I prepared a two-minute answer to explain my low scores. I must have sounded really rehearsed and nervous during my interview.

Mr. Case and Mr. Wilkinson are hired for positions at Money Movers. Mr. Martinez is not hired. He sues the company claiming that he was not hired because he is Latino. Who wins?

Result

Mr. Martinez would win. Title VII prohibits subjecting people to differing criteria based on national origin. Mr. Martinez was treated differently because he is Latino. Interviewers only elicited GMAT scores from African-American and Latino applicants. Therefore, he would have a strong claim under Title VII for national origin discrimination.

Legal Concerns for the Meritocratist Lens

The Meritocratist focuses on assessments of merit to which the Meritocratist can relate. If you think you may use the Meritocratist Lens, be aware of the following:

1. Assuming that a person who has not achieved like the Meritocratist is incapable of performing may lead to exclusions of persons in protected categories that are underrepresented in a company's workforce.

"I don't want to interview any applicants who haven't achieved the highest grades in school."

2. Focusing disproportionately on conventional predictors of job performance may ignore valid alternative measures of merit. Apparently objective standards of measure—such as number of years in the workforce or the number of hours logged on the job or the number of trips taken—may underestimate the skills and work-translatable experience of, for example:

   - Women who are returning to the workforce after an absence for child-rearing
   - People with disabilities for whom reasonable accommodations only recently have become available
   - People of different national origins in the process of adapting to American culture

Meritocratist Highest Expression

What the Best of the **Meritocratist Lens** Contributes to the Organization and Community

Creating Equitable Systems

The Meritocratist is a poster child for the notion that we are independent beings, each born with the capacity to choose our destiny and create our reality through everyday choices. Although the mountain may be steep and difficult to climb, the Meritocratist believes that we must summon the courage to attempt the climb. When the Meritocratist succeeds, she is convinced that she is reaping the rewards of her effort. In emphasizing personal responsibility for our successes and failures, the Meritocratist challenges us to resist the notion that our destinies are shaped by powerful forces outside of our control.

From this original stance, the Meritocratist sees the game of life as requiring everyone to compete against one another in organizations and in the larger society with the prize going in the end to the best—i.e., most competent—person. From a higher, more holistic perspective, the Meritocratist continues to advocate personal responsibility, but she moves from a position of blind faith in, or disregard about, the fairness of the game to a desire to ensure that the rules of the game are equitable for all. She realizes that organizations have built-in preferences for certain types of people who demonstrate certain types of cultural characteristics. Furthermore, the Meritocratist understands that organizational systems perpetuate the cultural qualities and styles of the people who originate and control them. The Meritocratist acknowledges that gaining acceptance, recognition, and opportunity is more difficult for individuals who do not mirror the accepted cultural style of the organization.

For example, a colorful and extroverted interpersonal style may close the door to more senior opportunities within an organization for person A, while the door is opened by the more measured and reserved style of person B. Both individuals may have the same capabilities required to perform the job, but they have very different interpersonal styles that have been fostered by their different cultural identities. If awarded the opportunity, employee B may believe that talent and hard work earned the opportunity, unaware that her interpersonal style was of a better "fit" with the organization's culture. Employee B may never consider that the opportunity was not totally based on merit and that Employee A was eliminated from consideration due to a criterion that had nothing to do with actual job performance. Organization life is filled with examples of how cultural identity-group styles influence recognition, advancement, and opportunity.

In its highest expression, the Meritocratist Lens willingly plays a role in changing formal and informal systems so that the organization measures competence from a perspective that includes the acceptance of a broader range of cultural styles. She comes to believe that the use of any of the styles within the new broader set of cultural norms can produce similar results, and she is not satisfied until the gap is considerably narrowed between those employees who have benefited from the "fit" of their cultural style and those who have not. Then, and only then, the Meritocratist now realizes, will everyone be allowed to compete fairly and to taste success based on individual initiative.

Meritocratist Quotes

"The country has changed during the near-century of the NAACP's existence, but the organization has stayed the same. It still preaches the gospel of victimhood and reliance on government, instead of self-reliance. One longed to hear the testimonies of Tiger Woods or Venus and Serena Williams—how they prospered not by focusing on the color of their skin but by the swing of a club or tennis racket in games that have been almost exclusively dominated by whites. In recent interviews, Woods and the Williams sisters spoke of persistence and never accepting defeat, of long hours and of fathers who loved and encouraged them. More than legislation, black families, like all families, need a father in the home. The politics of race gets the Democrats' votes but does little for the people who need to be told that their salvation does not lie on the road to Washington. Race politics doesn't communicate that the poor among them can make it just as their middle- and upper-class black brothers and sisters have done—through hard work, intact families and never accepting defeat as the final answer."

Cal Thomas, "The Compassion Tour Does the NAACP,"
Online Magazine: *Jewish World Review*, July 14, 2000.
www.Jewishworldreview.com/cols/thomas071400.asp.

"If Bush wins in November, Rice is likely to be his national security adviser and Powell his secretary of state—African Americans both. That may not mean that the Republican Party is once again truly the Party of Lincoln—but it does mean it's not your old man's GOP either... Powell and Rice send precisely the right message. They may owe a measure of their charisma to their racial identity and personal sagas, but they are not in the least black spokespeople. If they wind up in a Bush administration, it will be on account of ability and experience, not because they represent a particular constituency or a racial agenda."

Richard Cohen, "Diversity: It's Not All Phony"
The Washington Post, August 3, 2000, A29.

"God gives food to every bird, but does not throw it into the nest."

Montenegrin Proverb

"The individual who can do something that the world wants done will, in the end, make his way regardless of his race."

Booker T. Washington, *Up from Slavery: An Autobiography*.
(New York: Doubleday, 1901), 114.

"My parents taught me the founding principles of this country, the principles of freedom and opportunity, the value of hard work, the need to ensure that every man and woman is compensated fairly for their hard work."

Elaine Chao, Secretary of Labor, "Profile on Elaine Chao," Associated Press, January 12, 2001.

"What is success? I think it is a mixture of having a flair for the thing that you are doing; knowing that it is not enough, that you have got to have hard work and a certain sense of purpose."

Margaret Thatcher, *Great Quotes from Great Women*, ed. Peggy Anderson. (Illinois: Celebrating Excellence Publishing, 1992), 15.

Multiculturalist

Multiculturalist Archetype

Meet Dr. Loraine Berry

Loraine Berry is a vice president of diversity for a manufacturing company with 20,000 employees. She is considered quite accomplished in her profession and was offered several other opportunities before accepting the job at her current company. She is responsible for developing the company's strategic plan to incorporate diversity into its business processes and human resources management systems. At present, the company is considering initiating overseas operations or acquiring an overseas company as a way of lowering production costs and competing globally. The chief executive officer of the manufacturing company recognizes that this makes it all the more important for the company to understand and be able to manage a culturally diverse workforce.

Loraine works closely with the departments of human resources, advertising, and corporate image, as well as with vendor programs in executing her responsibilities. With her extensive knowledge and excellent interpersonal skills, she has been able to assume a highly influential role with the managers of these departments, as well as with the chief executive officer. She recently made a presentation to him and won his support to institute a bonus program for senior managers who meet diversity-related goals that she and the human resources department established last year. For the most part, these managers are opposed to the initiative because they believe that the diversity goals interfere with accomplishing business results, such as meeting sales and production quotas.

On a number of occasions in the year since she arrived, Loraine has managed to disturb her senior colleagues, with actions such as the introduction of diversity goals and the recent bonus program for senior managers. Another of her initiatives was to establish an organization culture advisory committee, consisting of representatives from the different racial, ethnic, and cultural groups in the workforce, whose purpose is to advise her on the need for new organizational systems, policies, and practices designed to be inclusive of all groups. While the committee is only advisory in nature, most of its recommendations have been adopted for implementation and, in several cases, have been perceived by the senior-line managers as creating "busy work" for them while making it increasingly difficult to get the "real work" done.

Loraine's activities and initiatives have been described as dangerously out of touch with the demands of running a business and are a source of deep concern to many of her senior colleagues. They say that since she has no bottom-line accountability, it is easy for her to add new requirements, change standards, and shift measurements without sufficient thought about the impact of these changes on business activities.

Loraine believes their complaints are standard resistance from "dinosaurs" who will be left behind as the company moves forward with the changing times. She thinks that most of the managers in the company do not appreciate how the future of the company depends on successfully implemented diversity initiatives. It is imperative, for example, that the company recruits workers from all over the world to staff and manage international operations; that the company understands and is able to comply with international laws and requirements that will affect global operations and global sales; that the company demonstrates its understanding and appreciation of racial, ethnic, and cultural diversity to its customers and employees who represent these different populations.

Loraine has identified a small group of "new-thought" managers and created a fast-track program to get them into rotation for senior jobs. In this way, she eventually will have support from company leaders who understand how important diversity is to the future of the business as it attempts to broaden its products and customer base in an age of increased global competition.

Loraine demonstrates a strong preference for the Multiculturalist Lens.

Multiculturalist Profile

The Multiculturalist celebrates and honors the diversity of cultures, emphasizing their value to our national character and history. Through this lens, there is a reconsideration of traditional history and recognition of the contributions that each culture has made to our national heritage.

The Multiculturalist strongly supports and works for the retention of the customs, languages, and abilities of people who come from other cultures, as well as those ethnic minorities who have been a part of this country since its beginnings. In contrast to the Assimilationist's image of America as a melting pot, the Multiculturalist sees it as a mosaic or kaleidoscope of different ethnicities. This mosaic contributes to the whole while still preserving and developing the qualities that are distinct to each culture. The Multiculturalist wants to prevent the transformation of distinct ethnic groups into Anglo homogeneity.

The Multiculturalist believes the world would be very dull if everyone looked, spoke, thought, and acted the same. She moves effortlessly through a mix of ethnic landscapes, intrigued by varied cuisines, dress, music, smells, languages, rituals, dwellings, and religious traditions. She likes the idea of combining the influences of many different cultures and races to create a true world view.

The Multiculturalist thinks that we must establish new systems, policies, values, and customs that are inclusive of all cultures. She abhors ranking systems that judge or compare cultures to one another, preferring to see them as unique with each one having contributions to make and gifts to share. She feels strongly about the rightness of this position and often has a kind of zeal that is experienced as intense.

In the work environment, the Multiculturalist wants to incorporate all cultural perspectives and experiences into every aspect of organization life. She understands the value of creating and sustaining an organizational culture that values diversity, and she knows how to use diversity as a competitive advantage. It is her firm belief that today's organization needs culturally diverse employees to adequately understand, serve, and leverage cultural niche markets and emerging markets.

The Multiculturalist leverages organizational systems to implement her beliefs and ensure diversity within every part of the business enterprise, from the boardroom to the shop floor. She supports programs such as affirmative action and targeted recruiting from institutions that are culturally diverse. She advocates strongly for affinity groups that provide support, networking, and career strategies for success to those employees in the cultural minority. She urges that the informal and formal policies and norms of the organization shift to be more inclusive and reflective of the multicultural workforce—that the style of communication, dress codes, social activities, celebration of holidays, even the food being served in the cafeteria, should all be reevaluated based on multicultural criteria.

The Multiculturalist uses difference in cultural perspective as a competence when hiring if she believes that this will contribute to a work team's performance, even though the candidate being considered may not have all the traditional prerequisite experience. The Multiculturalist argues that the standards are biased and that they were created in an era of monocultural reality. To be truly fair, the Multiculturalist argues, we need new standards and criteria that take into account what different cultures have used in assessing competencies.

The Multiculturalist wants organizational change *now* and can be insensitive about the fact that people need time to adjust, reorient themselves, and deal with the resistance that may arise from being part of a multicultural workforce. The Multiculturalist can be insensitive about treating people first as members of their racial, ethnic, or cultural groups, and only then as individuals.

A Multiculturalist customer might say, "I will spend my money in an organization that embraces cultural diversity and models it at all levels of the organization by employing a diverse workforce, delivering products and services to meet specific cultural needs, and reaching out to the communities in which it employs its workforce." The Multiculturalist customer is always scanning the environment to assess how businesses are doing on the cultural competency scale. She is very aware of how people from different cultural backgrounds are being treated and can usually identify the weaknesses and challenges inherent in the organization's understanding and use of diversity as a competitive advantage.

In the community, the Multiculturalist, like the Integrationist, works hard to bring racial understanding to everyone. Unlike the Integrationist, however, the Multiculturalist is not focused on the black/white issues of the 1960s and 1970s but rather on the acknowledgment and synthesis of varied ethnic and cultural contributions. The Multiculturalist typically understands that our society is in transition from viewing diversity exclusively in black-and-white terms to recognizing the need to adapt to a truly multiracial populace. However, at the same time, she can fail to see whites as a cultural group, completely missing the needs of populations within the white group based on class, and she can de-emphasize the need for people of color to develop increased sensitivity and understanding within their own groups.

The Multiculturalist Lens has gained prominence and influence in making today's classrooms and workplaces comfortable for those whose primary culture is not European. The Multiculturalist is active in ensuring bilingual education, and she has remained a soldier in battles over affirmative action. Her rallying call is that minority groups will constitute the majority of people residing in the United States by 2020, according to the U.S. Census Bureau. Multiculturalists are working to refashion this country, our communities, and basic institutions in ways that reflect and respect our cultural diversity.

Multiculturalist Strength and Shadows

There are many attributes to the Multiculturalist Lens. Some of the primary Strengths and Shadows of the lens are listed below.

Strengths

Multiculturalists:

- Cherish and encourage an America that includes and honors all cultures without emphasizing the importance of one over the other

- Understand that, in the words of poet Audre Lorde, "it is not our differences that divide us; it is our inability to recognize, accept, and celebrate those differences"

- Remind us that America has been pluralist from the start and that it would not have prospered and developed its rich heritage without the contributions of all ethnicities

- Help the rest of us to get beyond our narrow perspectives and develop a more expansive worldview

- Know how to create inclusive work teams that incorporate all perspectives and experiences

- Help create and sustain organizational cultures that value diversity and understand how to use diversity as a competitive advantage in the global marketplace

Shadows

Multiculturalists:

- May be overly focused on cultural differences and unwilling to identify and commit to common values, goals, standards and norms for the organization

- Can overemphasize racial, ethnic, or cultural group membership, making individuals feel depersonalized and seen only as part of a group rather than as individuals

- May contribute to divisiveness in the workforce by being excessively critical of white, middle-class, heterosexual men of European descent simply because they represent the historic majority and ruling class in our society and organizations

- May not always tie initiatives to clear business goals

- May not recognize or be skilled at managing the change process

- May appear as preachy, self-righteous, and impatient

Historical Perspective

The roots of multiculturalism go back to the early stages of our union. In addition to the original inhabitants, many other ethnicities came in search of security, opportunity, and freedom in America. Words of our greatest leaders and thinkers remain to illustrate how long this ideal has existed: President John Adams spoke of a "wonderful mixture of nations," author Herman Melville saw America as an "ethnographic panorama," and poet Walt Whitman viewed the country as a "nation of nations."

Horace Kallen introduced the idea of cultural pluralism in 1915 in his article "Democracy Versus the Melting Pot." Examining the roots and legacies of Multiculturalist thought, author Stephen Steinberg explains that:

[Kallen's] vision of America was of a "democracy of nationalities," where ethnic groups would share an overriding loyalty to the nation and participate in its political and economic life, but still be free to cultivate their ethnic differences.

Kallen likened the emerging populace to a symphony orchestra, arguing that union would be achieved not through uniformity but through a harmony among the parts. Kallen's premise, and that of cultural pluralists ever since, is that "democracy involves not the elimination of differences but the perfection and conservation of differences."

Immigration to the United States has been slowly increasing since the 1940s, after a decline during World War II. According to the U.S. Census Bureau, the immigrant population has slowly increased over the past thirty years from 9.7 million, or 5.4 percent of the population, to 14.1 million, or 6.2 percent in 1990.

Over the years, the ethnicity and culture of immigrant groups have changed. Recordkeeping with respect to immigration began in 1820. The trend until 1970 was that most foreign born came from Europe. However, in the past thirty years, European immigrants accounted for only 2.7 percent of the 15 million newcomers. As of 2000, 28.4 million foreign born were living in the United States. This figure represents 10 percent of the total population. Of this percentage, 50 percent of the immigrant population comes from Latin America and 25 percent from Asia; put differently, 75 percent of the immigrant population comes from non-European countries.

In the 1980s, companies began to realize that many different cultural groups might want different products or services from those currently offered to the mainstream—or might buy more mainstream products and services if these were advertised in ways that appealed directly to them. This was the beginning of cultural niche marketing, which has become a major source of revenues for many businesses.

Cultural niche marketing has served to reinforce the idea that America in the twenty-first century is truly a multicultural country. The binary lens of a black-and-white society no longer works because it attempts to simplify complicated issues of cultural identity and ignores our tremendous diversity. Affirmative action involves Americans of all races. The question of bilingual education affects all citizens. The creation of the multiracial category on the census has an impact on people of all shades of color. Each of us is affected and enriched in countless ways by the multicultural realities of the world in which we live as contemporary Americans.

The Multiculturalist Lens at Work

Motivation and Career Advancement from the Multiculturalist's Perspective

The Multiculturalist cares deeply about creating inclusive workplaces in which individuals from all racial, ethnic, and cultural groups are welcomed, respected, and appreciated. If given the opportunity, she works tirelessly on changing the organization's policies and norms to reflect different cultural influences rather than Eurocentric traditions. She excels at positions calling for interaction with organization members or customers representing different racial and ethnic groups. The Multiculturalist also is interested in, and effective at, creating culturally diverse coalitions and work teams.

When the Multiculturalist is a member of a cultural minority, her career advancement strategy is likely to begin with the recognition that there are few or none of "my kind" in the upper ranks of this organization and that the company needs more diversity in these ranks. She emphasizes this when she announces her interest in being considered for an opening to those in decision-making positions. She networks with those who feel the same way that she does about the importance of diversity and asks them for their support.

When the Multiculturalist is a member of the dominant group in the organization, she begins with the recognition that there is not enough diversity in the ranks of management and senior management. She thinks in terms of the need to make a concerted effort to seek out individuals from different membership groups and discover what it would take to get them interested in serving in these positions. She focuses on the need to create a more inclusive culture, starting at the top of the organization.

Impacts of These Strategies on the Individual's Advancement Potential

If an organization recognizes its need for more diversity in management and executive ranks and the Multiculturalist is appropriately qualified for such positions, these strategies have very positive consequences for the individual's career advancement. However, if the individual is the first member of a diverse identity group to become a part of upper management and has a style that does not fit easily with the predominant culture, she and the rest of the management team are in for a difficult adjustment period. If the organization does not recognize a need for more diversity and/or the individual is not appropriately qualified, these strategies are likely to backfire. Members of the dominant group of the management team are likely to feel burdened by the presence of someone who has been "foisted" on them in the name of diversity without having the appropriate qualifications to carry a fair share of the load. They find subtle or overt ways of taking their frustrations out on the individual.

Impacts of These Strategies on the Organization's Human Resources

All people of difference in the organization will have the experience of feeling more valued and included when these strategies are successfully implemented by, or on behalf of, well-qualified individuals from diverse membership groups. However, if the perception is that individuals were promoted primarily to add some diversity to management or executive ranks, rather than because the individuals were the best qualified, these strategies will have negative consequences. Members of the dominant group are likely to resent this evidence of reverse discrimination, and all members of the organization are likely to believe that standards have been lowered to satisfy legal or public-relations requirements. The action may be interpreted by all as an indication that the organization equates diversity with inferior capabilities. Other negative consequences may well include legal actions being taken against the organization.

Working with the Multiculturalist

If you are working with or managing a person who has a strong preference for Multiculturalist views, you are likely to find that the layers that are most important to them are those focusing on cultural diversity, specifically race, color, ethnicity, and nationality. The questions and concerns that the Multiculturalist emphasizes include:

- How can we eliminate prejudice so that you are free to thrive in our organizational culture and society?
- How can we preserve the best of your ethnic differences so we can leverage them to our competitive advantage?
- How can your group bring new business perspectives to our workplace?
- How can we learn from you so that we can be better prepared to do business in or attract customers from your country of origin?

You and the employee may be speaking from entirely different layers. If you are feeling defensive or confused during a conversation or there is tension between you, it may help to keep the following guidelines in mind:

- Acknowledge that the Multiculturalist's core motivation is to be inclusive of all groups, not to put down the historical majority in this country.
- If she is being insensitive in her remarks about the historical majority, or in treating you as a member of a group rather than an individual, tactfully tell her so.

- Recognize that the Multiculturalist often sees a business advantage to inclusiveness and is not always working a "hidden social agenda."
- Understand that the Multiculturalist believes passionately in the "rightness" of her position from both a business and moral perspective and may have trouble seeing the validity in the positions of other lenses.

Coaching the Multiculturalist Manager or Supervisor

A manager or supervisor with a strong preference for the Multiculturalist Lens can be so intent on developing social initiatives to create an inclusive organizational culture that she can have difficulty clearly linking such initiatives to business needs. She may have a tendency to de-emphasize traditional organization values and norms in favor of diverse cultural practices. With her priority on diversity, it may be difficult to focus on the skills and abilities of employees rather than on representation of different cultural groups when making decisions about employee assignments. In developing marketing and sales strategies, this lens may overemphasize inclusion and try to be "all things to all people."

Unmonitored and underdeveloped, the Multiculturalist stance can lead to charges of reverse discrimination and poor use of organization and human resources. Your job as a manager and leader in your organization is to coach the Multiculturalist so that she is competent, confident, and willing to use or modify the organization's systems on behalf of all employees.

Specifically, you can require the Multiculturalist to use the organization's systems in ways that:

- Establish and clearly communicate the business need for any social initiatives
- Ensure that all members of the organization subscribe to a set of common values and business practices that are recognized as the organization's way of doing business and that supersede the beliefs and traditions of subcultures within the organization
- Guarantee that diversity is used as only one key factor in the decision-making process, recognizing that it cannot be the primary decision-making criterion in lieu of other important business needs
- Target specific markets for the organization's marketing and sales efforts based on sound business analyses

The Multiculturalist and Organizational Systems

The Multiculturalist has a strong desire to change, enhance, develop, or eliminate organizational systems in the name of creating a valuing organizational culture. The Multiculturalist believes that these changes are vital to the future of the organization to compete in a multicultural and global environment. The

Multiculturalist can adopt a "righteous" moral fervor. When she combines moral persuasion with perceived business need, she can be quite a formidable advocate for change. At times, she can force the organization to fit perhaps unsuitably qualified people into opportunities and positions for the sake of diversity. This can leave the organization vulnerable to claims of reverse discrimination and bias.

Each of the lenses influences the organization's human resources systems in different ways. The essence of the ways in which the Multiculturalist Lens influences these systems is presented in each of the statements below. As you review these statements, think of the impact of the Multiculturalist stance on these same types of programs and activities in your work environment.

Multicultural Stance: "I will use the organization's systems to build and sustain an inclusive work environment that values people from all cultures. Today's global marketplace requires this type of culture and enables us to use diversity as a competitive advantage."

Recruiting: "I will recruit from a wide variety of institutions to create a culturally diverse applicant pool."

Hiring: "I will hire the most qualified talent to create culturally diverse perspectives in all aspects of our business."

Compensation and Benefits: "I will create programs that appeal to a variety of employees based on their needs and offer flexibility to employees to choose the benefits that most appeal to them."

Job Placement and Assignments: "I will assign employees with culturally diverse perspectives to each work group and utilize these different perspectives to create competitive advantage."

Building Effective Teams: "I will make sure that cultural diversity is a requirement for all of our teams."

Performance Management: "I will advocate systems that give managers direct feedback from all levels about how they are managing diversity, and I will hold them accountable based on the results."

Mentoring: "I will create policies and programs to ensure that our culturally diverse employees are receiving the proper career guidance at critical points in their careers, and I will hold senior leaders responsible for executing these programs."

Training: "I will make sure that the training programs are sensitive to the cultural diversity in our organization and use multilingual training and alternative forms of communication as appropriate."

Succession Planning: "I will advocate that all pathways to career advancement are open and actively recruit candidates who are culturally diverse."

The Multiculturalist and the Law

The Multiculturalist Lens could affect your business' bottom line in several ways. As you read the following hypothetical case, consider whether your organization may be manifesting the Multiculturalist Lens in similar ways.

The Case

Paul is a supervisor at a midsize marketing firm who faced the difficult decision of selecting between two mid-level employees for a promotion to manager. After considering the employment record, training, longevity, and recommendations of both employees, he decided to promote Vicki, an African-American female. Andrew, the other employee, came to talk to Paul:

Andrew: I just can't figure out why you promoted Vicki instead of me. I've been here longer, I've worked longer hours, I have more training—you've basically groomed me for this position since I first came here.

Paul: Andrew, I know that you have a good record with this company. But you know that we've been under fire for not promoting enough women and minorities. I just couldn't pass up the opportunity to promote an African-American woman.

Andrew: I understand that you've had a problem in the past, but why should I pay for that? You are basically telling me that hard work and dedication no longer count here.

Paul: That's not true. But Vicki has an impressive background. Whatever she lacks in experience is more than made up for in the new perspective she'll bring to management. Just be patient. Your turn will come soon enough.

Angry at being passed over for promotion, Andrew sues. Result?

Result

Andrew wins. Paul's multicultural lens led him to base his employment decision on Vicki's membership in two protected groups. As a result, Paul discriminated against Andrew by using Andrew's race as a factor against Andrew in making his employment decision. Using a person's protected status as a factor in decisionmaking violates Title VII of the Civil Rights Act of 1964. Ironically, one problem with multiculturalism may be stereotyping—assuming that a member of a minority will speak as a representative for the entire class of minorities, offering the "black perspective" or "female perspective."

Although this hypothetical case involves two applicants who are not equally qualified, it is not clear what the result would be if both candidates were equally qualified. The Supreme Court was presented with a similar case in *United States v. Board of Education of the Township of Piscataway*, 91 F.3d 1547 (3d Cir. 1996) (en banc), cert. granted 521 U.S. 1117 (1997). But the case settled before the court could issue a decision. The case involved a school board that applied its affirmative action plan in deciding to lay off a white employee instead of an equally qualified African-American employee.

Legal Concerns for the Multiculturalist Lens

To pursue the values of multiculturalism, the Multiculturalist is conscious of the cultural backgrounds of applicants and employees. If you think you may use the Multiculturalist Lens, be aware of the following:

- Using a person's cultural background as a factor in decisionmaking about hiring or job assignments may lead to conduct that may violate Title VII of the Civil Rights Act of 1964 or comparable state laws.

    "We really have too many white males in this department; of these two candidates, I'd prefer the [African-American/Hispanic/Asian-American] candidate."

Multiculturalist Highest Expression

What the Best of the **Multiculturalist Lens** Contributes to the Organization and Community

Creating Synergistic Governance

The Multiculturalist Lens, in its original stance, seeks to foster the valuing, inclusion, and celebration of all cultures. From a higher, more holistic perspective, the Multiculturalist understands that in addition to honoring our cultural differences we also must create governance mechanisms—laws, policies, norms—that enable us to govern our relationships across cultural differences and manage the dilemmas associated with living and working in a multicultural society effectively.

In its highest expression, the Multiculturalist Lens knows that sensitivity to and appreciation of our differences are not enough and cannot serve as the end game for our multicultural society. She recognizes that deeper understanding across cultural differences does not automatically translate into tangible or concrete guidelines to help us manage our daily cross-cultural interactions in schools, workplaces, and communities.

Appreciation does not tell us whose history to teach or how to craft an advancement strategy within an organization that avoids the appearance of reverse discrimination. Greater sensitivity does not instruct us in how to honor the spirit and intent of numerous civil rights laws on behalf of some individuals without infringing on the rights of others. Appreciation does not show us how to deal with the resistance to affinity groups on the part of some organization members. Greater understanding and valuing of our differences does not provide guidance on how to justly deny a promotional opportunity to an employee because the culture and nationality where the company does business does not accept or tolerate individuals from the employee's religious and cultural background. Celebration of diversity does not tell us where or when or whether policies should be colorblind or race sensitive.

As our diversity increases, so do the political, legal, and social dilemmas facing us. It is becoming more and more difficult to operationalize the ideals and image we have for ourselves as the land of equal opportunity for all—where no one is denied an opportunity based on racial, cultural, or ethnic identity.

The task before us is to move beyond appreciation and coexistence and determine how to manage ourselves as a multicultural society. From its highest expression, the Multiculturalist can help lead the effort to create synergistic governance structures that preserve our integrity and ideals as a nation while simultaneously recognizing the cultural values of the many racial, ethnic, religious, and national sub-groups that constitute the population known as "the American people."

Multiculturalist Quotes

"We must develop the ability to tolerate the creative chaos of many voices and opinions all expressing themselves at once; to not seek control over the thoughts or behaviors of others just because they are different from us; and to listen with respect and recognize the dignity of those with whom we disagree.... It is a first principle that each of us, and each of our many cultures, has valuable things to say and to contribute. Allowing everyone to do so is central to our liberty, our genius, and our evolution toward greater good."

Marianne Williamson, *The Healing of America*.
(New York: Simon & Schuster, 1997), 73.

"The United States really needs to find its soul. It has to be one that recognizes its strength in diversity. What makes a world power really great is being able to say we're rich because we have different kinds of people."

Maria Torres, *Race: How Blacks & Whites Think & Feel About the American Obsession*. (New York: The New Press, 1992), 333.

"In the next century, we will have an opportunity to become the world's first truly multiracial, multiethnic democracy. Today there are more children from more diverse backgrounds in our public schools than at any other time in our history, with one in five from immigrant families. For example, just across the Potomac River from our Nation's capital, Virginia's Fairfax County School District boasts children from 180 different racial, national, and ethnic groups who are fluent in more than 100 different native languages."

Bill Clinton, "The United States, A Nation of Diversity and Promise," Online Source: Electronic Journal of the U.S. Information Agency, Vol. 4, No. 2, June 1999. www.//usinfo.state.gov/journals/itsv/0699/ijse/clin.htm.

Seclusionist

Seclusionist Archetype

Meet Frank White

Frank is a forty-five-year-old white male. He is a line supervisor for U.S.A. Farming, a company located in the Midwest that manufactures farm equipment. He is considered competent, hard-working, reliable. Frank was born and raised in the small town where he works and has known many of his coworkers for more than twenty years.

U.S.A. Farming recently merged with a larger company whose main manufacturing plant is near Chicago, Illinois. The new company has an international presence, with plants operating in Mexico, France, England, and Germany.

Now that the merger is complete, new managers and senior leaders are beginning to arrive at the plant. The rumor is that many of the managers at U.S.A. Farming will be moved to other locations as part of a corporate strategy to rotate them throughout the entire company. Frank is nervous about this and was overheard saying to some coworkers that he hoped the new leaders were "good, white, Christian Americans." His friends gently teased him about the comment and made a few jokes back about how the good old days were over but maybe the new company would provide more opportunity for everyone. This reasoning did not comfort Frank.

A few days later, Frank met his new manager and was shocked to meet a Mexican man with a "heavy accent." Jorge had heard very positive things about Frank and told Frank that a willingness to relocate would enhance Frank's experience and increase his value to the new company.

Frank said he would not move and, when pressed, said the kind of community he lives in is important to his family. After the meeting, Frank told everyone that he would have a hard time working for someone who was so different from him and that he certainly could not move his family to an inner city or a foreign country.

He has heard that some of the new sales people are black or Asian. In addition to his worries about how all of this is going to affect him personally, Frank is concerned that all of their major customers, who are white, are going to have a hard time dealing with these nonwhite sales people. "Our customers are going to think we've been taken over," he said several times to friends.

Frank wonders where all of these new outsiders are going to live. One of the reasons that he moved his family into their present community was because he knew that it was made up of people with similar backgrounds and values to his. He believes that "those other people" can be bad influences on his family and does not want to risk exposing his kids to this danger.

Many of Frank's friends are appalled by his attitude and do not know what to do to help him. Frank says he either will try to wait this thing out until retirement or hope they offer him an early out. The worst-case scenario for everyone is that Frank might quit.

Frank demonstrates a strong preference for the Seclusionist Lens.

Seclusionist Profile

The Seclusionist is an individual who opposes all aspects of integration, intermarriage, and cross-cultural interaction where his group is not dominant. He believes that interaction among different races inevitably leads to conflict, and he often relies on historical and biblical sources to justify this perspective. While both whites and people of color can be Seclusionists, most people of color who hold the Seclusionist views tend more to be found at the extremes of the Culturalcentrist Lens.

One extreme of the Seclusionist Lens is the white person who is convinced of his racial superiority and his right to economic, political, and social dominance over all other races. This feeling of superiority springs from the notion that he is a part of the chosen race and that being a member of this chosen race accords him privileges and rights not to be granted to others. He opposes the notion of one world, or globalization, because it not only diminishes the authority of the United States but also increases the influence of Third World nations inhabited by people whom he considers to be inferior.

The Seclusionist fears that these other races are slowly encroaching on his rights and privileges and that "these people" will use their growing economic influence to shape the U.S. social agenda. He is angry because he believes that the government and other societal institutions have joined with "the others" in a complicit movement to overturn the natural order. The most extreme of the Seclusionists are antisocial and speak of racial holy wars.

The vast majority of white Seclusionists are far less outspoken or violent in acting out their beliefs. This Seclusionist locates himself quietly in white neighborhoods and communities and places his children in schools that reinforce separateness. He is likely to feel unnerved, even shocked, when a person of difference moves into his neighborhood. He fears for his safety and worries about maintaining the cleanliness of his neighborhood and the value of his property. However, he is not likely to confront the new neighbor directly; rather, he will ignore, isolate, and behave coldly toward the person of difference sending clear signals that the intruder is not welcome.

While the extreme Seclusionist feels obligated to educate his children by passing on overtly negative ideas and beliefs about "those others," the more passive Seclusionist will pass on the legacy of withdrawal as the way to survive comfortably in this mixed-up world.

The passive Seclusionist moves into the multicultural world to receive services from a multicultural workforce; if given the choice, he prefers to interact only with those of his own kind. He does not venture into the central city for the arts or other cultural activities and tends to have an underlying fear about his safety in urban settings. When working in a metropolitan area, he is likely to live miles outside of the city and commute long distances to live in homogenous environments with other whites.

At work, the Seclusionist seeks to avoid contact with people of different races and cultures. Whenever possible, he chooses jobs, departments, and/or office locations that will allow him to have the comfort of coworkers of his "own kind." He maintains his isolated stance, and when he feels at risk of exposure, he typically withdraws from the situation. The Seclusionist is very reluctant to give or receive feedback across cultural differences and is uncomfortable as a peer or subordinate of people of color.

He has no curiosity about or interest in cultural differences. Since he has little first-hand experience with other groups, he will most likely rely on stereotypical information he has heard over his lifetime. The nature of the type of data he has stored is likely to be negative, unless positive stereotypes are associated with the group—for example, "Asians are good at technical things."

As might be expected, the Seclusionist does not support his organization's diversity initiatives. When forced to go to diversity training, he will quietly pass the time thinking of or working on other things. Although the Seclusionist can hide his feelings adeptly and adapt smoothly to the new political correctness prevalent in today's organizations, he may openly challenge affirmative action and other diversity initiatives.

The Seclusionist customer prefers to be served by members of his own group. For example, a Seclusionist client may not want a person from "the other" group as his account representative. The Seclusionist customer will try to avoid social interaction with "the others" in public situations, asking to have his seat moved in a restaurant or his hotel room changed so he does not have to be located near people with whom he feels uncomfortable.

Such situations are fraught with tension and must be competently addressed when they occur, regardless of the rightness or wrongness of the Seclusionist customer's stance. The Seclusionist customer can cause serious problems for your organization if your employees are not well-prepared or trained to deal with the ramifications of this lens.

In the community, the Seclusionist supports ballot initiatives, political philosophies, and candidates that reflect his views. He speaks openly about his feelings in the privacy of his home with his neighbors, friends, and family. However, in most public situations, he will remain quiet for fear of exposure, given today's societal norms.

For the extreme Seclusionist, there are organizations he can join to actively express and act on his views, since, unfortunately, many hate groups have racial cleansing or the reclaiming of America as their agenda. The most extreme Seclusionist is as free to express his views under our Constitution as any other American citizen.

Seclusionist Strengths and Shadows

The primary Strengths and Shadows of the Seclusionist Lens are listed below.

Strengths

Seclusionists:

- Exemplify one of our most precious rights as Americans: freedom of thought and speech
- Hold a simple and very certain worldview about diversity, eliminating the need for any self doubts or complexity of thought on the subject
- Are extremely loyal to their "own kind"

Shadows

Seclusionists:

- Form exclusive communities of whites often based on fear, misunderstanding, or mistrust of "others"
- Are severely limited in their ability to be successful in today's culturally diverse workforce
- In extreme cases, perpetuate hatred and violence across racial groups

Historical Perspective

Most of our early leaders in this country, from George Washington on, believed in separatism for the races. From the 1770s through the Civil War, many respected and thoughtful Americans, including Thomas Jefferson and Henry Clay, were in favor of colonizing free blacks. The American Colonization Society was founded in 1816 for the purpose of expediting the emancipation of slaves and exporting them back to Africa. Active members of this society included James Madison, Andrew Jackson, Daniel Webster, and James Monroe. None of these individuals, nor other prominent figures of society, believed that a multiracial society could work well. A little known fact is that even Abraham Lincoln was interested in trying to separate the races. At one point, he initiated the Chiriqui project to settle black people in an area in Central America; at another time, he thought of making Texas a republic of black America.

Blacks also have pursued back-to-Africa movements throughout our history. These have not been successful, however, due to a lack of financial support and the discomfort encountered by those who did get to make the return trip with the politics, culture, and climate that they found in their original homelands. In the 1920s, the back-to-Africa movement reached its heyday with the imagination and support of Marcus Garvey. After his death, the movement declined.

Increasingly, over the last half-century with the ghettoization of many of our urban centers and the white flight to the suburbs, more and more people of different races have resided and socialized in separate communities from each other. While integration and affirmative action initiatives have resulted in whites and people of color going to school and working together to some degree, they still go their separate ways once the school bell rings or the hands on the clock reach five. This is especially true for the low-income, low-middle-income, and upper-income classes. Those of the upper-middle-income class seem to be somewhat more successful at integrating their neighborhoods and social activities on a voluntary basis.

The most extreme Seclusionist position of whites is exemplified in the secret fraternal society of the Ku Klux Klan, formed in the South following the Civil War. The Klan consists of white, American-born Protestants, who promote white supremacy and hostility toward all other groups. The Klan aims its hatred especially at Jews, African Americans, and Catholics. White Seclusionist groups argue that whites are the only race of people in the world who do not have a nation exclusively comprised of their own. They use this rhetoric to justify racially motivated acts of violence. Aryan Nations member Louis Beam states:

... the Greater White Racialist Movement intends to establish for our White Aryan Race what every other race on Earth has: A racial homeland.... Our order intends to take part in the Physical and Spiritual Racial Purification of ALL those countries which have traditionally been considered White Lands in Modern Times.

... We intend to purge this land-area of Every Non-White person, idea, and influence.

www.publiceye.org/eyes/whitsup.html

The Internet has become a haven and gathering spot for all kinds of hate groups to communicate and share strategies to reach a new generation of recruits to their various causes. Anti–affirmative action campaigns, anti-immigrant campaigns, and anti-diversity or multicultural campaigns attract the extreme Seclusionist, although the organizers usually disavow any connection to or sympathy with the Seclusionist views.

The Seclusionist at Work

Motivation and Career Advancement from the Seclusionist's Perspective

The Seclusionist cares deeply about doing his job well, supporting the company, and getting along with his coworkers—as long as they are white. He is likely to feel betrayed and, in some cases, fearful when he sees management begin to bring in "those other people." As the workforce becomes more culturally diverse, it "doesn't feel the same as it used to," and he begins to disengage. His work may no longer be as satisfactory as it was; he is not interested in participating in company social events; and his working relationships with fellow whites may become more subdued or reclusive.

His thoughts about career advancement tend to progress along the following lines:

> Those people don't belong in management. It's bad enough that they've taken over most of the entry-level positions, so that the place just doesn't have the same feel that it used to. Let's at least draw the line on management positions. These should be reserved for those of us who understand what this company is all about and how it should be run. We're the ones who can represent it at its best out in the business world as well. They just don't have the same know-how that we do.

Impact of This Strategy on the Individual's Advancement Potential

Like several other strategies, this one can have either a positive or very negative impact on the Seclusionist's advancement potential, depending on circumstances. In organizations where the leadership group is composed primarily of people who view the world through the Seclusionist Lens, this strategy would be vigorously supported and the individual would be viewed as a strong contender for a management position, provided that he possessed the necessary competencies. In organizations where the leadership group understands the value of diversity, expressing this kind of sentiment would put an end to the Seclusionist's advancement potential.

Impact of This Strategy on the Organization's Human Resources

Successful implementation of the Seclusionist's advancement strategy would have demoralizing and demotivating impacts on all people of difference in the organization, as well as on many other organization members concerned about equitable treatment for all employees. Most people want to believe that promotions in their organization go to those who deserve them most, regardless of factors such as race, gender, or ethnicity. Systematic exclusion of people of difference from management or executive ranks blatantly announces that this is not the case. When there is an obvious lack of diversity in management and senior ranks, the organization is vulnerable to lawsuits and public relations problems.

Working with the Seclusionist

If you are working with or managing a person who has a strong preference for the Seclusionist views, it is likely that he holds the views expressed below with respect to the layers:

> *Race*—I do not want to associate with those people. Why should I be forced to interact with them?
>
> *Ethnicity*—There is a cultural purity standard, but I know I can't say that out loud.
>
> *Class*—They are taking opportunities from us and it is unfair! The government is on their side.
>
> *Nationality*—Too many people from the wrong places are coming into our country and ruining it by taking what is rightfully ours.

You may be speaking from entirely different layers. If you are feeling defensive or confused during your discussion, this may be because you have prioritized your layers differently or other lenses may be operating unconsciously. If there is tension or a conflict situation that needs to be resolved, the following guidelines may be useful:

- Understand that the Seclusionist Lens may be deeply submerged in an individual's belief system and that he may have learned to keep his thoughts and feelings hidden in workplace discussions.

- Paraphrase often during the discussion to make sure there are no misunderstandings.

- In cases where you are dealing with an extreme Seclusionist, consider having a third party join the discussion so that there is a witness to what is said. Document the discussion. Remember that nothing is off the record and that you will be held accountable for anything you say.

- Be clear about your company's disciplinary policies before you engage in a discussion.

Coaching the Seclusionist Manager or Supervisor

A manager or supervisor with a strong preference for the Seclusionist Lens has difficulty understanding that in a competitive job market and economy, organizations need every talented and competent employee available. He may fail to recognize that the demographics of customers are shifting and a multicultural workforce is needed to respond to new markets and customers. The Seclusionist does not accept that the majority of society has concluded that cultural diversity leads to competitive advantage in business and to a greater interest and richness in human relations. He does not understand the consequences of his biases to the organization and may not believe that his future with the organization is at risk if he expresses or acts on these biases.

Unmonitored and underdeveloped, the extreme Seclusionist stance could lead to charges of bias, litigation, high turnover, low morale, and poor use of human resources. Your job as a manager and leader in your organization is to coach the Seclusionist so that he is competent, confident, and willing to use or modify the organization's systems on behalf of all employees.

Specifically, you can require the Seclusionist manager or supervisor to use the organization's systems in ways that:

- Recognize the importance of and help develop cultural niche market opportunities.
- Serve all customers courteously and responsively regardless of race, color, ethnicity, or nationality.
- Recruit, hire, develop, and promote employees based only on their qualifications to do the job, not on their racial or cultural identity.

If the Seclusionist employee cannot comply with these requirements, you have little choice but to use your organizational systems to discipline or terminate.

The Seclusionist and Organizational Systems

The Seclusionist has a strong desire to use the organization's systems in ways that will perpetuate a monocultural/monoracial perspective. The Seclusionist is likely to isolate "others" in certain areas of the organization to create a comfortable buffer zone between himself and people of difference. He is adroit at using available organizational systems to achieve this isolation effect in subtle ways, preferring to avoid the risk of being a vocal advocate for his perspective. When the Seclusionist does become visible and vocal in the business environment, he can have a devastating impact on brand identity, the public image of the company, and employee morale.

The essence of the ways in which the Seclusionist Lens influences the organization's human resources systems is presented in each of the statements below. As you review these statements, think of the impact of the Seclusionist stance on these same types of programs and activities in your work environment.

Seclusionist Stance: "I will use the organization's human resources systems to perpetuate opportunities for the dominant culture and reduce the opportunities for others to thrive in our organization."

Recruitment: "I will recruit from schools that are predominantly white."

Hiring: "I will establish formal and informal criteria to eliminate people of color from the selection process."

Compensation and Benefits: "I will reward the efforts of the majority group above those of other groups."

Job Placement: "I will place people in jobs where they fit and are with people who are like them."

Building Effective Teams: "I will choose people for my team that I feel comfortable with."

Performance Management: "I will use the performance feedback system to document unprofessional behavior or incompetent behavior of subpar employees."

Mentoring: "I will mentor people who are most like me and with whom I feel comfortable."

Training: "I will offer training to the right people who have the natural ability to be successful in our organization."

Succession Planning: "I will ensure that the right people remain in the pipeline and on the pathway to senior leadership."

The Seclusionist and the Law

The Seclusionist Lens could affect your business' bottom line in several ways. As you read the following hypothetical case, consider whether your organization may be manifesting the Seclusionist Lens in similar ways.

The Case

Terri Hugenois, a black West Indian immigrant, works for Zencon Incorporated as a computer programmer. She is on track to make senior programmer at the end of next year. She has been reassigned to Mark Simpson's team so she can acquire additional skills needed before she is promoted. Terri is the only minority person on her new team. Prior to her arrival on the team, Mark had very informal meetings with his team members in which they joked about the latest episode of "Cops" and made nasty comments about minorities arrested on the show. Since Terri's arrival, the group has become more serious, and people are afraid to make comments about minorities. Worried that group morale has been affected, he decides to reassign her to a group that has three minorities and is supervised by an Asian-American woman. He calls Terri to his office to discuss the move.

Mr. Simpson:	Look, Terri, I have decided to transfer you to a different group.
Ms. Hugenois:	Why? Have I done something wrong?
Mr. Simpson:	No. I just thought I could find a better fit for you. You would do much better in a more diverse group.
Ms. Hugenois:	Are you moving me because I am black?
Mr. Simpson:	Terri, I think it is better for everyone if they work with people that make them feel comfortable. I like your work, but I just don't think it is a good fit.

Terri sues Zencon claiming that the company reassigned her because she is black. Who wins?

Result

Terri wins. Title VII prohibits employment decisions made based on race. The only reason he offered for transferring her is her race. Thus, she would have a strong claim under Title VII for racial discrimination.

Legal Concerns for the Seclusionist Lens

The Seclusionist openly makes certain assumptions about the value of "like-kind" people associating with each other. If you think you may use the Seclusionist Lens, be aware of the following:

- Taking race or national origin into account in hiring people or assigning job responsibilities violates Title VII of the Civil Rights Act of 1964 and comparable state laws.
  "I want people to work in teams where they'll be most comfortable, so I am going to assign the white employees to a white supervisor and the black employees to a black supervisor."

In rare instances, the law recognizes that a person's gender, national origin, or religion is a "bona fide occupational qualification" for a job. For example, you must be a woman to be an attendant in a woman's locker room.

Seclusionist Highest Expression

What the Best of the **Seclusionist Lens** Contributes to the Organization

Multiple Cultural Stakeholders

The Seclusionist Lens desires racial supremacy for the dominant cultural group within the society. In its original stance, the Seclusionist Lens employs a variety of strategies to accomplish this aim from passive retreat to sponsoring acts of intolerance or violence. From a higher and more holistic perspective, the Seclusionist Lens shifts from asserting cultural supremacy to being a passionate guardian of society as a whole along with other cultural groups.

This move toward a higher level of expression demands a dramatic shift in attitude—a shift much greater than that required with the other lenses. Such a shift would be motivated by the perception of a threat to the entire society that would force the Seclusionist to collaborate with the very groups of people with whom he would otherwise be in conflict. He would need to understand that cross-cultural interdependence and cooperation were linked to our very survivability as the human race.

From this higher perspective, the Seclusionist Lens would recognize issues that touch our lives in ways that do not differentiate among cultural groups—issues such as the proliferation of nuclear weapons, overpopulation, and the spread of infectious diseases—and that we need to involve all cross-cultural stakeholders in the development and implementation of superordinate goals that will resolve these issues.

Seclusionist Quotes

"To truly control its own life a race must also exercise exclusive and sovereign control over its culture, history, art and myths, its self image, soul, heart and mind, its view of its past, present and future, its purpose and destiny, nature and identity. No race can be truly free if another race exercises control over it, in whole or in part, in any of these areas"

Richard McCulloch, *The Racial Compact.*
(Florida: Towncourt Enterprises, 1994).

"We basically accept that there are three races—Caucasians, Negroes and Orientals. Caucasians can't date Orientals. Orientals can't date Caucasians, and neither of them can date Negroes."

Bob Jones III, president, Bob Jones University, "Bush Caters to the Bigotry of Bob Jones," *Washington Post*, February 28, 2000, A15.

"First, that racial separation is necessary for the long-term preservation of the Northern European race, the founding and still the majority American racial type, which I refer to as the Nordish race. It is a simple matter of either-or—either racial separation or racial death. Second, that the alternative to racial destruction, the solution to the Nordish racial crisis, is racial separation. Not immigration restrictions, segregation, white supremacism or other half-measures, nor anything that need harm other races or violate their legitimate rights and interests. None of these things can save us. Only separation can. Separation is the preservationist imperative."

Richard McCulloch, "Separation: The Preservationist Imperative,"
http://www.racialcompact.com/preservationimperative.html.

Transcendent

Transcendent Archetype

Meet Ari Keating

Ari is the superintendent of history for an urban school district that has a highly multicultural student base. His responsibility is to coordinate all of the curriculum, standards, and activities for the history departments in his district. He has an undergraduate degree in philosophy, a master's degree in theology, and a Ph.D. in history. Ari chose education as his career because he deeply believes that human beings must have positive values, a sense of mission, and a willingness to serve others to make the world a better place. He believes that there is no better use of his God-given talents than to educate young minds.

Until recently, he enjoyed motivating teachers, finding new and exciting methods and tools to use in the classroom, creating higher standards, and moving history into the core curriculum. Recently, however, Ari was suddenly thrust into the middle of a cultural battle to determine the perspectives from which history should be taught in his district. Conservative school board members and parents want to see traditional history based on Christopher Columbus, the founding fathers, and American heroes like George Washington, Thomas Jefferson, and Betsy Ross at the center of the curriculum. Parents of children of color believe that this slant on American history is biased and negates the powerful influences of Native, African, Asian, and Hispanic Americans on the development of the country. Some parents are calling for cultural centric views to be incorporated in the curriculum; others want to see a special history curriculum developed and taught from the perspective of multiple cultures.

This was all very difficult for Ari to manage, mostly because of the anger and conflict that was voiced at several open community meetings generated by the situation. Ari believed that all of the perspectives were important and that a way could be found to incorporate and balance different views. He spent hours on the phone and in person talking with parents, teachers, and students about their concerns and expectations.

He tried to facilitate a town hall meeting to engage everyone in dialogue on this topic, trusting that they could find common ground and a sensible solution. The meeting quickly degenerated into a shouting match, and Ari was amazed at how angry and determined people were about holding onto their views. Every time someone tried to focus on race, ethnicity, and culture, Ari would try to move the discussion to a higher level to talk about the universal oneness of humanity. Several times Ari implored people to keep an open heart. Ari told the group that, during times of crisis such as these, there was an opening for powerful results to occur that were beyond what people could imagine and that he believed the current debate was part of a greater scheme to help everyone increase their level of understanding and appreciation of what education was all about. Ari believed that important lessons were being learned at deep spiritual levels during the debate and people, including himself, might not understand what was transpiring until some time later. However, none of Ari's insights moderated the anger of the people at the meeting.

Ari has spent a great deal of time in meditation, prayer, and deep thought since the meeting waiting for an answer. Meanwhile, his administration has lost faith in Ari's ability to deal with the problem effectively. From the superintendent's perspective, Ari failed to take charge of the situation, did not look for best practices from other districts facing similar problems, allowed too much participation from parents, did not understand the financial implications of the options, and did not think through the implications of implementing a new curriculum without state approval. From the perspective of the parents, Ari unfairly raised their expectations by leading them to believe they could change the curriculum. Ari himself thinks that the issues needed to be addressed and that dialogue was taking place that increased people's sensitivity to and awareness of cultural diversity. He wishes that the superintendent, the board, and the parents were not so upset and that they were willing to give more time for some new possibilities to arise.

Ari demonstrates a strong preference for the Transcendent Lens.

Transcendent Profile

The Transcendent focuses on our universal identity as human beings and our divine interconnectedness with all things. This lens believes that each soul is evolving through its particular life experience as part of a grand unknowable mystery in accordance with divine destiny. The Transcendent believes people are bound together on a spiritual quest that involves transcending their individual lives to recognize the universal human potential that exists in each of us.

The Transcendent's perspective is too broad and too flooded with light to have a preoccupation with race or personality traits. According to the Transcendent, we must respect and honor different races and cultures, but view them only in the context of our spiritual oneness.

The Transcendent Lens can be divided into two major categories: religious and spiritual. The religious Transcendent views people as God's children and believes that God or the Universe assigns each of us a particular skin color and cultural identity to experience life and actualize our humanity from this perspective. He acknowledges that, because of this, it is important for us to learn to appreciate these differences. On the other hand, the religious Transcendent often feels that his life experience is shaped more by his condition as a human being under religious guidance than by the specifics of his racial or cultural background.

The spiritual Transcendent views the physical body as the vehicle through which we gain greater wisdom and evolve into higher spiritual beings. He strives for what DuBois calls "a loftier respect for the sovereign human soul" and a nation in which people are free to grow spiritually and to gain a better understanding of our purpose in life. The Transcendent argues that our universal/divine identity as human beings is our primary identity. Each of us has a right to claim equal recognition on the basis of this universal human identity and potential and not on the basis of a racial or ethnic identity. Like the Color-blind Lens, the spiritual Transcendent focuses on our similarities and hopes we can grow beyond racial and cultural identity and the divisions we have allowed ourselves to attach to it. The Transcendent finds the common thread among people of diverse backgrounds and expects that people from different cultures and experiences are capable of finding a similar purpose.

In the quest to facilitate oneness, the Transcendent may smooth over conflicts and minimize the impact of historical legacies of distrust. Because he sees the best in each of us, he may avoid the hard work of managing our darker tendencies to act with intolerance across our differences. With the Universe or God "on his side," he can sometimes be perceived as self-righteous and moralistic; he can be a formidable adversary.

As an employee, the Transcendent sees himself as on a mission, fulfilling a higher purpose in life. He may never feel at home in highly competitive, top-down, bottom-line work environments where people seem to play out a daily soap opera of hidden agendas, office politics, and interpersonal one-upsmanship. He is more likely to be attracted to occupations and organizations that are involved in development or helping services. Transcendents often work as counselors, trainers, human resources professionals, community relations officers, teachers, field workers in development agencies, foundation employees, and other helping professions and service arenas.

The Transcendent believes that the way to organizational success is to align the organization with higher guiding principles. He is less concerned with the governance structure, internal rules, and politics, and more focused on vision, values, and mission. His concern is whether the organization is living up to its potential and having a positive impact on society.

The Transcendent is sensitive to the difficulties employees face in the workplace due to their racial or cultural minority status, but he does not sponsor or support initiatives that create wedges or increase misunderstandings among different groups. He favors dialogue, inquiry, and fellowship rather than confrontation as the principal mechanisms to achieve greater harmony and understanding. When employees are feeling angry or upset, the Transcendent may wish to move to imagining the possibilities of a new future too quickly before some people have released their pain and frustration about the past. The Transcendent's tendency to live in the moment with an eye toward "actualizing a better future either in this life or on some other plane" can be irritating for those employees still mired in real-world conflicts and challenges. In addition to generating anger in such cases, the Transcendent's perspective also generates cynicism and disbelief about its naiveté.

The Transcendent generally enjoys working with other Transcendents because of their shared beliefs. They understand and support each other's interest in knowing and valuing the whole person, including his or her spiritual identity. If there are several of them working together and they use new-age terminology and concepts in their conversations, they are likely to be perceived as "the flakes" or "space cadets" by their coworkers.

The Transcendent customer wants to do business with an organization that acts on social concerns, makes products and services that do not harm people or the environment, and treats employees with dignity in the workplace. He is concerned about issues such as the exploitation of foreign workers, the production of goods in oppressive environments, and the manufacture of products that harm the environment.

The Transcendent is likely to be committed to socially responsible investments, looking for companies that are progressive in the ways they treat human beings and the planet. He is interested in investing his money in companies that make social responsibility a key aspect of company business. He appreciates and is loyal to a company that donates money to some worthy community program or group, sets up a special internship program that provides opportunities for people who otherwise would be neglected, or establishes a corporate philanthropic program to fund projects that help people in need.

In the community, the Transcendent is often allied with the Victim Lens in the attempt to seize the moral high ground and use it as leverage to pressure organizations to do the "right thing" with respect to the well-being of employees, the public, and the environment. The Transcendent would rather have the social dialogue focus on issues of justice, equality, fairness, dignity, and what is morally right rather than on diversity for diversity's sake. He sponsors and participates in cross-cultural exchange programs, confronts government organizations that are accused of demonstrating culturally-based bias toward community members, organizes boycotts against a company that has discriminated along racial or ethnic lines, or takes other actions—including volunteering to serve on committees, participating in rallies, and donating his money—to show his support for diversity in the name of social justice.

Transcendent Strength and Shadows

Among the many attributes of the Transcendent Lens are the primary Strengths and Shadows listed below.

Strengths

Transcendents:

- Promote and model tolerance and acceptance of all beings
- Focus on the opportunities and possibilities of today and tomorrow rather than on the grievances of yesterday
- Can inspire us to forgive the history between us which includes hurtful and harmful actions
- Help us heal ourselves and our relationships
- Remind us of the connections that bind us together most deeply
- Help create organizational cultures that emphasize global community

Shadows

Transcendents:

- Can be impatient and dismissive when they think others are staying "stuck" in their hurt and anger over how they have been treated
- May not be able or willing to recognize the forces of oppression that still exist in our organizations and society and may allow such conditions to continue to exist without taking action to eliminate them
- May be unwilling or unable to help surface and address the conflicts and tensions that exist among people for whom differences in histories, experiences, and opportunities are extremely important

Historical Perspective

Transcendent thinking in this country has been shaped by a strong Christian tradition blended with the spiritual influences of Eastern philosophies and other faith traditions. William Penn, the renowned Quaker leader, was one of the first Americans to articulate the transcendent perspective. In 1682, Penn delivered an address to a group of American Indians, in which he subtly merged Christian and Native American thought as follows:

The Great Spirit who made me and you, who rules the heavens and the earth, and who knows the innermost thoughts of men, knows that I and my friends have a hearty desire to live in peace and friendship with you. Our object is not to do injury and thus provoke the Great Spirit, but to do good.

www.san.beck.org/WP12-Foxandpenn.html.

In the early nineteenth century, William Ellery Channing, a leading Unitarian, spoke ardently about "the spirit of human brotherhood," emphasizing that "there can be no peace without but through peace within." Channing had a profound influence on Ralph Waldo Emerson, founder of the Transcendentalist movement. Emerson wrote of the importance of developing spiritual insights, "accomplished by the spontaneous teaching of the cultivated soul."

Although the Christian tradition remained the dominant strain in American society throughout the nineteenth century, Eastern religious and spiritual ideas began making inroads into U.S. cultural thought. In 1893, a diverse ecumenical gathering entitled "The Parliament of the World's Religion" was held in Chicago. Hindu swamis, Native American elders, and leaders of the world's major nature religions, among others, gathered to share their perspectives on religious and spiritual belief systems.

In the latter half of the twentieth century, respected Christian leaders like Martin Luther King, Jr., began to connect their religious tradition with the belief in human equality that had been voiced by such figures as Emerson and Indian leader Mahatma Gandhi. As King called on volunteers of all races to end racial segregation, he urged them to "Pray daily to be used by God in order that all men might be free" and to "Strive to be in good spiritual and bodily health."

In more recent years, the Promise Keepers, a Christian men's organization founded in 1990, has required its members to reach "beyond any racial and denominational barriers to demonstrate the power of biblical unity."

While the Christian religious emphasis has remained a strong force in one track of transcendent thinking, an equally important influence in the last few decades has been that of Eastern philosophy. Drawing on both Eastern philosophy and earlier transcendent thinking in this country, pop culture icons like James Redfield, Oprah Winfrey, and Deepak Chopra have fueled a spiritual growth movement that has been gaining momentum since the 1960s. Echoing the words of Emerson, James Redfield, author of *The Celestine Prophecy*, writes of "a new spiritual awakening" in which "we all evolve toward the best completion of our spiritual missions." Winfrey emphasizes the importance of "each individual having her or his own inner revolution." Chopra captures the heart of the transcendent perspective when he writes "essentially we are spiritual beings who have taken manifestation in physical form."

The Transcendent Lens at Work

Motivation and Career Advancement from the Transcendent's Perspective

The Transcendent Lens is motivated by a sense of mission and spiritual quest. He approaches his life and his job from the perspective that he is where he is supposed to be as part of a divine plan. The Transcendent is concerned with learning whatever lessons the Universe/God has planned for him day by day and with contributing to the greater good. As long as he believes that his job is helping him to make a meaningful contribution and that the organization is acting in socially responsible ways, he will give his best efforts to his job and the organization.

Given his spiritual beliefs, the Transcendent does not think in terms of career advancement. His expectation is that the higher powers will arrange for him to be placed wherever he is supposed to be to make the contribution that he is supposed to make in accordance with the divine plan. If he is meant to take a management role in the organization, it will happen. If not, so be it.

Impact of This Strategy on the Individual's Advancement Potential

The impact of this strategy on the Transcendent's advancement potential depends on a number of factors, including how exceptionally qualified he is for management positions, how openly and frequently he expresses the Transcendent belief system (and how wide a gap this creates with respect to his "fit" with the culture), and how unwilling or unable he is to manage the political dynamics that operate in the organization.

Impact of This Strategy on the Organization's Human Resources

If the majority of individuals in an organization were to adopt this same belief system, totally new selection, development, and promotion systems would need to evolve—based, perhaps, on honoring and promoting shared values.

Working with the Transcendent

If you are working with or managing a person who has a strong preference for the Transcendent Lens, the layers that you are likely to hear emphasized in conversations with him will include religion, spirituality, and personal style. The themes for each of these layers are likely to sound like this:

> Religion—We are all God's children.
>
> Spirituality—We have a deeper identity and purpose, and our race, culture, and

ethnicity are only tools to aid us on our journey of self-discovery and attunement to the universal and the divine.

Personal Style—We all have the choice and the responsibility to align ourselves with higher values and principles and to treat others with fairness and dignity.

Remember, you may be speaking with this individual from entirely different legacies and layers. If you are feeling defensive or confused during a discussion, or if there is tension or conflict that needs to be addressed, it may help to keep the following guidelines in mind.

- Understand that a belief in the importance of spiritual ascendance and in the interconnectedness of all people is the core motivation for the Transcendent.

- Help him understand that, while he may be able to dismiss or minimize the discriminatory experiences that people of different racial and cultural groups have had in the organization, these are still very real and hurtful for them.

- Try to stay focused on the sincerity of the message about tolerance and love for all human beings and not get turned off by the zealous manner in which the message may be delivered.

Coaching the Transcendent Manager or Supervisor

A manager or supervisor with a strong preference for the Transcendent Lens has difficulty identifying and addressing discriminatory conditions pertaining to hiring, job assignments, and promotion opportunities because he simply does not focus on these aspects of organizational life. He also shies away from addressing and resolving racial, ethnic, cultural, or other tensions that exist among different groups of employees, trying instead to get them to see that "we are all one." He may not recognize that racial, cultural, and ethnic identities are important to many people, and he often becomes impatient with people who are not able to see beyond differences or let go of past grievances.

Giving negative feedback to employees is something else that is difficult for the Transcendent manager or supervisor because he prefers to focus on and support the divine essence of each individual. As part of this effort to support this essence, the Transcendent manager might create subjective criteria for employees who need special help. This might begin with bending the rules or ignoring policy in order to help one individual who needs a break. Soon the same thing has happened with a second and a third person. Before long, the Transcendent has created an inconsistent approach to managing that sends confusing messages to employees and puts the organization at risk.

Unmonitored and underdeveloped, the Transcendent stance could lead to charges of inconsistency and bias in applying organizational policies, eruptions of tension among employees of different racial and cultural groups, low morale, and possible litigation. Your job as a manager or a leader is to coach the

Transcendent so he is competent, confident, and willing to use or modify the organization's systems on behalf of all employees.

Specifically, you can require the Transcendent to use the organization's systems in ways that:

- Acknowledge the differences in treatment that have been experienced historically by different racial and cultural groups in the organization and ensure that hiring, placement, development, and promotion systems are administered fairly and equitably for all.

- Respond to the needs of different racial and cultural groups to be supported by targeted initiatives that will enable them to be successful and advance within the organization.

- Ensure that organizational policies are based on clearly understood guidelines and implemented with consistency, not on a case-by-case basis.

The Transcendent and Organizational Systems

The Transcendent wants the organization's systems to support its values and visions. He uses the systems as a catalyst to encourage the best in each individual, so that everyone has a fair chance to reach his or her highest potential.

The Transcendent Stance: "I will use the organization's systems to develop the potential of every employee and to empower people to act on our organization's most deeply held values."

Recruiting: "I will recruit people who share our values and who are committed to our vision."

Hiring: "I will hire people who share our values and will use their talents and abilities on behalf of our vision and mission."

Compensation and Benefits: "I will compensate people in the best way we can, balancing their needs and dignity with the organization's mission and resources."

Job Placement and Assignments: "I will place people in jobs where they can make contributions to and serve the greater good."

Building Effective Teams: "I will create a team that has all kinds of people on it who can bring the perspectives we need to achieve our goals and mission."

Performance Management: "I will support people in whatever way I can to help them accomplish their personal and organizational goals."

Mentoring: "I will help people understand how the organization works and serve as an advocate for them. I will also help the organization to better understand the individuals whom I am mentoring."

Training: "I will use training to help people learn how to behave in ways that are consistent with our values and mission."

Succession Planning: "I will ensure that those who are in the pipeline for management and executive positions believe in and model the values and vision on which this organization is founded."

The Transcendent and the Law

The Transcendent Lens could affect your business' bottom line in several ways. As you read the following hypothetical case, consider whether your organization may be manifesting the Transcendent Lens in similar ways.

The Case

Matlock and Henderson, a large consulting firm in the Boston area, requires managers and all other senior level executives to attend a retreat each year. All employees who attend the retreat are paid for the days they spend at the retreat. Meg West, human resources manager, has decided that Nema Sinchai, a spiritual leader from Thailand, will conduct this year's retreat. During the five-day retreat, participants are scheduled to spend approximately three hours in deep meditation and are taught different Buddhist chants. Tammy Jones, a devout member of the New Christian Movement, is disturbed by the retreat activities and choice of retreat leader. She schedules an appointment to see Meg.

Ms. Jones: Is there a way we can have someone else lead the retreat? As a Christian, I am uncomfortable with the meditation and spiritual enlightenment exercises.

Ms. West: I do not understand. The retreat is not religious. It is simply an exercise in bringing the firm into spiritual oneness with the universe. This retreat is exactly what the firm needs to clear the negative energy that has pervaded it since management's decision to lay off employees.

Ms. Jones: I cannot attend if we are doing Buddhist chants. All this new age stuff is totally against the teachings of my faith.

Ms. West: The Buddhist religion is not new age. This retreat is beyond religion; it is about spirituality. But I'm willing to do this: come to the retreat. There will be substantial parts that have nothing to do with the Buddhist chants. If you want, you can step out of the program during the other parts. Maybe others will want to join you.

Ms. Jones: I appreciate that, but the whole thing still makes me really uncomfortable. I'd rather not come at all.

Ms. West: That's where I have to draw the line. If you don't come for those five days, I can't pay you for those five days.

Tammy sues the company for failing to compensate her for the five days she missed because of her refusal to attend the spiritual retreat. Who wins?

Result

Probably the company. Title VII requires that an employer make reasonable accommodations for the religious beliefs and practices of its employees unless it will cause the employer undue hardship. Tammy was within her rights to say that she objected to what she perceived as an infringement of her own religious practices and beliefs. However, Meg responded appropriately by offering to "reasonably accommodate" those practices and beliefs in offering to excuse her from the parts of the program to which she reasonably could object. When Tammy rejected that accommodation, she went further than the protections afforded by Title VII.

Legal Concerns for the Transcendent

The Transcendent emphasizes our common bonds to the exclusion of our distinguishing characteristics. If you think you may use the Transcendent Lens, be aware of the following:

- Overlooking legitimate concerns or grievances that one employee has against another in the interest of reaching an amicable resolution may result in failing to respond adequately to complaints about misconduct that violates Title VII or other federal or state antidiscrimination laws.

Transcendent Highest Expression

What the Best of the **Transcendent Lens** Contributes to the Organization and Community

Fostering Humanity-Centric Love

The Transcendent Lens believes in the power of personal enlightenment, assuming that once we are in an enlightened state, we will rise above the limitations that we have imposed on ourselves due to our racial and cultural differences. In the meantime, however, our increasingly diverse cultural lifestyles and experiences are contributing to ongoing conflicts over which values, philosophies, beliefs, and agendas are appropriate to pursue within our organizations, society, and the world. To live peacefully across significant differences such as these, we need to develop a sustained ability to converse with one another, understanding and appreciating the commonality of our human experience.

From its higher and more holistic perspective, the Transcendent Lens can provide inspiration and guidance to help us evolve into a "human-centric" community driven by universally accepted norms and values that we can incorporate into the fabric of our daily lives. This perspective says we are all members of one human family united in a common heritage and divinely inspired destiny, and that our similarities far outweigh our differences on almost every dimension.

Religion, psychology, and science all provide theories and constructs that seek to explain the fundamental paradox: our individual uniqueness and our universal oneness. To the Transcendent, universal oneness means that each of us is a spark of life force from the same divine experience. We are all fueled by a mysterious energy, often called "the human spirit." This energy sustains all of us, regardless of our cultural backgrounds, as we grow, learn, love, and achieve our way through life, experiencing its joys and pains, striving to understand its purpose and meaning.

While the Transcendent continues to seek personal enlightenment, from its higher perspective, this lens also concerns itself with facilitating an understanding of our universal oneness with others. He acknowledges nuances of variation from one belief system to another but believes key ideas transcend these differences; love is one of the most important of these ideas. He has a deep desire to find ways to realign our institutions with universal principles that foster unconditional love from this humanity-centered perspective.

To accomplish this, the Transcendent must let go of the need to proselytize, an attribute associated with the original stance of this lens. He must be willing to move away from allegiance to insular beliefs within his own religious or spiritual paradigm and identify and foster universal values in community with others.

There is a deep longing for reconciliation and healing across our cultural differences. However, contemporary social and organizational challenges are so complex that no one religion or spiritual perspective alone can fully address these challenges or heal the painful wounds within the human family. The Transcendent serves as a catalyst to that end by guiding us on our journey to find the intersection of the common good and common ground. This is the point at which our motivations and methods are driven by what we know in our hearts and minds to be universally true and accepted.

In its highest expression, the Transcendent looks for ways to inspire us to realize that it is not enough to be successful in our own lives; we need to give something back to the human community for today and for future generations. In a time when so many of us are facing spiritual depletion within our organizations and communities, the highest expression of the Transcendent guides us to fill some of the void that is a by-product of contemporary organizational life.

Transcendent Quotes

"…We shouldn't fear that if race lost all its value as a distinction among people, we would suddenly have nothing to share. Human beings are deeper and more protean than that. And the development of an American civilization or culture worthy of that depth depends on our letting go of races as its organizing principle."

Jim Sleeper, "Letting Go of Race." *Atlantic Unbound*. August 21, 1997. www.theatlantic.com/unbound/bookauth/sleepint.htm.

"I am talking about each individual having her or his own inner revolution. I am talking about each individual coming to the awareness that 'I am Creation's son. I am Creation's daughter. I am more than my physical self. I am more than this job that I do. I am more than the external definitions that I have given myself. I am a mother, but I am not just a mother. I am a husband, but I am not just a husband. I am a daughter, but I am not just a daughter. Those roles are all extensions of who I define myself to be, but ultimately I am Spirit come from the greatest Spirit. I am Spirit.'"

Oprah Winfrey, "Inner Revolution," an interview with Gary Zukav, January 2000, www.zukav.com.

"The authentic self is the soul made visible."

Sarah Ban Breathnach, *Simple Abundance*. (New York: Warner Books, 1995), foreword.

"I offer you peace. I offer you love. I offer you friendship. I see your beauty. I hear your need. I feel your feelings. My wisdom flows from the Highest Source. I salute that Source in you. Let us work together for unity and love."

Mahatma Gandhi, *Prayer for Peace*. www.quoteaholic.com

"Each of us is here to discover our true Self...that essentially we are spiritual beings who have taken manifestation in physical form...that...we're not human beings that have occasional spiritual experiences...[rather that] we're spiritual beings that have occasional human experiences."

Deepak Chopra, *The Seven Spiritual Laws of Success*.
(California: New World Library, 1994), 97.

Victim/Caretaker

Victim/Caretaker Archetype

Meet Rene Johnson

Rene is a thirty-seven-year-old African-American woman. She works for a large government agency as a branch chief of security operations, and her division inspects briefcases and packages and assigns visitor badges in the lobby of the main building. Rene has been employed by this agency for seven years.

In the past two years, she has applied for three promotions and has not been selected for any of them. Rene believes that her race is the principal reason she has not been selected. Her white counterparts have been promoted ahead of her, even though they have less time on the job and similar work experience. She is angry and has contacted an attorney to investigate her claims of discrimination.

Four years ago, Rene's supervisor told her that to be more competitive she needed to finish her college degree. At the time, she had completed two years toward a bachelor's degree in business management. Rene spends quite a bit of her time outside of work volunteering to help at-risk people in her neighborhood and community. Because of this involvement, she does not have time to attend classes. She has taken one class per semester since receiving her supervisor's recommendation, but she has not completed the course work to earn a degree.

In her last performance review, Rene was told that she needed to improve her report-writing skills and that she ought to consider making a lateral move to another location to expand her knowledge of security operations if she was interested in advancement. Rene does not believe any action on her part will increase her chances of being selected to fill a supervisory position. She is convinced that the people in the organization are prejudiced.

Rene regularly confronts her supervisors and other government employees about what she describes as the agency's hostile work environment. She has written letters to senior agency officials describing the bias she experiences, and she spends her lunch and free time venting about her situation to anyone who listens. She raises the issue of discrimination at all public forums and has been to the Equal Employment Office to file several complaints. At this point, Rene's supervisor is reluctant to give her any more direct feedback on her performance because he is concerned that she will name him in a complaint that could damage his career.

Off the record, a friend told Rene that no one wants to work with her because she has a negative attitude, blaming her lack of a promotion on her race. Her friend told her to consider making a fresh start elsewhere. However, Rene says she will not give "them" the satisfaction of leaving. As far as she is concerned, they "owe her" for all she has been through. As long as she stays, they will have to look at the impact of their "racism"; she is willing to suffer for "the cause." Rene makes an effort to tell new African-American employees all the bad things that have happened to her and advises them to watch their backs because similar things will happen to them.

Rene demonstrates a strong preference for the Victim/Caretaker Lens.

Victim/Caretaker Profile

The Victim/Caretaker Lens looks at oppression and exploitation from two sides of the same coin. From the Victim's side, the issue is one of "being done to"; from the Caretaker's side, it is one of "making up for." The roles of Victims and Caretakers are interdependent, their relationship circular and complex. The Victim tends to become engaged in caretaking activities along with non-victims to fight for equality and justice. Both the Victim and the Caretaker tend to believe that skin color, ethnicity, and country of origin are primary factors in people's lives, and that members of racial and ethnic minorities in America have had very little control over their destinies.

The Victim tends not to trust the integrity of institutions or systems that she does not control. Her history and present-day experience teach her that these systems are biased and intolerant of her cultural or racial difference. Because of this, she often considers prejudice against her group as the cause for whatever negative experiences she has in life—not getting good grades in school, not getting selected for the varsity team, not getting admitted into the college of her choice, not being offered a job she really wants, not getting the desired promotion, not having the loan approved—before she is willing to consider the possibility of individual factors, such as the lack of certain capabilities or the presence of unpleasant personality factors.

The Victim assumes that there is bias and then waits to be proven wrong. Members of the majority group must first demonstrate that they are not prejudiced, or in any other way acting like the Victim's stereotype of the majority group, before the Victim will risk interacting with them in any meaningful way. This often frustrates well-intending members of the majority group or members of groups different from the Victim, who merely want to be seen and treated as individuals—an ironic reversal of what members of racial and cultural minorities typically experience.

The Caretaking Lens has its roots in a passion for justice and equality, a belief in brotherhood and/or a commitment to a religious or spiritual path. The Caretaker feels that, where there is incivility, prejudice, or need, she has a responsibility to act on behalf of those who do not have the opportunities or resources that all of us deserve. Like the other lenses, the intensity of caretaking varies. Caretakers and Victims who become Caretakers may find their niche in government, law, community affairs, social services, health care, volunteerism, and other helping professions. Some are more visible than others, walking at the very front of the parade for social action. Some write legislation while others write letters. Some make movies and some build houses. Whatever their role, the motivation of a felt obligation to others and a need to help is basically the same. The Caretaking Lens is embodied in public entities like Head Start, affirmative action projects, Social Security, Peace Corps, International Monetary Fund, and civil rights organizations.

In work situations, the Victim blames the system or others for individual performance problems and avoids looking at her own contributions to workplace challenges. If the Victim is also a Caretaker, she expresses a genuine and compassionate concern about any inequities in the organization's systems and wants to volunteer on diversity committees or special task forces to make the organization's systems more equitable. The Victim often risks her image within the organization to confront management. She raises uncomfortable issues without fear of embarrassing organization leaders, and she uses the system in every possible manner to present her complaints and/or suggestions.

The Victim believes that if one member of her group has received a promotion, then they have all in some way succeeded and contributed to the individual's advancement. There is a strong feeling of group pride when someone has beaten the odds and "scored big" with a promotion. There is also strong pressure on this individual to come back and extend a helping hand to others. If this bond is broken, there can be ramifications, such as loss of prestige and isolation within the individual's membership group. In some instances the pressures can be so intense that the Victim has refused promotions because she does not feel comfortable managing or supervising those who were once her peers.

The Victim tends to believe that no matter how much education or experience she has or what skill level she achieves, members of the dominant culture will prevent her from gaining opportunities. Sometimes the Victim feels that she needs to overachieve to receive any advancement or justify any recognition that does come her way. With her assumption of bias in the workplace, the Victim may not believe that she is a real stakeholder in the organization and think, instead, that she simply is being tolerated or, worse still, exploited to help the dominant culture succeed.

The Victim is aware of the inconsistencies, contradictions, and biases that are a part of the organization's history and can point to very specific examples of how the system unfairly creates barriers for members of her group and other cultural minorities. The Victim is aware of how members of her group are being treated in other organizations. The news is filled with reports of companies being sued and settling on class action suits that pertain to discrimination in the workplace. The Victim believes that, to some degree, the same behavior is present in every organization. It is only a matter of time before the next organization or even her company is caught.

As customers, the Victim/Caretaker spends her money in an organization that has a track record of social justice—one that does not exploit its workforce, has members of minority groups in its management ranks, and takes an active role in addressing social concerns in the communities in which it is located. The Victim is one of the lenses that is most sensitive to any kind of slight or disrespectful attitude that occurs in the consumer process. She has spent most of her life refining the radar needed to detect such affronts and is highly attuned to the ways in which racial and cultural minorities are often singled out. For example, the Victim is sensitive to sales people spending less time with them or to being followed in stores to ensure that she does not engage in shoplifting or other illegal activities.

The Victim is hypersensitive to the ways in which she is perceived and treated in the community. In school systems, the Victim believes that her student gets less attention from teachers and is meted out harsher sanctions for similar or lesser violations of the rules. When availing herself of community services, the Victim is certain that she has to wait longer than others and is being treated as a second-class citizen because of her race, culture, color, ethnicity, or nationality. She assumes that these are the reasons why she did not get the apartment rental or the loan for which she applied. She expects to be profiled by the police or to receive harsher sentences for crimes similar to those committed by members of the majority group. The sad fact is that there is enough reality in the experiences of racial and cultural minorities to reinforce these assumptions so that the Victim never has to reexamine her belief in the prejudice and unfairness inherent in all systems and institutions.

The Victim has watchdog organizations that monitor these kinds of situations, as well as informal networks that get the word out quickly when incidents occur. Sometimes the Victim is comfortable with, and makes effective use of, legal and regulatory avenues to pursue her concerns. With civil rights laws on her side, she can have a significant impact on organizations that are acting in biased ways. Many caretaking civil rights groups look for patterns of mistreatment in employment and consumer transactions. They can be quite effective at shining the media spotlight on the offending organization and encouraging boycotts until the deficiency is corrected.

The Victim/Caretaker can be religiously or spiritually motivated and often depends on religious institutions to bring spiritual views and political activism together. All major religions have charity and service as core concepts. Churches, synagogues, and temples have been involved as catalysts for demonstrations, boycotts, protests, acts of civil disobedience, marches, and other events to call attention to discriminatory actions. The Victim/Caretaker participates in civic meetings, town hall events, volunteer programs, and other community-based initiatives aimed at promoting social justice.

Victim/Caretaker Strength and Shadows

The primary Strengths and Shadows of the Victim and Caretaker Lens are listed separately below.

Strengths

Victims:

- Help us to focus on issues of social injustice
- Inform us of the inequities that still exist today in our workplaces and communities
- Encourage us to move out of complacency and take a proactive stance to eliminate all forms of exploitation and discrimination

Caretakers:

- Demonstrate genuine concern and caring about other human beings
- Inspire deeper levels of understanding of, and interest in, the collective welfare of society
- Help us rise above self-interest to support those who do not have the opportunities and resources that everyone deserves

Shadows

Victims:

- Blame societal or organizational factors for their position in life
- Tend to be unwilling to take personal responsibility for their job performance
- Can have negative impacts on an organization's time and financial resources by initiating unfounded legal claims
- May prejudge members of the dominant culture as not worth trusting, investing in, or relating to

Caretakers:

- Can act in self-righteous and paternalistic/maternalistic ways
- May disempower people by assuming that they should receive special treatment instead of requiring them to "pull their own weight"

Historical Perspective

The story of America has been one of the oppressor and the oppressed since the first English immigrants arrived here to free themselves of the oppression they had experienced. Throughout our history, despite our outward stability, we have existed as the powerful versus the powerless, the exploiter and the exploited, with the oppression perpetuated by one group—those who were white, European-descended, American-born, heterosexual, middle- and upper-class American men.

Black/white polarity has dominated American discourse on oppression, and the history of African Americans has received the lion's share of attention in discussing social injustice. However, they can stand as symbols of other groups who have not been given the opportunity to have their voices heard as deeply or fully. We cannot forget, to name a few, the atrocities perpetrated on the Native Americans, the exploitation of Chinese railroad workers, the struggle of Mexican farm workers, the systematic subjugation of women, the internment of the Japanese, the dismissal of anyone too "different."

At times, the oppressed have responded to their condition in the classic American way of public dissent. Public outcry has been an American reaction to oppression since the dumping of tea into Boston Harbor. Martin Luther King, Jr., attempted to lead the civil rights movement in the manner of Gandhi—peacefully but unremittingly.

Other groups have taken up protest with the United States government. The American Indian Movement (AIM) was organized officially in 1968 under the leadership of Dennis Banks and Clyde Bellencourt to deal with the allegations of police discrimination and the arrests of American Indians in Minneapolis and Saint Paul. Since its inception, AIM has been involved in various protests from those targeted at the Bureau of Indian Affairs for implementing what AIM considered to be improper policies to those focused on sports organizations and sports media for their use of Native American names and symbols for sports teams and their mascots.

"Minneapolis and St. Paul, unlike nearly every other major U.S. metropolitan area, had Indian populations large enough to register on the radar of city government, the press, and the public. One of AIM's first projects was to create an AIM patrol. They raised money to equip cars with two-way radios, cameras, and tape recorders so they could monitor arrests by the police department. When the AIM patrol heard police dispatched to certain bars or street corners, officers would be met by Indians in red jackets carefully observing their actions. It was a tactic similar to Black Panthers' campaigns to monitor police in Oakland, California, and other cities."

Women have fought a long and difficult battle for their rights as citizens. In 1840, Lucretia Mott and Elizabeth Cady Stanton were not allowed to attend an Abolitionist convention because they were women. They swore that they would hold their own convention and did so, convening the first women's rights rally in 1848 in Seneca Falls, New York. Seventy-two years and many rallies and conventions later, women finally won the right to vote with the ratification of the Nineteenth Amendment to the Constitution of the United States.

Victims today continue to protest on behalf of social change, even after legal milestones have been established. From the Victim's perspective, the laws may have changed, but hearts, minds, and behavior are slow to follow.

Just as there have been Victims throughout our history as a country, there have been Caretakers, from Harriet Beecher Stowe to Lyndon Baines Johnson and Jimmy Carter. The administration of Franklin Delano Roosevelt (FDR) was mainly responsible for setting the standard of government help to citizens in hardship. As a part of FDR's New Deal, the Social Security system of services and payments was established to help support the aged, unemployed, disabled, and other categories of needy citizens. Funded by payroll taxes paid by workers and employers, it is our national caretaker. Abolition of this system has been attempted with the argument that it was supposed to be a temporary measure during hard times.

A segment of the populace now suggests that some Victims have outgrown their status; that we have now achieved a comfortable enough distance from outright racism to stop giving the benefit of the doubt to all descendents of oppression and require them to pull their weight, fight their necessary life battles, and develop their best qualities. This segment argues that the groups victimized in the past now should be able to contribute to society and achieve social mobility despite former obstacles. They say that the American way is to *earn* success and *merit* opportunity rather than have them conferred because ancestors suffered from oppression in the past.

This segment challenges the motivation of Caretakers, suggesting that they might harbor an unconscious need to play the hero or heroine in the battle for social justice to reinforce their own ego and self-esteem. Caretakers may feel good about themselves, but they may unwittingly be robbing others of the empowering experience of self-sufficiency.

The Victim at Work

Motivation and Career Advancement from the Victim/Caretaker Perspective

The Victim/Caretaker Lens is motivated by the desire to right social wrongs, especially those that are targeted at racial and cultural minorities. She may be more focused on seeking out and publicizing such wrongs than on doing the job for which she was hired. While the Victim tends to blame substandard job performance on others or the system, the Caretaker is more likely to accept personal responsibility for her performance and want to improve it. Both the Victim and the Caretaker are eager to serve on any kind of committee or task force dedicated to identifying and resolving biases and inequities in the organization's hiring, training, compensation, promotion, or disciplinary systems.

The Victim and the Caretaker have different career advancement strategies. The Victim tends to think in terms of having been unfairly passed over for promotions in the past. She expects the organization to make amends for this; if it does not do so, she may initiate legal action when the next promotional opportunity comes around.

The Caretaker is focused on the fact that the organization has not treated certain racial or cultural groups fairly in the past with respect to advancement opportunities in the organization. She wants to redress this wrong by making special efforts to find qualified individuals from these racial or cultural identity groups for future management positions. If the organization cannot find any such candidates who are qualified in terms of style attributes, the Caretaker wants to establish a special mentoring track to prepare technically qualified individuals as quickly as possible.

Impacts of These Strategies on the Individual's Advancement Potential

Victim's Strategy: In most cases, this strategy serves as the death knell for the individual's career ambitions in the organization. In rare instances, when an organization is beset by legal problems related to charges of discrimination, the strategy might serve to advance the individual. However, it is unlikely that she will win many friends in the process or be taken very seriously in the new position.

Caretaker's Strategy: The impact of this strategy on individuals depends heavily on the manner in which it was implemented. A quiet effort undertaken to identify several well-qualified individuals from different membership groups and mentor them to ensure a better fit between their styles and the organization's culture would have a strongly positive effect on the individuals' advancement potential for the future. A well-publicized banner effort, carried out in the name of affirmative action, would have the opposite result.

Impacts of These Strategies on the Organization's Human Resources

Victim's Strategy: A range of consequences could result from this strategy if it became public knowledge, from widespread scorn for the individual who was promoted based on this strategy to initiation of a number of additional lawsuits. One unfortunate consequence could be that individuals who were experiencing real discrimination in their own situations with respect to work assignments, performance evaluations, or promotions would become even more reluctant to bring these concerns to the attention of the organization.

Caretaker's Strategy: The impact of this strategy depends on how it is carried out. A quiet effort that results in well-qualified individuals from different membership groups being promoted sends out the signal that the organization believes in and acts upon the twin values of competency and diversity. This can serve as a morale booster for employees, especially those from different membership groups. A loudly publicized effort is likely to be perceived as "reverse discrimination" by some members of the organization and as a statement about the inferiority of certain membership groups by all.

Working with the Victim/Caretaker

If you are working with or managing a person who has a strong preference for the Victim Lens, you are likely to hear an emphasis on the layers of race, nationality, ethnicity, socioeconomic class, and religion in interactions with him or her. Specific themes include:

- Bias against my race and culture is a daily part of my life.
- Because I was not born in this country, I feel that I am not looked on as a legitimate American by the majority culture.
- My style and many of my customs and traditions are viewed as inferior.
- Our economic worth as a race or cultural group has been diminished because of the exploitation of our ancestors, who either provided free labor or were exploited during the development of the country.
- Our religious institutions provide a philosophical and political base for mobilization to cope with the challenges of bias that we face.

While the Caretaker Lens speaks more for those whom she perceives have been oppressed and mistreated, she echoes the same sentiments.

You may be speaking from an entirely different set of layers with a Victim/Caretaker. If you are feeling defensive or confused during your discussion, or there is a need to resolve tension or conflict between you, the following guidelines may help:

- Recognize that the protests and complaints of Victims and Caretakers arise out of a deep-seated sense of injustice and a desire to right past wrongs.
- Listen empathically to their feelings of anger, frustration, and hopelessness.
- Do not ignore the concerns they express about inequities simply because they have complained about things in the past; they may be bringing some very real issues to your attention.

- Take time to understand their perspective on issues facing their community.
- Do not shy away from giving needed performance feedback to them because of a fear of reprisal or being perceived as "biased."

Coaching the Victim/Caretaker Manager or Supervisor

A Victim/Caretaker manager or supervisor may have difficulty understanding that the subject of oppression and discrimination is a very complicated one in which the labels of oppressor/discriminator and oppressed/discriminated against can quickly change, depending on the dimensions considered. For example, a white man may be perceived as the "discriminator" and a black man as the "discriminated against." However, if the white man is gay and the black man is heterosexual, the labels may become reversed. This lens needs help in taking a broader view in discussions about victimization and discrimination.

In supervising employees or interacting with customers, the Victim/Caretaker manager must understand that any excusing of individual actions based on such factors as race and color is a paternalistic and disempowering way of treating others. On the other hand, she also must be able to recognize that emerging global markets can be cultivated and cultural niche markets developed without the organization being exploitative or paternalistic in the process.

Unmonitored and underdeveloped, the Victim/Caretaker stance could lead to an overemphasis on social initiatives versus organizational performance, charges of bias in terms of preferential treatment to racial and cultural minorities, litigation, and poor use of organization and human resources. Your job as a manager or leader is to coach the Victim/Caretaker so that she is competent, confident, and willing to use or modify the organizational systems on behalf of the full range of employees in your organization.

Specifically, you can require Victim/Caretaker managers or supervisors to use the organization's systems in ways that:

- Recognize and support the needs of all members of the organization, not just those who are members of their own racial or cultural identity group
- Ensure that everyone who is hired or promoted meets the criteria that the organization has established for the opportunity as opposed to using moral persuasion or criteria based on social justice
- Encourage and reward individual initiative, not group membership.
- Establish an organizational culture in which employees are empowered with the necessary authorities and resources to take responsibility and be accountable for their actions
- Work to cultivate emerging global markets and cultural niche markets in ways that are nonexploitative and respectful of the cultures involved

The Victim/Caretaker and Organizational Systems

The Victim/Caretaker Lens is highly sensitive to inequities within the organization's systems and how these systems create barriers for some and advantages for others. She has a strong desire to reform or enhance systems so that they are more equitable for all. She may think that, since the organization's systems historically have worked against racial and cultural minorities, the systems should be used today as tools to rectify past wrongs and level the playing field. With her perspective, the Victim/Caretaker can create challenges for the organization by moving too far away from the use of objective criteria in administering the systems and depending too heavily instead on group membership as the criterion for selection or advancement opportunities.

The essence of the ways in which the organization's human resources systems are influenced by the Victim/Caretaker Lens is presented in each of the statements below. As you review these statements, think of the impact of the Victim/Caretaker stance on these same types of programs and activities in your work environment.

> **The Victim/Caretaker Stance:** "I will use the systems to increase opportunities for members of my group/racial and cultural minorities to succeed within the organization."
>
> **Recruiting:** "I will go to schools where I know there are people from my group/different cultural identity group(s) struggling for a fair shake and the right opportunity."
>
> **Hiring:** "I will hire people who otherwise would be overlooked and not given a fair chance to prove their competence."
>
> **Compensation and Benefits:** "I will make sure that members of my group/racial and cultural minority groups receive the same compensation and benefits as members of the majority culture and that we/they are not being exploited or shortchanged."
>
> **Job Placement and Assignments:** "I will ensure that members of my group/racial and cultural minority groups are not excluded from choice assignments and opportunities."
>
> **Building Effective Teams:** "I will make sure that the 'good-ole-boy' network does not block members of my group/minority groups from being considered for team membership."
>
> **Performance Management:** "I will establish a fair and equitable performance management system so that a supervisor who is biased or uncomfortable with me/racial or cultural minorities cannot harm my/their career(s) with unfair negative evaluations."

Mentoring: "I will help members of my group/racial or cultural minority groups obtain knowledgeable and successful mentors. I will institutionalize mentoring as an organizational system to force majority culture members to include us/minorities in the mentoring process."

Training: "I will ensure that we/minorities have access to the education, training, and development opportunities that will have a direct impact on our/their advancement."

Succession Planning: "I will involve our people/racial and cultural minorities in the succession planning process and see that they are included in adequate numbers in the succession planning pipeline. I will monitor the number of people from our group/minority groups who make it to senior positions."

The Victim/Caretaker and the Law

The Victim/Caretaker Lens could affect your business' bottom line in several ways. As you read the following hypothetical case, consider whether your organization may be manifesting the Victim/Caretaker Lens in similar ways.

The Case

Kimberly, a supervisor at a restaurant, decided to terminate Michael for three unexcused absences within two months. Michael protested:

Michael:	I know I had three unexcused absences. But this isn't fair. I'm usually on time and my attendance is good. There are other people here who've had unexcused absences, and you're not firing them.
Kimberly:	Never mind them. Their situation is different. They're here as part of a county program to promote hiring of people who've been unemployed. For some of them, it's their first job.
Michael:	The only difference that I can see between me and my coworkers is that I'm white and they're not.
Kimberly:	Actually, there's another difference. You've had three unexcused absences and you had a prior warning. No one else has more than one.

Michael sues his employer alleging that his termination was an act of discrimination under Title VII. Who wins?

Result

The company wins. Unexcused absences are a legitimate nondiscriminatory reason for terminating an employee. Supervisor Kimberly's "Victims and

Caretakers" mentality could have created a problem for the company, when she said she was deliberately treating the nonwhite employees differently because "for some of them, it's their first job." However, in the final analysis, she treated those employees differently because they did not have as many absences as Michael, not because they are of a different race or color.

Legal Concerns for the Victim/Caretaker Lens

The Victim/Caretaker is particularly concerned for those perceived as oppressed. If you think you may use the Victim/Caretaker Lens, be aware of the following:

- Bending the rules to favor those perceived as oppressed might result in inconsistent treatment that could lead to a claim of discrimination.

  "When I don't show up for work on time, I get reprimanded. Why don't [African-American/Hispanic/older] employees get reprimanded like I do?"

Victim/Caretaker Highest Expression

What the Best of the **Victim/Caretaker Lens** Can Contribute to the Organization and Community

Collective Settlement, Healing, Reform, Forgiveness

The Victim/Caretaker Lens, in its original stance, seeks freedom and justice for all races and cultures to end the adverse impact of historical and present-day oppression. From a higher and more holistic perspective, the Victim/Caretaker continues to seek freedom and justice but, in addition, strives to achieve an appropriate blend of collective settlement, community healing, institutional reform, and forgiveness.

From this higher perspective, the Victim/Caretaker promotes the belief that when any group is persecuted and/or marginalized, we are all negatively affected because of the cycle of retribution. The cycle begins with the dominant group, which holds the reins of institutional power, acting with hatred or intolerance toward one or more subordinate groups. To counter this reaction, subordinate groups, who feel persecuted or discriminated against, rebel and seek retribution. The Victim/Caretaker recognizes that we need to change our focus from blame and revenge to settlement, healing, and forgiveness, and ultimately, true reform.

Moving from retribution to reform can be a challenge for the Victim/Caretaker because she can become mired in the overwhelming pain associated with subordinate status in the organization and society. To make the move, she must allow the justness of her cause to motivate her toward personal and collective empowerment. She must be willing to act in concert with members from the dominant group who share her passion for justice. Together with them, the Victim/Caretaker is able to explore ways to resolve painful chapters in our collective societal history so that we can all envision and work toward a new reality.

To settle disputes, all participants must agree that a settlement is necessary in the form of reparation and/or atonement. The settlement frees the community from past injustices and negative energy and allows the institution to institute corrective and preventive reforms. These reforms create protections so that the same types of injustices cannot recur.

In its highest expression, the Victim/Caretaker knows that institutionalizing values such as dignity, equality, and fairness may come at a high price but that our inability to extend these values to all members of our organizations and society will exact an even higher price. Without these values, we will not be able to forgive. Without forgiveness, there can be no healing; without healing, there can be no end to the cycle of retribution. When the Victim/Caretaker operates from its highest expression, seeking redemption and justice, the result can be societal and organizational transformation.

Victim/Caretaker Quotes

Victim Quotes

"With most Asian Americans having immigrated to the U.S. after 1965 under selective standards, our socioeconomic status provides useful but misleading statistical ammunition for those who celebrate Asian success without acknowledging that Asian Americans face pervasive workplace discrimination and receive lower incomes than whites at every level of education and experience."

Andrew Chin, "Elaine Chao: Poster Child for the 'Model Minority' Myth," January 11, 2001, www.modelminority.com/politics/used.htm.

"In an America where most people of color continue to experience the indignity of racial discrimination on a daily basis, your constant impulse has been to blame the victims. You're fond of telling us it's all in our heads. Racial minorities suffer not from oppression, but from "low expectations".... We Asian Americans will not be used to deliver that message. Sure, we've had our success stories. But we've also known poverty, exclusion, disenfranchisement, dislocation, and internment. We continue to face violence, workplace discrimination, and social marginalization on account of our race."

Andrew Chin, in an open letter to President-elect George W. Bush, January 13, 2001.

"After noticing that 'the black students were the worst students on campus,' he [John McWhorter, an associate professor of linguistics at Berkeley] concluded they were held back by three "defeatist thought patterns":

- the Cult of Victimology, which leads blacks to blame their problem on racism;
- the Cult of Separatism, which makes blacks think that whatever whites do, they should do the opposite; and
- the cult of Anti-Intellectualism, which holds that scholastic excellence is a white thing."

Jack E. White, "Are Blacks Biased Against Braininess?," *Time Magazine*, August 7, 2000.

"It comes as a great shock to see Gary Cooper killing off the Indians and, although you are rooting for Gary Cooper, the Indians are *you*."

James Baldwin, speech at Cambridge University, February 17, 1965. www.xrefer.com/entry/168354

Caretaker Quotes

"Remember no one can make you feel inferior without your consent."

Eleanor Roosevelt, *Great Quotes from Great Women*. ed. Peggy Anderson. (Illinois: Celebrating Excellence Publishing, 1992), 3.

"It ought to be axiomatic in this country that every man must devote a reasonable share of his time to doing his duty in the . . . life of the community."

Theodore Roosevelt, "The Duties of American Citizenship," Buffalo, New York, January 26, 1883: www.tamu.edu/scom/pres/archive.html.

"You cannot hope to build a better world without improving the individuals. To that end each of us must work for his own improvement, and at the same time share a general responsibility for all humanity, our particular duty being to aid those to whom we think we can be most useful."

Marie Curie, *Great Quotes from Great Women*. ed. Peggy Anderson. (Illinois: Celebrating Excellence Publishing, 1992), 23.

The Eleventh Lens

Introduction

The ten lenses provide a framework, but they also expose our distorted and incomplete vision. There is yet another perspective: an emerging Eleventh Lens, comprising the highest expressions of each of the other ten lenses, that can liberate us from the boundaries of these lenses and propel us toward healing ourselves, each other, and our planet.

The Eleventh Lens envisions the earth and its inhabitants as inextricably blended in a chorus of universal harmony that is both diverse and self-sustaining. The harmony depends on every voice and the quality of its contribution; it is threatened only by the exclusion or destruction of any of its parts. The chorus is powered by an invisible universal force that moves us from separation to connection, from independence to interdependence, from discord to unity.

The metaphor for the Eleventh Lens is "One Song, Many Voices," and its purpose is to find one's own voice within the chorus of life and practice responsible life actions that support wholeness and harmony. The web of life balances our individuality and our interconnection. From inside the web each of us can see:

> I am one voice singing in the choir
> One flame burning in the fire
> I am one wave rolling in the sea
> One voice in the sea of humanity

The Eleventh Lens is supported by concepts rooted in the physical, biological, ecological, technological, and spiritual domains. These constructs teach us that our prosperity and survival depend on our ability to understand the connectedness of all living things, to embrace our differences, to collaborate with each other, and to see the world as full of opportunities and riches for all.

Eleventh Lens Core Beliefs

People and the Earth Are Inextricably Linked

Four core beliefs form the basis of the eleventh Lens.

First, people and the earth are inextricably linked. Discoveries about the nature of biological systems reveal the presence of a mysterious underlying force that creates and sustains all life forms of the universe and causes them to interact in ways that produce the optimal conditions for continued growth and evolution of the universe as a whole. For years, some biologists held the view that the earth was dead. Today many microbiologists—including Professor Lynn Margulis, coauthor of *The Gaia Theory*—have submitted ample evidence that, in fact, life on earth is maintained through a series of highly complex and interdependent systems that hold life in the balance at the microscopic level.

There is a narrow margin for error in the variables that support life on this planet. Oxygen, sulfur, nitrogen, and carbon concentrations; temperature, pressure, salinity of water; and other variables—all are controlled in a delicate balance that maintains the links in the life chain.

What or who accomplishes this perfect balance of elements? The biologists' answer to that question is that a global network of protozoa, bacteria, and other microscopic entities modulates and regulates with incredible precision. Indeed, there is a "world wide web," and it has been working for some 3.5 billion years—enabling, supporting, and sustaining the conditions necessary for life.

The Gaia hypothesis was first posited in the 1960s by James Lovelock when he was involved in devising experiments to test for life on Mars for the Jet Propulsion Laboratory and the National Aeronautics and Space Administration. Although the Viking lander found no evidence of life on Mars, Lovelock's thinking about the earth was transformed. Instead of a planet playing host to a variety of life forms, he began to think of earth as a planet constantly transformed by a "self-evolving and self-regulating living being." Lovelock bestowed the name "Gaia" on this living system in honor of the Greek goddess who caused the living world to come forth from Chaos. While not all scientists would agree with Lovelock's hypothesis, there is an ever-increasing body of research to support it.

Those who inhabited this country before European immigrants arrived understood that there could be no separation between people and the earth—the earth was a living thing and all living beings are related. The majority culture has not adopted or acted on that belief over the intervening centuries, but we are beginning to understand once again that there can be no separation.

Diverse Ecosystems Are Strong and Durable

The second core belief is in the strength and durability of diverse ecosystems.

The value of diversity in ecology is not an argument—just a question of degree and intensity. Bill McDonough, the Dean of the School of Architecture at the University of Virginia, is a "green designer." His aim is to design and build in ways that integrate humankind's role in the web of life. He works to find methods that use resources responsibly and provide consumers with options of sustainable materials. A key point in his work is diversity. He says, "nature adores diversity."

Diverse ecosystems are strong, durable, cyclical, unified, and interdependent. In a stand of elms that has been invaded by Dutch elm disease, the result is catastrophic. However, in that same area of woods consisting of elms, oaks, pines, birch, maple, and other species, the diverse forest is resilient with a long life expectancy. One element may fall out of the cycle and be missed, but because of the diversity, the absence is not fatal to the whole. In recent years, the study of ecology has taught us that there is no such thing as a local environment. What happens to the diversity of life within the rain forest has consequences for the future quality of life worldwide.

These themes in biology and ecology suggest a blueprint for honoring diversity in human communities. When diverse cultures, histories, customs, ideas, and gifts are honored and incorporated, the community as a whole is enriched. By stark contrast, we can imagine the consequences if the Nazis had succeeded in their plan for a "final solution"—one monoculture of Aryan Europeans. We can only imagine what riches in art, culture, music, science, poetry, philosophy and human expression would have been lost!

Whatever We Do to the Web, We Do to Ourselves

The third core belief is that we cannot separate ourselves and our actions from the web. Revolutionary discoveries in quantum physics, "the new science," support the biological and ecological evidence for an invisible and forceful web of life. Interdependence and relationship reemerge as key factors. In seeking to determine the nature of subatomic matter, scientists are finding that they cannot isolate particles but can understand them only in relation to each other. There is no independent thing; instead, the fundamental elements of all creation exist in interrelationship. On a physical level, we are part of an invisible, interdependent whole.

All Is One

The fourth of the core beliefs is that all is one. The eleventh Lens defines a way of life in which physics, metaphysics, science, and religion converge. Themes of connection, interdependence, and mutuality that emerge from hard and social sciences echo teachings that have been articulated for millennia. Buddhists speak of "oneness"; Christians of the need to "love thy neighbor as thyself";

the fundamental daily prayer of the Jews praises God as one.

Hispanic Asian Caucasian Arab Indian African

Muslim Hindu Christian Jew

Men and Women

Me and You

Every heart beats to the rhythm of Humanity

A story is told about a traveler who asked a wise one, "Why do people come in such great diversity?" The wise one replied, "Because we are all made in God's image." If God has infinite diversity and we accept that we are spiritual beings in his image, then we come to know God's mystery and unconditional love by growing in intimacy with all people and all beings. From this perspective, another's difference is a gift to me; my opportunity to know God is enriched by another made in God's image. The web of life is incomplete without the spiritual element, whatever form we wish to give it. In the diversity, richness, and multiplicity of all life forms, we come to know the higher form and see our logical and spiritual place in the chorus.

Moving Toward the Eleventh Lens

The Eleventh Lens calls on us to embrace the mystery and diversity within ourselves and in those who are different. A biological tribe educates its members with the skills of survival according to the tribe's standards, customs, and laws. A key element of survival is how to relate to others from differing tribes, races, and cultures and to protect physical and psychological safety. Eleventh Lens vision requires that we choose intentionally to retain those influences from our tribe that are positive and to discard those that are not, even at the risk of experiencing ridicule and alienation from the tribe. It may be necessary for us to sound a discordant note while the band plays on. Many of those who have begun to operate from the Eleventh Lens describe their experience as being out of tune with their family, race, culture, or society, because they are challenging tribal thought and the core mental constructs that uphold existing social norms, political discourse, and economic structure.

Author Ken Wilber is credited with developing a unified field theory of consciousness—a synthesis and interpretation of psychological, philosophical, and spiritual traditions. He notes that a dramatic shift occurs when we experience "the emergence of the capacity to take on the role of the other, at which point the egocentric perspective shifts to sociocentric." Wilber says that from the sociocentric perspective we are closer to a world-centric stance—where we gain a wider consciousness that shines beyond the confines of me and mine. Individuals who see the world through the Eleventh Lens believe that, once free of the habitual norms and practices of the other lenses, their interior world opens up, they experience inward vision often described as a voice within, and their intuitions guide them through new and exciting spiritual and psychological terrain.

When we experience life from the perspective of the Eleventh Lens, we find that we are living by a set of values that provides an ethical compass to guide our thoughts, intentions, and actions. This is because we are given the responsibility and privilege of acting in accordance with the mysterious life-serving force, which is creative and intelligent by nature. It is our birthright as inhabitants of the universe to access this life-serving force. In return, we each serve life by aligning our thoughts, intentions, and actions with this force that unifies all life. Sister Corita Kent, a graphic artist who gained attention in the 1960s, featured this quote in a serigraph: "Every soul is like a tiny drop without which the whole world would thirst." To liken a soul to a drop of water is this artist's way of emphasizing the value of each element in the web of life.

My race, my religion
And nationality
Are gifts I bring
To humanity

Holding Paradox

Many of us have been well conditioned by our religious and cultural inheritances to maintain a puritanical insistence on black-and-white, right-and-wrong viewpoints. The Eleventh Lens broadens our vision to incorporate multiple perspectives on reality. Study the circle of paradoxes shown below. Six paradoxical statements are placed opposite each other in the circle: "We Are The Same—I Am Unique; One Right Way—Multiple Truths; Individual Orientation—Institutional Orientation; Future Possibility—History of

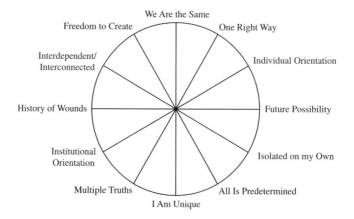

Wounds; Isolated on my Own—Interdependent/Interconnected; and All is Predetermined—Freedom to Create."

Which idea in each of these dyads is true? From the perspective of the Eleventh Lens, the answer is "both." Each of us is unique, yet we are all human beings with common interests and needs. There is a right way and there are multiple truths. We are individuals and we are a part of institutions. There are future possibilities and there is a history of wounds. We are on our own and we are interconnected. All is predetermined and we have the freedom to create. We can listen for the rhythm of these and other paradoxes: day and night, black and white, dark and light, earth and sky. The oppositional "either/or" polarizes, but we can hear the power of "and" to unite.

A kabbalist rabbi was asked, "What's the meaning of paradox—you know, the kind that blows your mind?" She answered, "Yes." The ability to think laterally and to hold paradoxical experiences simultaneously with ease and grace is essential for the Eleventh Lens. As our minds expand to hold seemingly contradictory themes, we develop a flexibility and resilience in our thinking, acting, and being. As we move from "either/or" to "both/and" thinking, we develop compassion and appreciation for all people and all beings. As poet, singer, author, and spiritual leader Maya Angelou says, "I am a human being; nothing human can be foreign to me."

The Use of Dialogue

You may understand the concept but still wonder how we increase our capacity for paradoxical thinking. One approach is through the practice of the dialogue process that involves sitting with others in a circle and engaging in reflective conversation with the help of some specific guidelines. Dialogue of this sort can be a powerful tool for self-awareness. As you sit in the circle where viewpoints are being expressed that are contrary to those you hold dear, you have the opportunity either to react defensively or to be aware of your reactivity and consider the paradox that is present. Using the circle of paradoxes as an example, you can imagine that you are in a dialogue where people in the room are representing each of these perspectives. As a witness you might hear one person speaking of his personal history of wounds, while another articulates her vision for a powerful future. Which is right? If you find yourself voting for one or the other, you may get stuck in polarized thinking. However, if you can see the whole and embrace the perfection of each viewpoint, given the unique perspectives of the people who are voicing them, you have the opportunity to hold the paradox and increase the flexibility of your thinking. You have the opportunity to find both the wounded and visionary parts within yourself and honor both of them.

What if you are the one holding a strong opinion in the dialogue circle? For example, you believe that there are multiple truths while the person opposite you insists on one true way. When you are mentally and emotionally tied to this one perspective, it is more challenging to practice paradoxical thinking and to find what is right, good, and whole about the other person. It can help to literally step out of your position by moving physically and changing your position to gain a new perspective. You can ask yourself if there is a third position that would embrace the needs, fears, and aspirations of both perspectives. When you can detach from your own dearly held viewpoints long enough to see validity in the opposition, you have made great strides toward peace. You have also found that small place within that recognizes the humanity of people with opposing views.

Obstacles to Using the Eleventh Lens

The Scarcity Myth

Throughout history, atrocities have been committed for the sake of financial gain. We see evidence over the last 5,000 years of people exploiting and oppressing those who are different and vulnerable. The Egyptians used the Hebrews to build their pyramids. The Romans massacred thousands in their efforts to conquer the world. The first settlers in the New World slaughtered the native peoples to control the land and secure their fortunes. Slave traders stole Africans from their homelands to exploit the land and make it more productive and profitable. Greed and competition are often identified as the motives for these brutal acts of oppression, and these certainly are present. However, a deeper fundamental structure drives the greed, and that is an underlying belief in the myth of scarcity.

The scarcity myth can be expressed as follows: "There is not enough for all of us; I must survive, therefore, I must have power over you, enslave you, or murder you to eliminate you as a threat. I must fight you for my survival." The consequences of the scarcity world view are devastating. A wise Holocaust survivor once said, "...when you allow one people to define themselves as superior to another, the logical consequences are gas chambers and the burning of bodies. Don't let it happen." He did not have to conjure an image to illustrate the consequences of unchecked social and political power, for he had experienced them—devastation of entire peoples and cultures.

There are nearly 6 billion people on the planet. One in six of us goes hungry each day. Sweatshops allow us to use other people for work that is outlawed as subhuman. We continue to objectify and exploit those who are different in our desire to maximize profit. In pursuit of financial reward, we have given ourselves permission to exploit the land and pollute rivers, aquifers, soil, and air—the fundamental elements that are the stuff of planetary survival.

The predatory nature of most creatures in the food chain is appropriate and, in fact, necessary; on the human domain it is neither. The scarcity mentality is a fundamental misconception that, like the belief in a flat world, has been repeated enough and flourished so long that we are unable to see the truth. Our world resources go beyond "enough" to "abundant." There is abundant food, water, shelter, energy, and material for us to meet our basic needs with dignity and grace.

There is no food shortage because of necessity; there is a lack of political, social, and economic motivation to develop the infrastructure needed to get the food to hungry people. There is no energy crisis; everyday we receive 8,000 times more energy from the sun than we need, yet there is a crisis of creativity that has prevented us from harnessing available energy in ways that are environmentally sustainable and cost efficient. There is a crisis of ethics that allows uneven distribution and usage of energy based on the wants of some rather than the needs of all.

Victor–Victim–Vampire Cycle

The scarcity myth keeps us from seeing reality and living our birthright. It is a view that promotes disconnection, xenophobia, domination, win-lose competitiveness and, ultimately, violence. It destroys beauty and diversity. A vicious cycle is established of victor/victim/vampire as a result of the myth. We see this at work wherever there is ethnic conflict. Germany, defeated in World War I, became the vampire of World War II. Ethnic cleansing in Kosovo, apartheid in South Africa, Muslim-Jewish antagonism in the Middle East: in all of these brutal stories, we see people entangled in a push-pull-push drama of mutual destruction. The victors can exercise power actively over their victims, change the system to their advantage, or simply watch events play out as passive bystanders. The victims can fight back, internalize shame and powerlessness, or become the vampires/perpetrators of the next generation. Another option we all have to these recurring patterns of history is to break out of the cycle, dismiss the scarcity myth once and for all, and embrace the Eleventh Lens wholeheartedly.

Values of the Eleventh Lens

A simple but profound ethic emerges from the values and truths of the Eleventh Lens, which can be summarized as follows:

- I am connected to others and the earth.
- My life is essential to everything else; at the deepest level what I think and do matters.
- A holistic perspective of totality requires looking both inward and outward to experience oneness.

- Diversity is vital to survival; sameness prevents growth.
- Subordination, exploitation, or oppression of any culture, group, or element injures all.
- There is abundance—enough for all.
- Either/or excludes; both/and includes.

Achieving the Perspective of the Eleventh Lens

The perspective of the Eleventh Lens emerges from combining the highest expressions of each of the other lenses. At its lowest level of expression, each lens exhibits intolerant behaviors. As the lens develops, it moves through a stage of tolerant behaviors, followed by a third stage of valuing behaviors. The fourth and highest stage of expression involves inclusive behaviors. Examples of the behaviors at each step in this model for each of the ten lenses is found in the chart titled "Individual Lenses' Paths to Inclusive Behaviors." The following guidelines may help if you are interested in moving toward the highest expression of your lenses:

1. Recognize the inherent limitations in the original stance of your own and the other nine lenses.
2. Determine what appeals to you personally about the perspective of the Eleventh Lens. What will keep you motivated when the journey gets tough?
3. Capitalize on the strengths of your lens, using them as the stepping stones in the progression from the original stance to the highest expression.
4. Learn more about the dialogue process and use it whenever you can to increase the flexibility of your thinking and your ability to hold paradoxes.
5. Acknowledge and appreciate the strengths that other lenses contribute to your personal, work, social, and community life.
6. Invite someone from a different racial or cultural group to have conversations with you about your different perspectives and experiences with respect to organization or community life.
7. Invite someone whose lens is different from yours to have conversations about your similarities and differences, what you admire about each other's perspective, and how you can help each other take the steps from original stance to highest expression.
8. Take the time to develop a clear picture of what it looks like to you at each step in your journey toward the highest expression of your lens. How will you know when you are at the intolerant, tolerant, valuing, and inclusive levels of expression of your lenses? How will you acknowledge and celebrate your progress?

The Influences the Eleventh Lens
Would Have on An Organization

If your organization were operating primarily from the stance of the Eleventh Lens, you would be likely to observe some of the following characteristics:

- There would be a shared vision of what the organization desired to become that incorporated the values and core beliefs of a humanity-centered institution in line with the world view of the Eleventh Lens.

- The organization would respect the perspectives and interests of its multicultural stakeholders as it sought to maintain and expand on its current customer base.

- Business would be developed and conducted using universal standards of excellence.

- There would be equitable human resources management systems that treated all members of the organization fairly and with dignity.

- The control systems would be in place to give people all of the resources and authorities necessary to do their jobs well and then hold them accountable.

- The organizational culture would incorporate a broader range of standards and norms, offering a much greater freedom of multicultural expression.

- Formal and informal processes would be in place to encourage and support relationships across all racial and cultural lines.

As a result, people would:

- Want to belong to the organization and show allegiance and loyalty to it.

- Demonstrate a strong sense of ownership and pride in the organization's activities.

- Know that they were respected.

- Feel personally empowered and motivated to contribute their best.

- Be able to demonstrate their individuality while simultaneously acknowledging and honoring their racial and cultural identities.

- Be able to let go of grievances and engage in true healing processes with each other.

In summary, organizations working from the Eleventh Lens are creative, successful, resilient, and diverse. They are employers of choice, fostering loyalty, spirited morale, and high retention rates among their employees. Viewed by Wall Street as standard bearers for the twenty-first century, they attract investment capital. They are valued by their customers, who are loyal to them, and appreciated by the communities in which they are located.

A Final Note

Life within the scope of the Eleventh Lens is already ours by birthright. We need only open ourselves to whatever changes are necessary to allow the values and truths of the Eleventh Lens to govern every aspect of our lives, moving us from separation to connection and from discord to unity. These truths are the stuff of the web of life, the basic notes in our chorus. It is time for each of us to sing out!

Introduction to "The Path to Organizational Inclusiveness"

One way of looking at an organization's approach to diversity is to describe behaviors and organization practices along a continuum, from:

- Intolerant (putting others down, excluding them, basing policies and procedures on stereotypes and prejudices) to
- Tolerant (putting up with others, giving them token acknowledgement, making sure that policies and procedures comply with legal requirements) to
- Valuing (recognizing and valuing others' contributions, responding to special needs voiced by employees in establishing policies and procedures) to
- Inclusive (seeking out the opinions, needs, and contributions of others, being authentically interested in other racial and cultural groups, anticipating the needs of different groups of employees and establishing progressive policies and procedures to meet these needs).

At the intolerant end of the continuum, organization employees are likely to feel unrecognized, unvalued, and unwilling to be as productive, creative, and collaborative as they could be. At the inclusive end of the continuum, they are likely to feel just the opposite and be enthusiastically motivated to give the best that is in them.

There are three contributing factors to consider in assessing where an organization is along the continuum to inclusiveness: individual employee behaviors; manager and supervisor role behaviors; and the systemic practices of the organization, in terms of its internal human resources management systems, its external customer interface, and market development systems.

On the following pages, you will find examples of how each of the ten lenses would contribute to intolerant, tolerant, valuing, and inclusive work environments in the individual employee behaviors.

Individual Lenses' Paths to Inclusive Behaviors

	Intolerant	Tolerant	Valuing	Inclusive
Assimilationist	Refusing to recognize the validity of other people's cultural beliefs and practices Insisting that people do things "the American way"	Acknowledging the validity of other people's cultural beliefs and practices, but being unwilling to take part in implementing and/or celebrating them	Showing interest in other people's cultural beliefs and practices Participating in the implementation and/or celebration of these different practices	Incorporating different cultural beliefs and practices into one's own belief system and practices
Colorblind	Denying the reality of racial or cultural differences among individuals	Acknowledging the reality of racial or cultural differences but insisting that they make no difference in individual life/ work experiences or relationships	Recognizing and appreciating how racial or cultural differences are an integral part of individual identities	Exploring with others how racial or cultural differences have influenced one's life/ work choices and experiences
Culturalcentrist	Denying differences within one's own racial or cultural group Isolating one's self or group from other racial or cultural groups in the workforce	Acknowledging differences within one's own racial or cultural group when confronted with these Working side by side with members of other identity groups when necessary	Recognizing and appreciating individual differences within one's own cultural identity group and within other racial and cultural groups as well—especially within those groups with which there are feelings of identity or sympathetic connection	Collaborating with individuals from other racial and cultural groups—especially from those groups with which there are feelings of identity or sympathetic connection—to build on individual differences when working on organizational projects

Intolerant	Tolerant	Valuing	Inclusive
Elitist			
Denying that one's status in the organization has been achieved with the help of one's connections, social standing, or lineage Putting down—or not having anything to do with those members of the workforce who do not come from the same background or have the same standing in the organization/society	Acknowledging that one's background and connections have served as advantages in career advancement and that other members of the workforce have not experienced the same advantages	Paying attention to the input of those who do not come from the same privileged backgrounds Showing interest in and appreciation for their different talents and contributions	Proactively seeking the ideas, help, and support on various jobs or organization projects from individuals who do not share the same social status or standing
Integrationist			
Focusing only on concerns related to black/white relationships and equity issues in the workplace Insisting on the need for black and white coworkers to associate closely with each other during work hours and at social events sponsored by the organization, whether others want to do this or not	Extending attention to the needs and relationships of other racial and cultural identity groups in the workplace Recognizing that coworkers of different races and cultures may not be ready to associate with each other as completely or quickly as the Integrationist would like to see happen	Recognizing that, for many people, cultural pride and group identity are extremely important and that integration is perceived as a threat to maintaining these aspects of one's identity	Moving beyond stereotypes and developing more meaningful and authentic working relationships with coworkers from different racial and cultural identity groups

(cont.)

Intolerant	Tolerant	Valuing	Inclusive
Meritocratist			
Placing all credit or blame for different achievement levels among coworkers on individual competencies or deficiencies, or on race, gender, or ethnicity without considering the impacts that race, gender, etc. may have had	Acknowledging that different levels of family support, socio-economic background, or educational opportunities result in unequal starting places for people in the game of organizational life and that this often has as much to do with coworkers' achievement levels as do their skills, abilities, and ambition levels	Recognizing that coworkers from different cultural identity groups may have different ways of defining competencies and merit	Supporting coworkers who demonstrate different kinds of initiatives, competencies, and accomplishments rather than just those defined as "the right ones" by those who traditionally have held leadership positions
Multiculturalist			
Insisting that the organization focus on diversity issues related to race, culture, ethnicity, or gender above all else— including business needs Making critical remarks about all white, middle-class, heterosexual men of European descent because they represent the historical majority	Recognizing that overemphasizing diversity can be experienced by others as depersonalizing them if they believe that they are being seen only as "women," "African Americans," "Latinos," "gays" Not making critical remarks about any individuals just because they are members of a particular identity group	Acknowledging the complexities involved in balancing business needs and creating organizational systems to support multiculturalism	Participating actively in organizational efforts to create a common set of business practices and cultural norms that incorporate multiculturalist values but supercede the beliefs and traditions of diverse sub-cultures within the organization

	Intolerant	Tolerant	Valuing	Inclusive
Seclusionist	Making insulting or hostile remarks about people in the workforce from other racial or cultural groups Blaming them for productivity, quality, or service problems whether or not they had anything to do with these problems	Remaining separate from other racial or cultural groups in the workforce whenever possible, but without directly antagonizing them Acting politely whenever one is required to work directly with those of other racial or cultural groups	Remaining separate from other racial or cultural groups in the workforce whenever possible, but acknowledging the contributions they make to the organization	Pulling together as a team with all members of the workforce, regardless of racial or cultural identity, especially in times of crisis
Transcendent	Denying the importance of differences with respect to race, culture, ethnicity, or gender for many coworkers Proselytizing with coworkers about spiritual enlightenment	Recognizing that racial and cultural differences are critically important to some people and that coworkers may be turned off or threatened by zealousness in talking about individual enlightenment and the "oneness of all"	Acknowledging and appreciating the diversity of religious/spiritual contributions made by different identity groups	Incorporating different cultural beliefs and practices into one's own belief system and practices with respect to individual spiritual enlightenment

(cont.)

Intolerant	Tolerant	Valuing	Inclusive
Victim/Caretaker			
Blaming the system, other individuals, or other cultural identity groups for one's (victim) or other people's (caretaker) performance problems, organizational standing, problems with coworkers, and/or general dissatisfaction with life	Acknowledging that the individual owns part of the problem and will need to make some changes, rather than expect all changes to be made by the organization to remediate the situation Recognizing that the requirement to "pull one's own weight" can be a sign of respect for an individual's capabilities rather than an attempt to ignore historic inequities	Expressing one's anger, hurt, or resentment to the people involved and then working with them to achieve a mutual understanding of what needs to be done on both parts to improve the situation (victim) Facilitating meetings to express emotions and agree on what should be done to settle issues (caretaker)	Empowering one's self (victim) or helping others to feel empowered (caretaker) by taking responsibility for job performance or the situation, clarifying what the goals and expectations of others are, obtaining the necessary resources and support, and working well with others to perform the job or fix the situation in a timely and effective manner

Tools and Concepts
Overview

The final four chapters in this book offer concepts and tools to help managers apply what they have learned about lenses to their organizational roles. Many of the topics covered in these chapters have been touched on at different points in the book. In these last four chapters, the topics are explored in depth.

While the subject of "fit" with the organization's culture has been mentioned in the Motivation and Career Advancement sections of earlier chapters, Cultural Fit and Career Advancement discusses this topic in more detail and offers some provocative thoughts with respect to the hidden criteria involved in career advancement.

Using the "Ls" to Improve Communication with Employees in a Diverse Workforce presents more comprehensive aspects of how to use the concepts of legacies and layers in building relationships with employees, as well as some additional tools for effective communications in both personal and professional relationships.

Looking Through the Lenses at Your Human Resources Management Systems takes you step by step through the process of assessing the influence of specific lenses on your organization's systems. The chapter contains specific guidelines for planning and implementing the change process to accomplish this goal.

Finally, Checklists for the Lenses includes a series of checklists, one for each of the ten lenses, that offer you suggestions about how to operate more effectively from the perspective of your lens.

Cultural Fit and Career Advancement

Introduction

Which of these statements most reflects how you believe people move up in organizations?

- It's not what you know; it's who you know that counts.
- You need to show that you've got the smarts to do whatever the job requires.
- If you work hard and play by the rules, you'll eventually succeed.
- If you have the right image, you'll go far.
- You need to fit in with the organizational culture and style.
- Some combination of the above.

Most people would say "some combination of the above," and they would be right. What is interesting to note is that the weight placed on these different factors seems to vary as one moves up in the organization. For the most part, presumed competence implied by a resumé with the relevant education, skills, and experience and, sometimes, connections will get you in the door of the organization. As you demonstrate your "smarts" and your willingness to work hard, you are rewarded by promotions within your technical classification and even into first- and second-line supervisory positions.

However, after this point, advancement usually becomes less about competence, which you are presumed to have, and more about how well you "fit" with the organizational culture. Fit has to do with two things: 1) how closely your identity characteristics match those of the predominant membership group(s) of the organization; and 2) how well your style aligns with the organization's cultural norms. The specific mix of these two dimensions affects the pathways of mobility to the upper levels of the organization.

When senior leaders in various organizations have been asked to show their job descriptions, they generally respond by saying "there isn't one." In response to the follow-up question, "How did the organization know that you were the most qualified individual for the job?" individuals usually mention things like their tenure, exposure to different parts of the organization, past successes, and proven ability to motivate employees. When asked what happens when two or three people in the organization have the same level of experience, tenure, and success, the response is, "The selection is based on comfort or on how well the person is known and liked or how well-connected he is in the organization." However, it usually takes a lot of probing to get an individual to talk about these qualities because they are more about group membership and style and less about competence.

To illustrate this point, you might ask a group of people to list the legal criteria to become president of the United States. After some discussion, people usually agree that the legal criteria to be president of the United States include being 35 years of age or older, having been born a U.S. citizen, and not having been convicted of a felony. A second question to ask is, "Based on these criteria, who in the room is eligible to be president of the United States?" Most of the time, the majority of people in the room will raise their hands. However, when asked a third question, "How many of you believe you could be elected president of the United States?" very few people will raise their hands.

The Hidden Criteria

The reasons for this are twofold. First, most of us have not had the experiences that would provide us with the competency to perform in the role of president. Second, most of us are aware at some level of the hidden criteria. You can get people to identify these hidden criteria by asking them to look back in history and name the types of qualities and characteristics that past presidents have possessed. Individuals typically identify characteristics such as: white, male, lawyer, married, family man, military experience, a leader, charismatic, strong, articulate, northeastern, wealthy, Christian, physically fit, outgoing personality, and extrovert. While there are exceptions to the rule, their comments are mostly correct. A final step in this experiment is to ask people to place these characteristics into one of three categories: Competence, Membership Identity, and Style.

They are usually surprised to see how many of the criteria are driven by style and membership. They are more aware of how many different kinds of people would not necessarily be seen as presidential material based wholly on membership and style characteristics.

Organizations operate in a similar manner. At some point, most of the candidates for senior positions are included in the pool for potential advancement because they meet or have exceeded the competency and experience requirements for these positions. Typically, the ultimate decision about who is awarded the opportunity comes down to how well the individual's membership identity and style "fit" with the organization's culture. It is these attributes that garner internal political support for the individual.

Membership Identity

Membership identity includes characteristics such as gender, race, age, nationality, ethnicity, socioeconomic class, religion, and sexual orientation.

Membership in the various groups into which we are born profoundly affects how we experience the world—what we are exposed to, where and how we are educated, our styles of communication, our levels of confidence, our expectations of how we should be treated and what we should achieve, how comfortable and skilled we are at interacting across various class levels. In turn, these attributes—especially those immediately obvious to others, such as gender, race, age, class, and physical or mental challenges—profoundly affect how others experience us.

The more our membership identities mirror those of the dominant membership group(s) of the organization, the better the fit, and the more likely we are to have the potential to advance to senior levels of the organization, depending on our style characteristics.

Style

Style incorporates both tangible and intangible factors. The more tangible elements include our work practices; our ways of interacting with those above us, our peers, and those at lower levels of the organization; how we manage conflict; how we dress; how we speak at meetings and make presentations; whether we socialize with colleagues; and how we handle the political dynamics of the organization. The intangible elements, which can be inferred from our behaviors, include our beliefs, attitudes, trustworthiness, and core values.

In *Men and Women of the Corporation*, social scientist Rosabeth Moss Kantor introduced the notion of "homosocial reproduction." Her premise was that those at the top of the organization (typically, older white males of European descent) inadvertently "reproduce" themselves when they are promoting individuals to senior positions because they can trust and feel most comfortable with those who are most like themselves.

Different organizations and industries are likely to require very different style attributes for advancement into senior ranks. For example, to advance as a senior leader in the military requires a very different style from that needed in retail or the service industry.

The question for individuals seeking advancement to upper-middle and senior-management levels of the organization becomes: "Do I have the necessary style characteristics to fit into this organization's leadership club? Do I have the same kind of personal image as others at the top of the organization, so that my peers and other internal and external stakeholders will feel comfortable with me?"

Below are examples of some style attributes. As you review the items, think about which attributes are more highly regarded in your organization. Also, think about how some of these attributes may be biased toward various cultures.

- An outgoing self-confident manner
- Articulate
- A reserved, thoughtful style of speaking
- Direct eye contact
- Firm handshake
- Straightforward; able and willing to address conflict directly
- Preferring to avoid conflict
- Educational background
- Reserved style of dress
- Colorful style of dress
- Finest of designer labels and materials in clothing
- Extremely knowledgeable about travel, fine arts, performing arts, wines, good food, restaurants, literature, music, movie history, sports, local or national teams, stocks, history, the political dynamics of the organization, the industry, the business world
- Interested in socializing outside of the workplace
- Politically active
- Well connected
- Workaholic

The Impact of "Fit" on Advancement

Perceptions about how individuals adapt, respond, and succeed in an organization are unconsciously embedded in all our interpersonal interactions and organizational systems. They have a strong influence on the organizational culture; in turn, organizational culture influences how competency, membership identity, and style are viewed and acted on by the organization. Often, membership identity and style are discussed as if they were competencies. There is also a tendency to change one's perception of competency based on the group membership identity and style of an individual. For example, an Asian employee might be a competent leader, but his leadership style may be different from the traditional leadership style of the organization. He may be deemed deficient as a leader simply because his style does not mirror the organization's leadership style.

Depending on how broadly or narrowly an organization defines "fit," certain groups of organization members are advantaged and others are disadvantaged. The unfortunate part of this organizational dynamic is that it usually operates on an unconscious level, making it far more challenging for some employees to navigate through the organization and advance at the same pace as others.

People who are disadvantaged instinctively know that this is the case, but do not necessarily understand the issue of "fit." Depending on their level of self-confidence and cultural awareness, they either will ascribe their lack of advancement to deficiencies with their job performance or interpersonal skills, or they will label the situation as a "glass ceiling" involving organizational biases.

Applying the Idea of "Fit" to Career Advancement in Your Organization

The first step in using the concept of "fit" to support your own or your employees' career advancement is to have an accurate and comprehensive understanding of how your organization defines "fit" and how your own membership identity and style attributes are similar to and different from this definition. You may find the following questions helpful as you develop this picture.

1. What are the predominant membership identity characteristics in terms of:
   - Race
   - Gender
   - Ethnicity
   - Nationality
   - Age
   - Religion
   - Socioeconomic class
   - Sexual orientation
   - Marital status
   - Parent/non-parent status
   - Other

2. What are the predominant style attributes in terms of:
   - Verbal and nonverbal interpersonal relating style
   - Dress and appearance
   - Speaking/presentation skills
   - Educational background
   - Work habits
   - Conflict management
   - Interests, knowledge areas
   - Sociability
   - Political activity
   - Other

3. What are the similarities and differences in your group membership identity and style characteristics from those that you have listed in response to questions 1 and 2?

4. (If you are mentoring someone else) What are the similarities and differences in this person's group membership identity and style characteristics in comparison to those of senior management?

5. Are there individuals in upper level positions who belong to different membership identity groups and/or demonstrate very different style attributes? If so, what do you think were the key reasons for promoting them into these ranks?

6. What conclusions can you draw from your responses to the questions above that might support or improve your (or your mentee's) chances for career advancement in this organization?

It is often far easier to understand these hidden criteria when you are counseling someone else about them. When you are trying to assess your own "fit" with the organization, especially in terms of some of the more subtle style attributes, it helps to have someone else whom you trust and respect serve as your mentor and confidant.

Once you have completed your assessment, the second step is to determine which of the following courses of action would be most realistic:

- Continue to pursue career advancement opportunities without worrying about organization "fit"—either because your membership group identity and style attributes are consistent with those in leadership positions or because the organization is actively pursuing more diversity in its top ranks.

- Identify the style attributes that you are willing and able to change to bring these into more alignment with the style attributes of those in leadership positions, and then pursue advancement opportunities.

- Acknowledge that, at least for the foreseeable future, your group membership and style characteristics are so different from those in leadership positions that it is unlikely that your candidacy for senior management openings will be treated seriously.

Although this third course of action may seem severe to you or your mentee, at least it will be clear that the reason for not being able to progress further in the organization has to do with criteria that have nothing to do with your job-related competency and are beyond your control. Hopefully, this will leave you or those whom you are advising with the self-confidence to pursue opportunities with other organizations where there will be more of a "fit."

Using the "Ls" to Improve Communication

Introduction

Communication problems are frequently identified as one of the major sources of job dissatisfaction by employees and their supervisors at all levels in the organization.

Some of the most frequently reported communication problems between managers and employees revolve around the issues of:

Real or Perceived Inequities

- "Unfair" practices with respect to compensation, benefits, or prerequisites
- "Playing favorites" with respect to job assignments, vacation scheduling, or overtime options
- Promotions that do not appear to be based on objective criteria

Lack of Clarity about Responsibilities and Authorities

- Not being clear about performance expectations or priorities
- Not having the appropriate decision-making authorities or resources to perform a job well
- Being micromanaged without any flexibility to do the job in one's own way

Lack of Operational or Organizational Information

- Managers not giving staff members enough information about the rationale and requirements for various work assignments, organization plans, or personnel changes
- Peers keeping each other in the dark about activities in their different functional areas that might affect each other
- Subordinates not telling supervisors about problems in a timely manner

Lack of Timely Two-Way Communications

- Not soliciting input from employees before making decisions that will have direct impacts on them
- Not responding to suggestions from employees in a timely manner

Lack of Recognition or Timely Performance Feedback

- Supervisors, managers, or peers not giving each other positive feedback for a job well done
- Supervisors, managers, or peers not providing timely on-the-job coaching to correct performance problems

Being Blamed or Made to Feel Incompetent When Discussing a Problem

- Supervisors or managers focusing on "killing the messenger" rather than on fixing the problem and benefiting from lessons learned
- Supervisors, managers, or peers putting down each other's suggestions before considering what might be useful about them

Lack of Inclusion

- Not being acknowledged as a valued member of the organization or a part of the team

While these types of communication problems are difficult to work through with any supervisor, peer, or subordinate, they can become even more difficult to resolve when they occur between two individuals from diverse backgrounds.

When individuals are viewing the world through the same lenses and layers, they are much more likely to understand what is being said and, more importantly, what is meant. They use similar language and examples; their vocal tones and inflections are understood easily; their facial and body gestures are familiar. As background commonality diverges, people become much more likely to misunderstand each other's words and nonverbal communication, and the meaning of messages may become seriously distorted.

Earlier chapters introduced the "Diversity Ls"—lenses, layers, and legacies. This chapter suggests some additional ways in which you can draw upon the "Ls" to understand and communicate with employees, peers, or supervisors when race, ethnicity, gender, or other issues of diversity are contributing to your communication problems.

Lenses, Layers, and Legacies

To review definitions:

- **Lenses** are the *filters* through which we consciously and unconsciously view diversity issues

- **Layers** include all of the obvious and not so obvious *individual characteristics* that make each of us who we distinctly are at any given time in our lives—skin color, gender, age, physical appearance, physical and mental abilities, ethnicity, cultural background, socioeconomic background, sexual orientation, marital status, education, religious or spiritual beliefs, political affiliations

- **Legacies** are the *historical events and situations* that are important to us as members of different races, genders, cultures, religious and ethnic groups, political groups, and so forth. We may have personally experienced these events or situations or we may have heard about them in stories handed down to us by our parents, grandparents, and great-grandparents. We bring these legacies with us in our interactions with each other. Examples of legacies for different racial and cultural groups include:
  - The discovery of land on this continent by early European groups and their settlement on lands that had been inhabited previously by Native Americans
  - The capture and transportation of Africans from that continent to become slaves in this country
  - The holding and processing of immigrants at Ellis Island
  - The redistribution of land as a result of the Spanish-American Wars
  - The use of Chinese immigrants to build railroads across this country
  - The internment of Japanese citizens during World War II
  - The Civil Rights March on Washington and Martin Luther King's speech, "I Have a Dream"

Looking Inward, Listening, and "Languaging"

In addition to the three "Diversity Ls," here are three important "Process Ls" used in improving communications among you and individuals from diverse backgrounds:

- **Looking inward** to better understand the lenses, layers, and legacies that most influence *you* in these interactions
- **Listening** to the individual on three levels:
  - To hear the content of what is being said
  - To understand the feelings behind the words and get the full meaning of the message
  - To identify the worldview and key values that motivate the individual as an organizational member
- **"Languaging"** your message in ways that are respectful of the other individual's lenses, layers, and legacies, so that your message has the potential to be heard as you intended it to be heard

---

Individual Exercise:

1. Review the list of common work-related communication problems described in the Introduction of this chapter. Select one that is of concern to you and involves someone from a diverse background. This individual might be a supervisor, peer, or subordinate. Describe the situation briefly on a separate sheet of paper. (*Note: If there is a communication problem involving someone from a very different background from yours that does not fit into any of the categories identified above, feel free to use this instead*).

Refer back to this situation in completing the remaining exercises in this chapter.

Step 1: Looking Inward

Each of us contributes 50 percent to the success or failure of any communication with another individual. Here is an example of how one manager looked inward to identify how his lenses, layers, and legacies were contributing to a communication problem he was having with a staff member:

James was having an ongoing performance problem with Karen, a member of his staff who was a single mother and late to work at least once or twice each week. Once she was there, she produced good work and was liked by other members of the staff. However, James was concerned about the precedent she was setting for other staff members. The first time that James brought up the problem with Karen, she explained that her regular babysitter had been sick and she was having trouble finding a backup sitter to take her two kids to school each morning after she left for work. Three weeks later, James brought the problem up again with Karen. During this meeting he found it hard to maintain his patience when she brought up the same excuses and cut her explanations short, telling her to work out her problems and be on time or else. The meeting ended with Karen in tears and James feeling dissatisfied with the way he had handled the discussion.

When James thought about it from the perspective of lenses, layers, and legacies, he realized that:

- The lens he used most frequently to look at work situations was that of Assimilationist. He expected all members of his staff to fit in with the cultural norms he had established, including those of being on time for work.
- The key layers of himself that he brought to this situation were: 1) that of a married man with a wife who was a freelance consultant able to schedule her work to accommodate their children's school schedule; and 2) that of a religious man who believed that divorce or having children out of wedlock was not right
- As an African-American man, the legacy he had inherited from his upwardly mobile middle-class family was one of making the most of equal opportunities but still being very wary of any kind of confrontation with a white woman.

This self-assessment helped him see how the lens, layers, and legacy that he brought to the situation were extremely different from those Karen brought. He realized that his Assimilationist Lens was driving him to think that there could be no exceptions to the rules; that the particular layers of himself prevalent in this situation were preventing him from being able to understand and empathize with Karen's problem; and that a part of his legacy made him very uncomfortable about having to bring up a problem with her or any other white woman. The next day he asked Karen to meet with him again. He told her that he had been disappointed in the way that he handled their meeting the day before and that he wanted to work collaboratively with her in coming up with a better solution to the problem. Karen suggested that they bring up the issue at the next staff meeting, explain why she needed to be late at times, and discuss how she could make up for this lost time whenever she was able to do so. A situation that might eventually have resulted in the loss of a good employee, or at the very least in complaints about unequal treatment of employees, was resolved in a far more effective way.

Think about the situation you described.

1. What lens(es) do you think you are looking through to view the situation?
2. What are the strengths of that lens? How do these strengths contribute to this situation?

3. What are the shadows of that lens? How do these shadows contribute to the situation?

4. What are the layers of yourself that you think are most important in this situation?

5. How are these layers similar to and different from the layers that the other individual brings to the situation?

6. What is the legacy that you bring to this situation?

7. How is this legacy similar to and different from the legacy that the other individual brings to this situation?

Step 2: Listening to the Other

Listening is one of the most important and difficult skills to master as a manager (and human being!). Most of us have one or more of the following bad habits when it come to listening:

- Pretending to listen when we are not
- Interrupting
- Anticipating what the other person will say
- "Rehearsing" our response to what the person is saying
- Focusing only on the words and not the feelings behind the words
- Being judgmental about what the other person is saying ("You should have...")
- Devaluing the speaker's feelings ("It's not that bad" or "You'll get over it")
- Playing "shrink" ("Your problem is...")
- Giving advice
- One upping ("That's nothing compared to what I went through when I was handling that project with him...")
- Refocusing the conversation on yourself ("I know just what you mean... I'm having the same problem with...")

---

1. Which, if any, of these bad habits do you notice in the people with whom you work most closely?

2. Which of these bad habits do you claim for yourself?

When we are truly engaged in listening to another individual to improve our working relationship, we need to listen on three levels. The first level involves listening for the content of what the person is saying. What are the main points that s/he is making? What are the key issues and concerns being voiced? Are there clues with respect to the lens which the individual is using to view the situation?

Some of the positive habits which help us to listen more effectively at this level include:

- Paying full attention while the other person is speaking—not thinking about other issues or rehearsing our responses
- Asking questions to get more information—not just advocating our own position
- Sharing the "air space"—not dominating the conversation
- Letting the speaker finish without interruptions
- Not anticipating what the speaker will say
- Summarizing the speaker's points in our own words to check the accuracy of our understanding

The second level of listening involves tapping into the emotions that the speaker is experiencing so that we get the full message. Is there anger behind the statement? Are there indications that we have pushed the individual's "hot buttons" by what we said? Does the person seem anxious or afraid to say what is really on his or her mind? Is the speaker enthusiastic about what he or she is saying?

Some listening habits that help us at this level include:

- Showing attentive body language—maintaining appropriate eye contact and occasionally nodding our heads; not fidgeting or doodling
- Making comments that show we value the speaker—acknowledging points made, not devaluing the speaker's feelings
- Listening to really understand, without judging or criticizing
- Listening "with the heart as well as the head" to hear what is behind the words

The third level of listening is to help us understand more about the whole individual. What is his or her "worldview" in terms of the lens, layers, and legacies used? What might the individual's values be? What motivates him or her to contribute to the organization? What are the bridges that connect us as one human being to another?

This level of listening is the most difficult—and the most rewarding. There are no easy tips to follow, just one major caveat: We have to constantly remember that we are making assumptions, based on the clues we gather as the individual talks, and the validity of those assumptions always needs to be verified before we act on them.

In the example offered at the beginning of this chapter, as James listened to Karen in the meeting the next day, he was able to understand the following things about her "worldview":

- The lens she used to look at the work situation was that of a Multiculturalist in the sense that she believed that different staff members had different needs regarding work schedules and that these differences could be accommodated in acceptable ways with some creative thinking.
- Her status as a single mother was the central fact of her existence at this time in her life, with her children's welfare her primary concern.
- She believed that the productivity and quality of her work when she was there more than made up for her late arrivals.
- She was strongly motivated to perform well and maintain good working relationships with her coworkers and James so that she could continue to have work that she enjoyed doing and job security.
- She felt angry and helpless about James being so upset about her lateness and afraid of losing her job after yesterday's meeting.

James was able to begin connecting with Karen on the human-to-human level by recognizing how important their children were to each of them. He could see that they both placed a high value on quality work performance and teamwork. Finally, he could empathize with her feelings of helplessness by remembering a time when he had felt this way. As he built these bridges in listening and responding to her, it was far easier for him to support and follow through on the ideas she suggested for resolving the situation.

Think about the situation you have described.

1. Have you had the kind of conversation with this individual where you were willing to listen at all three levels as described above?
2. If not, are you willing to have a conversation of this kind with the individual in the near future? How will you initiate this?
3. If you have had this kind of conversation (or after you had it):
   a) What are the main points that the individual has made? What are his or her key issues and concerns and what would he or she like to do about them?
   b) What are the emotions and feelings that the individual has about these issues and concerns? How were these expressed?

c) What emotions and feelings do you have about these issues and concerns, as well as about how these were expressed?

d) How would you describe the individual's worldview? What did you learn about the lens, layers, and legacies that are most influential for him or her in this situation? Were key values or motivational themes expressed?

e) What similarities are there between your worldview and that of the individual? What are the bridges that you can build to connect the two of you as human beings?

Step 3: Languaging

Once you have looked inward to identify the lenses, layers, and legacies that you bring to your interactions with the individual from a different background, and you have shown yourself to be willing to really listen to what the individual has to say, the third process "L" involves becoming more aware of your use of language. There are two different aspects to consider with respect to effective "languaging."

The first has to do with the use of sensitive and noninflammatory language. Most of us know what the most offensive words and phrases are that have been used historically to refer to racial, gender, religious, and other differences. However, other expressions that we have learned to use have no real negative significance for us but can be extremely offensive to others. When we use either blatantly offensive language or the more subtly offensive expressions, we most likely push the other person's "hot buttons" and dramatically lessen the potential for improved communications.

It is important as a manager to become as knowledgeable as possible about such words and phrases and to be vigilant about not using these terms or allowing them to be used by other staff members.

The second aspect of effective languaging has to do with getting your message across, especially when you have a message that may be difficult for the other person to hear. The keys to accomplishing this include:

- Using *descriptive* language (words that describe the behavior, action, or situation factually) rather than *evaluative* language (words that describe your opinions or judgments about what happened)

- Making "I statements"—that is, talking about your feelings and reactions to the situation

- Being clear about what you would like to have change

One effective technique to help managers resolve a problem with an employee is called the "DES" Script. The guidelines for using a "DES" Script are:

D: Describe the Behavior of the Person

- Be specific—What did the person actually do or not do?
- Talk about behaviors which are observable—not about the person's motivation or attitude
- Use factual language that describes what you saw or heard—Do not use "red-flag" words that label, evaluate, or attack the other person and that are likely to stir up negative reactions
- Be accurate about how often the behavior happens—Do not say "always or never"
- Be brief—Do not give a "parental scolding"
- Be selective—Do not "dump" a lot of stored-up issues all at once

E: Express Your Feelings—The Impact of the Behavior on You

- Use "I Statements"—not "You Statements"
- Be genuine—Do not exaggerate or minimize how you feel
- Be honest—State your real reaction, not something that might "sound better"
- Do not worry about whether the impact has been "significant" enough from the other person's viewpoint
- Describe what the impact of the behavior has been on your personal rights with respect to time, money, resources, relationships, or work effectiveness
- Be descriptive, not moralistic
- Do not leave your feelings out of the message—This is a common mistake and greatly lessens the effectiveness of your message

S: Specify What You Are Requesting of the Other Person

- The behavior change desired—if you know what this is; if not, a request for some time with the other person to solve this together
- The steps you would like to take together to resolve the issue
- Remember that you are making a request, not a demand

Think about the situation you have described

1. What, if any, "hot buttons" do you think you might have pushed in past conversations?

2. What words or phrases have you used historically when you talked or thought about people who belong to this group?

3. What words or phrases is it particularly important for you to avoid using when you talk with or about this individual?

4. How could you express your concern to this individual using a "DES" Script:

   D:

   E:

   S:

5. What are the most important points for you to remember from this chapter to help you improve your communications with employees from different backgrounds?

Looking through the Lenses at Human Resources Management Systems

A Continuum to Consider When Thinking about Organization Change

When it comes to diversity within organizations, the dialogue about how to change usually plays out on a continuum. At one end are those who believe that it is the responsibility of employees to change aspects of who they are to fit into the existing organizational culture. At the other end are those who believe that it is the responsibility of the organization to change its culture to accommodate the cultural differences represented by employees. The same continuum of views applies to the interface between customers and the organization. However, businesses are less resistant to making organizational shifts to respond to the needs of their customers or clients because there is a clear link to potential profit or cost effectiveness in these cases.

These opposing perspectives play out in various aspects of the company's organization and are inherent in how key human resources systems are created and executed. Each lens has a particular perspective on how it views the organization in relation to the continuum and where it would like the organization to be on the continuum.

The lenses are grouped on the continuum as follows:

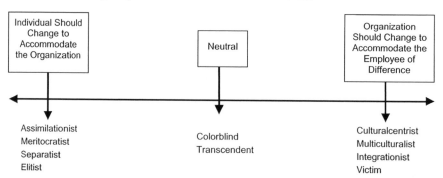

In addition to the lenses, the history and success level of the organization affects how and where leaders place themselves and their organizations along this continuum. Those leaders who have been responsible for the development and maintenance of the organization's current culture will tend to adopt the attitude, "If it ain't broke, don't fix it."

Leaders at the other end of the continuum believe that the organization could be even more successful if it leveraged its cultural differences related to its workforce and customer base. They argue that in order to respond to converging business forces such as shifting demographics, increased cultural pride, globalization of the workforce and customer base, increased pressure and oversight from social advocacy groups and new civil rights laws, organizations need to proactively shift their cultures to be more inclusive. Only in this way, they believe, will the organization be able to remain competitive and avoid legal and public relations problems related to charges of bias.

In this chapter, you are asked to identify some key human resources management strategies that your organization most needs to accomplish over the next three to five years and develop an implementation plan for improving the capacity of your human resources management systems to support these strategies. As you work through the questions in this chapter related to the lenses that govern these systems, keep in mind where each lens is located on the continuum of expectations for individual and organization change. This will help you to think about realistic strategies as you develop your implementation plan.

The Lens Model for Assessing Your Human Resources Management Systems

All organizations can be looked at as a combination of socio-technical systems. The technical systems consist of the equipment, materials, work processes, and procedures that turn raw materials or information into the products or services that the organization exists to produce. The "socio" systems focus on the people side of the business, particularly the human resources management systems designed to keep the organization functioning smoothly and effectively.

The human resources management systems include:

- Recruiting and Hiring
- Compensation and Benefits
- Job Classification and Job Placement
- Team Development
- Performance Management

- Mentoring
- Training and Development
- Succession Planning
- Employee Relations

Each of these systems plays a major role in the organization's growth and success. There are many ways to assess your organization's human resources management systems and determine whether they are performing their functions effectively. When you are depending on diversity as a strategic competitive advantage, one of the most useful ways to assess these systems is to use the Lens Model for Organizational Change.

The model consists of the following steps:

1. Determine the three to five human resources management strategies that you most need to accomplish over the next three to five years
2. Identify the human resources management systems that have the most direct bearing on these strategies
3. Determine the lens(es) through which each of these systems is being managed and implemented
4. Identify the strengths that the particular lens contributes to the system's capability to support the accomplishment of the strategies
5. Identify the "shadows" or the ways in which the particular lens detracts from the system's capability to support the strategies
6. Determine the ways in which you want to expand and improve on the system's capability to support the strategies
7. Identify the key levers that will help in improving the system's capability
8. Develop an implementation plan to carry out your improvement goals
9. Monitor implementation progress
10. Measure improvements/accomplishment of strategies

Each of these steps is discussed in the following pages. After each step is explained, there are questions for you to consider if you want to apply this model to your own organization or work unit.

1. Determine the Human Resources Management Strategies That You Most Need to Accomplish

Strategies exist to support your organization's business strategy and goals. These are developed to take advantage of, and respond to, whatever is happening (or about to happen) in your business environment. For example, a strategic scan of your external and internal business environment has identified one or more of the following trends:

- A new technology is becoming available that will dramatically change your production process.
- Customer expectations for 24-7 service responsiveness are increasing rapidly.
- The demographics of your customer base in four out of ten locations are changing from predominantly white to a mixture of African American and Asian.
- The candidate pool for high-tech positions has decreased by 15 percent over the last two years, and there are three new major competitors for the remaining candidates.
- Housing costs in the area have skyrocketed to the point that those in frontline jobs can no longer afford to live near the operation.
- Over one-third of your most senior technical contributors and first-line supervisors will be retiring in the next five years.
- Your workforce is becoming more and more diverse, with 18 percent of entry-level employees comprised of African Americans, Latin Americans, Vietnamese, Koreans and other diverse groups.

Each of these trends could have major impacts on your organization over the next few years. In most cases, you would want to develop business strategies and goals to respond to these findings. Examples include:

- Incorporate the new technology into your production process to achieve a 12 percent savings in labor costs
- Develop the capacity to provide 24-7 customer service
- Maintain the customer base in the locations where the demographics are changing
- Compete successfully for the most qualified candidates in a highly competitive market
- Ensure frontline coverage of operations around the clock
- Ensure a timely transfer of knowledge and skills from senior personnel before they retire
- Develop an organizational culture which recognizes and values diversity

Three of these business strategies directly correlate with human resources management strategies:

- Develop a competitive recruitment strategy to obtain the most qualified candidates in a highly competitive market
- Develop a succession plan that ensures the timely transfer of knowledge and skills from retiring senior technical contributors and first-line supervisors to their designated successors
- Develop and implement a training program that will provide all employees with the self-awareness, sensitivities, and skills required to understand and value diversity

In the other cases, human resources management strategies would have to be developed to help achieve the business goals—

- Establish new job classifications that incorporate the use of the new technology. Gain union support for the new classifications. Develop and implement programs to train employees to operate the new technology.
- In conjunction with the installation of new information technology, develop and implement a plan to have live coverage for 24-7 customer service.
- Ensure that some of the staff in the four business locations where the customer demographics are changing are representative of the same demographic groups.
- Increase the sensitivity and skills of all staff in these locations so that they will be able to provide responsive service to all customers.
- Initiate programs to enable essential frontline staff to purchase homes in the local area.

Applying the Model: Question

Using the explanations and examples above to help you consider your own organizational situation, what are the most important human resources management strategies for your organization to accomplish over the next few years?

2. Identify the Human Resources Management Systems That Have the Most Direct Bearing on Strategies

It is usually easy to identify the systems that will have the most direct bearing on the key strategies that you have selected. In the first three examples at the top of this page the systems would include:

- Recruiting and Hiring, Compensation and Benefits
- Succession Planning, Mentoring, and perhaps Training and Development
- Training and Development and perhaps Team Development

In the next five examples, the systems include:

- Job Classification and Job Placement, Compensation and Benefits, Employee Relations, and Training and Development
- Job Classification and Job Placement, and perhaps Compensation and Benefits, Employee Relations, and Training and Development
- Recruiting and Hiring, Job Placement, and perhaps Training and Development
- Compensation and Benefits

Applying the Model: Question

Which of the systems have the most direct bearing on the strategies that you have identified as most important for your organization?

3. Determine the Lens(es) Through Which Each of These Human Resources Management Systems Is being Managed and Implemented

The lenses through which a system is managed and implemented will have a significant impact on that system's effectiveness in supporting an organization's business goals. The impacts of each lens on different systems have been described in the earlier chapters of this book. On the following pages, examples of the influences of the different lenses on each of the systems have been grouped together for easy reference.

HRM Systems	Lens	Typical Influences
Recruiting and Hiring	Assimilationist	Hire people who will fit in with who we are and be willing to do things our way
	Culturalcentrist	Hire more of our kind
	Meritocratist	Hire only those who have already proven themselves elsewhere
	Colorblind	Hire whoever is qualified to do the job

(cont.)

HRM Systems	Lens	Typical Influences
	Victims and Caretakers	Give preference to those who have special needs of one type or another
	Elitist	Hire those who have personal connections with us
	Multiculturist	Hire the most diverse workforce possible
	Seclusionist	Hire *only* those of our kind
Job Classification and Placement, Compensation and Benefits	Assimilationist	Leave our job classifications and compensation and benefits programs alone unless we need to make minor adjustments to be more competitive
	Meritocratist	Design these programs to attract, give incentives, and reward our best performers
	Colorblind	Ensure that job classifications reflect current market data, and compensate everyone equitably
	Victims and Caretakers	Develop special classifications to provide entry-level positions for those who are economically disadvantaged
Team Development	Assimilationist	Recognize that team building helps everyone fit in better
	Culturalcentrist	Recognize our own diversity and that of others
	Colorblind	Use team building to help us understand and value

(cont.)

HRM Systems	Lens	Typical Influences
		each person as a unique individual
	Elitist	Let different groups form and affiliate with each other based on common interests and experiences
	Multiculturalist	Employ team building to help us recognize and celebrate our diversity
	Integrationist	Break down the barriers among us and come to know each other as individuals
Performance Management	Culturalcentrist	Pay more attention to how African Americans (etc.) are managed and promoted in this organization
	Meritocratist	Acknowledge those who perform at top levels and encourage them to move up the ladder
	Victims and Caretakers	Do a more effective job of training to improve performance
	Seclusionist	Encourage better performance by separating genders/races/etc.
	Transcendent	Focus on present and future accomplishments, not past performance problems
Mentoring, Training and Development	Assimilationist	Develop people so that they will carry on the traditions and practices that have made this organization so successful

(cont.)

HRM Systems	Lens	Typical Influences
Succession Planning	Culturalcentrist	Develop more Asians (etc.) to increase their representation in senior positions
	Meritocratist	Develop those who have proven themselves worthy of our efforts
	Colorblind	Provide equal opportunities to mentoring, participation in training and development programs, and consideration as candidates for succession planning
	Elitist	Develop individuals whom we know we can count on because they come from "good stock" (our kind of backgrounds)
Employee Relations	Colorblind	Establish good working relationships with union leadership, based on our mutual goals for the organization
	Victims and Caretakers	Assume they will not listen to anything we have to say, so we might as well not even try
	Elitist	Replace anyone who is not civil and reasonable
	Integrationist	Foster understanding and better working relationships between management and union leadership
	Transcendent	Encourage the willingness to let bygones be bygones and start fresh from a win-win perspective

Applying the Model: Questions

What additional examples can you think of with respect to the influences that different lenses might have on different human resources management systems?

In the left-hand column below, list the key systems that you have selected in response to Applying the Model: Question on page 211. In the middle column, list the lens(es) that you think have the most influence on the management and implementation of each of these systems. In the right-hand column, describe the influence in a short phrase as was done in the examples above.

HRM System	Lens	Possible Influences

4. Identify the Strengths and Shadows That the Particular Lens(es) Contribute to the System's Ability to Enact the HRM/Business Strategy

Each lens brings its own strengths and shadows to individual, group, and system-level interactions. One of the strategies included as an example earlier in this chapter was:

"Develop a succession plan that ensures the timely transfer of knowledge and skills from retiring senior technical contributors and first-line supervisors to their designated successors."

The systems involved in implementing this strategy would include Performance Management (from the perspective of identifying potential successors), Mentoring, Training and Development, and Succession Planning. If these systems were managed and implemented through the Assimilationist Lens, some of the strengths we could count on management demonstrating would be:

- In-depth understanding of the organization's current way of doing business
- Strong pride in, and commitment to, the organization's ongoing success
- Personal friendships or, at least, nodding acquaintances with most of the individuals who will be retiring
- Personal knowledge of most of the individuals who will be considered as successors
- Strong opinions about who the successors should be—with more agreement than disagreement
- Knowledge of the right training programs to help individuals develop the needed skills

- The ability to mentor and coach individuals so that they can be even more effective at doing things "the right way"

- The ability and willingness to write up a formal succession plan for each key position

Some of the shadows we could expect management to demonstrate would be:

- An inability or unwillingness to consider what changes the organization might need to make in its way of doing business for tomorrow

- An inability or unwillingness to consider individuals who are very different from themselves and from those who hold the positions as potential successors—even though the talents, experience, and diverse perspectives of such individuals might be just what is needed

- An inability or unwillingness to allow potential successors the flexibility to learn what they need to know in their own way

Consider how these shadows would adversely affect the succession plan and the organization's future success, especially in light of some of the trends identified in the strategic scan of the business environment—new technology coming online, increasing customer expectations for more responsiveness, changing demographics in four business locations, and an increasingly diverse workforce.

Applying the Model: Questions

Identify the strengths that the lens(es) you have identified contribute to managing and implementing the systems on which you are working:

Identify the shadows that the lens(es) you have identified contribute to managing and implementing these systems:

5. Determine the Ways in Which You Want to Expand and Improve on the System's Capability to Support the Accomplishment of the Strategies

In our example, the ways in which it would be most important to expand on the Assimilationist Lens viewpoint and improve the capability of the relevant systems to develop an effective succession plan would be to:

- Increase the organization's ability to scan its business environment and use the data acquired to evaluate indicated changes in the organization's way of doing business

- Increase the diversity of the management team itself, as well as the diversity of supervisory ranks and senior technical positions

- Incorporate more "out-of-the-box" thinking in the organization's culture

Applying the Model: Question

What are the ways in which you want to expand and improve on the capability of the systems on which you are working, based on your assessment of the strengths and shadows of the predominant lens(es) by which the systems are managed and implemented?

6. Identify the Key Levers That Will Help in Improving the System's Capability

There are many different levers for organizational change. Some of the most commonly used include:

- Providing education about the "big picture," why the change is needed, what the consequences will be if the change does not happen, what will be involved in making the change
- Disseminating information about "best practices" in similar organizations
- Arranging for representatives of different organizational levels to talk directly with peers or make site visits to other respected organizations
- Providing opportunities for everyone to hear *directly* from their customers about customer satisfactions and requirements
- Changing formal and informal reward systems to support the change
- Providing behavior modeling by formal and informal leaders to change cultural norms
- Encouraging risk taking and new learning
- Offering timely training and coaching
- Providing specific details of how things will be improved once the change has been implemented
- Having well-liked and respected organization leaders talk positively about the change
- Bringing in new perspectives—in the role of new managers or an influential consultant

In the case of our example, the levers that might be most effective would be:

- Working with the management team members to help them understand the implications of new technology coming online, changing customer expectations and demographics, and increasing workforce diversity
- Bringing in new perspectives by bringing a new manager on board
- Arranging for members of the management team to talk with peers who faced the same challenges
- Providing a training program on creative thinking for the management team

Applying the Model: Question

Which of levers do you think will have the most positive effect on accomplishing your implementation plan for your strategies?

7. Develop an Implementation Plan to Carry Out Your Improvement Plan

If an implementation plan is effective, it assigns accountability to one individual to carry out each of the key activities required, as well as a "by-when" date for each of these activities. You may find the following format useful in developing your implementation plan:

Who	What	By When

Applying the Model: Question

What will you include in your implementation plan?

8. Monitor Implementation Progress and Measure Results

Applying the Model: Questions

How will you monitor implementation progress?

What will you measure to assess results?

Checklists for the Lenses

Introduction

On the following pages some of the most important guidelines for managers and supervisors to keep in mind are summarized and presented in checklist format. In developing the checklists, some of the different aspects of the manager's role have been taken into consideration, including:

- Being involved in the process of business environment scanning and the development of strategic plans—including the targeting of emerging markets or the cultivation of cultural niche markets
- Making decisions about product development
- Managing different aspects of customer relations
- Executing the human resources systems within the work unit
- Shaping the organization's culture

The checklists can be used in three ways:

1. As a development tool for your personal use
2. As an aid to understanding the problems you may be having with another manager or supervisor who operates from a different lens
3. As a coaching tool to use with those whom you supervise or mentor

Checklist for the Assimilationist Lens

To supplement the natural tendencies of your Assimilationist Lens, make special efforts to:

✔ Search for and identify differentiated business opportunities focused on emerging global markets and cultural niche opportunities.

✔ Stay alert to the subtle ways in which Western cultural arrogance can negatively affect business dealings with global customers and employees.

✔ Consider business requirements for the use of multiple languages to serve different customer groups and/or ensure safe, efficient use of equipment and materials by different work groups within the organization.

✔ Recognize that different identity groups may bring different values and beliefs to the workplace and that these need to be acknowledged and respected to avoid misunderstandings, frustrations, and even legal problems with customers and employees.

✔ Be able to explain the business requirements underlying any restrictions related to employee appearance and dress or to employees adhering to their cultural traditions or religious practices during the workday.

✔ Create a culture that recognizes and values differences, so that the diversity of the workforce can be used to contribute unique perspectives and innovative solutions to business challenges.

✔ On a personal level, seek to understand and appreciate the different beliefs, interests, tastes, traditions, styles, and practices that different identity groups contribute to the workplace culture.

Checklist for the Colorblind Lens

To supplement the natural tendencies of your Colorblind Lens, make special efforts to:

✔ Recognize that demographic and cultural niche markets do exist. Research and help to identify such markets to expand business opportunities.

✔ Support the development of advertising campaigns that will appeal to different identity groups when marketing different products and services.

✔ Acknowledge that people of color and different racial groups have identities, experiences, and circumstances that have contributed to their development, both positively and negatively. Recognize these differences rather than glossing over them in order to establish authentic working relationships with customers and employees.

✔ Help to create an organizational culture in which discriminatory circumstances and events based on color or race are quickly surfaced and effectively resolved.

✔ Be sensitive to the fact that individual customers or employees may be more comfortable talking with someone from the same identity group when problems arise.

✔ Include more than one individual from a particular identity group on a work team, crew, or task force whenever possible, so that there can be more of a sense of comfort and mutual support for the individuals involved.

✔ Recognize that racial conflict and discrimination *do* exist in our organizations, and do not deny or minimize these realities for the sake of maintaining pseudoharmony.

Checklist for the Culturalcentrist Lens

To supplement the natural tendencies of your Culturalcentrist Lens, make special efforts to:

✔ Research and pay attention to the potential for cultural niche markets other than those of your own identity group.

✔ Understand and act on preferences related to sales and customer service interactions for other identity groups as well as your own.

✔ Recognize the need for all members of the organization to subscribe to a set of commonly held values, beliefs, and business practices for any organization to be successful.

✔ Balance the need to recognize and celebrate the traditions and practices of diverse groups within the organization with the need to establish and support a common organizational culture that reinforces teamwork and organization performance.

✔ Be alert to the potential for antagonisms and conflicts to develop when employees in different identity groups want to emphasize their differences and remain separate from each other.

✔ Create bridges among members of your own and other identity groups through dialogue sessions, social events, and other informal contacts.

✔ Recognize that there is as much diversity within an identity group as among groups, and avoid putting pressure on individuals within your cultural identity group to think and act in a prescribed way.

Checklist for the Elitist Lens

To supplement the natural tendencies of your Elitist Lens, make special efforts to:

✔ Recognize that there is much to learn from developing economies and emerging markets.

✔ Pay attention to the value and importance of cultural niche markets that may comprise identity groups very different from those who historically have been defined as "the right people."

✔ Ensure that the voices of all customer groups are listened and responded to in matters related to business development and customer service.

✔ Establish and maintain employee development and training programs that help all employees make the fullest possible use of their potential to support organization and individual goals.

✔ Assess and use the skills, abilities, and interests of all employees, rather than assuming that "the right school" or "the right family" will reliably predict those employees who will "rise to the top."

✔ Recognize and address real or perceived inequities in the ways in which systems are administered or the ways in which individual employees are treated by managers.

✔ Understand that the circumstances that existed for you on your way up in the organization may have been very different from those faced by individuals of different racial and cultural groups today.

Checklist for the Integrationist Lens

To supplement the natural tendencies of your Integrationist Lens, make special efforts to:

✔ Develop and promote cultural niche markets that address the needs of many different identity groups, not just those of African Americans.

✔ Recognize that customers representing different racial and socioeconomic groups may not be ready to move as quickly as you would like with respect to associating closely with each other.

✔ Acknowledge that different identity groups often have different needs and preferences when it comes to specific products or services and that it is important to recognize and honor these differences to retain each group's business.

✔ Ensure that business needs and sound management practices serve as the foundation for any affirmative action efforts underlying recruitment, selection, hiring, development, and promotion processes.

✔ Be sensitive to perceptions or fears about reverse discrimination in recruitment, selection, development, and promotion processes.

✔ Accept the preference of some members of different identity groups to remain separate during lunch or other opportunities for socializing.

✔ Recognize that many people take a great deal of pride in their group identity and heritage and want to have this acknowledged rather than ignored in interpersonal communications.

Checklist for the Meritocratist Lens

To supplement the natural tendencies of your Meritocratist Lens, make special efforts to:

✔ Research and provide assistance to emerging global markets, rather than wait for them to come knocking at your organizational door fully developed.

✔ Provide the opportunity for less prestigious but more diverse supplier groups to demonstrate how they might provide the same quality products and services as quickly and cost effectively as their competitors.

✔ Notice and counteract any attempts by yourself or others to rationalize inequalities among employees on the basis of racial or cultural stereotypes.

✔ Identify cultural biases that exist in the organization's selection, development, and promotion practices, and help create more level playing fields in these areas.

✔ Ensure organizational support for those individuals who want to compensate for the lack of educational opportunities and skill development earlier in their lives by furthering their education and training now.

✔ Recognize that different identity groups may have different ways of defining competencies and merit; explore what these might be with members of different groups in your customer base and workforce.

✔ Be sensitive to the fact that different levels of family support, socioeconomic exposure, and educational opportunities result in unequal starting places in the game of organizational life.

Checklist for the Multiculturalist Lens

To supplement the natural tendencies of your Multiculturist Lens, make special efforts to:

✔ Recognize that emerging global markets and cultural niche markets can be developed with sensitive regard for existing cultural traditions. Work within your organization to develop this capacity.

✔ Target specific markets for the organization's marketing and sales efforts, based on sound business analysis.

✔ Ensure that all members of the organization subscribe to a set of common values and business practices that are recognized as the organization's way of doing business and that supercede the beliefs and traditions of subcultures within the organization.

✔ Focus on skills, abilities, interests, and achievements of employees, rather than on representation of diversity, when making decisions about assigning employees to work on special task forces, attend professional conferences, or participate in special organizational events.

✔ Be sensitive to, and counteract, remarks by yourself or others that are critical of white, middle-class, heterosexual men of European descent simply because they represent the historic majority and ruling class in our society and organizations.

✔ Help organizational members understand how diversity training and other sensitivity initiatives relate to and support business goals.

✔ Recognize that an overemphasis on diversity can be perceived as a depersonalizing experience if individuals believe that they are being seen only as a "woman," "single mother," "African American," "Latino," "gay," "older male," "physically-challenged person."

Checklist for the Seclusionist Lens

To supplement the natural tendencies of your Seclusionist Lens, make special efforts to:

✔ Understand the reality of global markets in today's economy.

✔ Be willing to learn about and develop cultural niche market opportunities.

✔ Recruit, hire, develop, and promote employees based only on their qualifications to do the job.

✔ Ensure that all organizational members demonstrate common courtesies and respect for the dignity of each other as human beings, regardless of race, gender, ethnicity, religion, age, or other differences.

✔ Counteract unbased claims of favoritism or reverse discrimination when individuals from diverse identity groups have been hired or promoted because of their qualifications.

✔ Foster cultural norms that support good working relationships among all employees, the open exchange of ideas, and the willingness to take risks.

✔ Recognize that many people are uncomfortable with the viewpoint they associate with this lens and prefer to think in terms of multiculturalism or integration.

Checklist for the Transcendent Lens

To supplement the natural tendencies of your Transcendent Lens, make special efforts to:

✔ Learn from the organization's history—its attempts to open up different markets, the successes and failures of different ventures, how it has ignored or taken advantage of different cultural niche opportunities—rather than dismissing it as inconsequential with respect to today's and tomorrow's business.

✔ Recognize that racial, cultural, and ethnic identities are important to many people and can be used positively in developing marketing and advertising strategies.

✔ Be sensitive to the fact that many customers and employees have much more difficulty seeing beyond visible differences to the "oneness of all" and need to have this difficulty recognized and accepted in their interactions with others.

✔ Help identify and quickly address discriminatory conditions pertaining to hiring, job assignments, promotion opportunities, performance reviews, and disciplinary actions.

✔ Be willing to surface and help resolve tensions that exist among employees from different racial, ethnic, cultural, socioeconomic, political, or other identity groups.

✔ Help to create a culture that recognizes and values diversity so that all individuals are willing to contribute their own unique perspectives on how to solve problems and improve business operations.

✔ Be aware that the tendency to become impatient with those who are not as able to see beyond differences or let go of past grievances can close these individuals down prematurely and make them unwilling to talk with you in the future.

Checklist for the Victim/Caretaker Lens

To supplement the natural tendencies of your Victim/Caretaker Lens, make special efforts to:

✔ Recognize that emerging global markets can be cultivated and cultural niche markets developed without the organization being exploitative or paternalistic in the process and work with your organization toward this end.

✔ Ensure that all interfaces with diverse groups of customers are characterized by the respectful recognition that customers know what they need and want.

✔ Ensure that all organizational efforts to increase the diversity of the workforce are firmly grounded in competency-based assessment and the recognition of individual merit.

✔ Establish an organizational culture in which employees are empowered with the necessary authorities and resources to take responsibility and be accountable for their actions.

✔ Where there are performance or discipline problems, provide coaching and a reasonable turn-around time; if the problems remain, follow through with the same consequences for all employees.

✔ Recognize that the subject of oppression and discrimination is a very complicated one in which the labels of oppressor/discriminator and oppressed/discriminated against can quickly change, depending on the dimensions being considered. Help organization members take broader views in discussions about victimization, discrimination, or oppression.

✔ Recognize that any excusing of individual actions based on race, color, gender, or age is a paternalistic and disempowering way of treating customers or employees.

About The Diversity Channel

The Diversity Channel believes that there is a direct positive correlation between inclusive organizations and four organizational goals:

- Increased customer satisfaction and market share
- Profitability
- Enhanced quality of work life for all employees, and
- Adherence to the intent and spirit of societal laws and ethics

To become a fully inclusive organization, one that exhibits the kinds of characteristics described in this book, organizations and the individuals in them need to move from where they are to the highest expressions of the lenses—*from intolerant to tolerant to valuing to inclusive behaviors*—along three dimensions: individual behaviors, management role behaviors, and systemic practices.

The Diversity Channel has designed a comprehensive Lens approach to support organizations as they respond to the challenges and leverage the competitive advantages of diversity in today's global market and workplace. The model we use is developmental in nature with practical strategies that individual employees, managers, and organizational leaders can understand and apply easily.

This Lens approach to organizational improvement makes use of diagnostic tools that assess behavior and systems. The assessments include those that look at the organizational culture and human resources management systems that affect employee motivation and productivity levels as well as those that focus on external systems that affect both customers and communities where your organization does business. The complete educational process can be disseminated through different channels, from on-site live training to e-learning to satellite broadcast. It can be supported by online, on-demand resources, including an extensive database of tips, strategies, and answers to diversity questions, as well as interactive webcasts, ask the consultant, cultural protocols, and best legal practices. A blended solution is customized to meet your organization's needs. Our mission is to offer a comprehensive, fully integrated systemwide approach to embedding the benefits of diversity in all aspects of your business strategy.

Afterword

In the year 2001, we sit at the dawn of a new millennium. Like it or not, those of us with the luxury of time and literacy to read *The 10 Lenses* have the responsibility, in ways small and large, to lead in the complex times we have inherited. Our inheritance of the last two thousand years is inextricably linked to the rise and force of three dominant aspects of the modern world: capitalism, technology, and cultural and ethnic diversity. Our understanding of and ability to manage the first two, capitalism and technology, far exceed our capacities in the third domain. For proof of this thesis, one need only look at the economic development currently stifled by violent conflicts, the origins of which lie in the inability to cope with cultural and ethnic diversity in different parts of the world. Less perceptible but no less real is the incalculable amount of psychic energy and human capital squandered inside work organizations as individuals attempt to manage their fear of differences inside our organizations. Now compare that with how quickly we have adapted to the Internet, and former communist regimes have embraced capitalism. Yet, it is how we approach and manage the reality of cultural and ethnic diversity, within and across national borders and in the workplace, that will determine whether the technology and the flexibility of capital markets become drivers of human progress or sources of conflicts and inequalities destined to devastate the world and its economies.

The 10 Lenses offers us a way of understanding how people have made sense of this two-millennia-old movement toward cultural diversity being an inextricable part of their reality. Mark Williams' research illustrates some fundamental truths. First, individuals differ in the perspectives they hold about the meaning of these differences and how they relate to their own group identities. Second, the reality of modern societies and organizations is that all of these perspectives coexist in the same countries, communities, schools, and workplaces. Third, the perspectives we hold are the product of experience and, therefore, subject to change and progressive evolution as the result of subsequent experiences. Fourth, context matters: in other words, how we manage these differences and the people who represent them will determine whether our diversity will lead to net benefits or deficits.

A Language for Managing Differences

Reading *The 10 Lenses*, I reflected on my own two decades of research and writing about cultural and ethnic differences in organizations. I revisited countless moments when my deep well of theory and research-based knowledge proved inadequate to create a constructive dialogue between a culturally dominant manager and his or her subordinate from a minority group, especially when that manager possessed the experience of a relationship with another member of that same minority group whose views and behaviors, i.e., lens, was aligned with his or her own. *The 10 Lenses* offers us a language for understanding and dialoguing about differences that has been largely absent until now. This may be one of the primary reasons why humans' capacity to cope with economic and technological change seems to have outstripped their ability to manage cultural and ethnic diversity. We have a language and a discourse for engaging issues of economic and technological change.

The 10 Lenses, and the research on which it is based, provides the tools that I believe are essential to creating a deeper level of understanding among people of diverse backgrounds and perspectives. This is most important for those of us privileged to provide leadership, whether to communities of individuals, large organizations, or small work groups. In moments too numerous to delineate in the space allotted here, we will be challenged to help others constructively engage across lines of differences. Our ability to help others see that their core differences lie not at the point of observable difference, but in the cognitive realm of how each makes sense of the differences and responds, will determine whether they exhibit a positive pattern of interaction or a negative one. Multiplied hundreds and thousands of times each day, these encounters create our experience of diversity.

Leadership, Organization, and Diversity

Any observer of contemporary life in organizations must conclude that cultural diversity is an unavoidable part of it. Even communities and societies once thought to be synonymous with homogeneity, such as the Rocky Mountain regions of the western United States, Japan, and Scandinavia, are finding that technology and economic progress necessitate the opening of their physical and psychological boundaries to those who are culturally and ethnically different. In particular, work organizations must of necessity absorb this diversity and manage it. How they do this has been the focus of my work over the last two decades.[1]

---

[1] Thomas, D.A., and Alderfer, C.P. (1988), "The Significance of Race and Ethnicity for Understanding Organizational Behavior," in *Review of Industrial and Organizational Psychology*, 3 vols., edited by C. Cooper. John Wiley & Sons, Inc.

Thomas, D.A., and Ely, R.J. (1996), "Making Differences Matter: A New Paradigm for Managing Diversity," *Harvard Business Review*, Vol. 74, no. 5.

Thomas, D.A., and Gabarro, J.J. (1999), *Breaking Through: The Making of a Minority Executive in Corporate America*, Boston, Mass.: Harvard Business School Press.

Ely, R.J., and Thomas, D.A. (forthcoming), "Cultural Diversity at Work: The Effects of Diversity Perspectives on Work Group Processes and Outcomes," *Administrative Science Quarterly*.

With my colleague Robin Ely, I have determined that while several approaches and responses to demographic, economic, and social forces in an organization's environment can lead to it becoming more culturally diverse, only a certain set of organizational conditions lead to diversity becoming a sustainable resource for individual and organizational renewal and effectiveness. In the course of learning from Mark Williams and absorbing the concepts presented in *The 10 Lenses*, I realize that the Eleventh Lens provides the perspective or cognitive stance held by leaders who successfully create organizations in which diversity becomes a resource for increased organizational and individual effectiveness.

Just as individuals who possess the Eleventh Lens are in the minority, so too are organizations in which the experience of diversity enhances individual experience and the work itself. Key attributes of these organizations include a focus on the development of employees; a belief that the organization creates the context for employees to achieve excellence; high tolerance for conflict and the expression of difference; and a focus on eliminating dynamics of dominance and subordination such as racism, sexism, and hierarchy that limit individuals' ability to engage and contribute fully. In this model of organization, diversity is to be experienced and not suppressed, and it is a source of learning and contribution that enhances the work process and product.

In each organization or work group where we find this paradigm in action, the leadership was central to its emergence. The journey to reach this state was often difficult, if not perilous, as choices were made about how to manage differences and openly engage their implications for rethinking assumptions about work, culture, and even leadership. The most evident and common qualities of these organizational leaders were: (1) the ability to see and articulate the connection between diversity and the work; (2) the capacity to openly engage and explore differences as they become salient in the life of the workgroup or organization; (3) a belief in and focus on the development of those whom they lead; (4) the capacity to meet others where they were with regard to differences and create dialogue of learning and exploration; and (5) a clarity of vision and mission that unifies the diverse individuals and forms a basis for venting differences.

The 10 Lenses brings into focus another and perhaps overarching quality of these leaders. They each possessed, in large part, if not fully, the perspective of the Eleventh Lens. Their expressions of personal values and stories of their individual journeys to understand diversity resonate with descriptions of the Eleventh Lens. Most notable in their leadership style is the ability to "hold paradox." They find little contradiction in believing that each person is a unique individual and that group-based difference of cultural and background shape individual and organizational behavior. They understand that creating a positive future requires acknowledging history, including historical wounds. They work continually to create alignment between the needs of the individual and the task requirements of the institution.

An Instrument for Leadership Development

The potential applications of the model presented in *The 10 Lenses* are numerous. Many readers will be impressed by its power as a tool for raising awareness. Mark Williams has already had a transformative effect on thousands of individuals through his seminars. I have experienced first hand the eye-opening nature of his live presentations. *The 10 Lenses* is destined to become a touchstone shared among friends and colleagues helping one another to make sense and cope with the diverse world in which they live.

I believe, however, that the ultimate and most important application of this model is as a tool for developing leaders. Leaders in the twenty-first century must be set on a path to the Eleventh Lens. This cannot be achieved by merely mimicking politically correct jargon or learning to tolerate but not engage differences. Neither can we assume that the Eleventh Lens will emerge swiftly enough in the course of time to meet the challenges that increasing cultural diversity poses for communities and organizations. Universities, professional schools, CEOs, and others charged with the preparation of future institutional leaders must create developmental experiences that guide and facilitate individual leaders acquiring the Eleventh Lens. Such experiences require mechanisms for self-assessment, frameworks that enable learning from one's own experiences and those of others, and opportunities for action planning, experimentation, and feedback. The model of the Eleven Lenses, the diagnostic instrument, and the guided learning journeys that have evolved out of Mark Williams' two decades of consulting and research in this area address each of these needs.

Conclusion

In twenty years as a researcher and university professor, I have seldom seen research that is immediately useful for improving practice. The work that forms the basis for *The 10 Lenses* stands as one exception. As a result, it removes much of the excuse many leaders offer for not having created better environments in which diversity might flourish. Thanks to Mark Williams, we now have a language for creating dialogue and perspective that allows us to engage on a more fundamental level than before. We also have a tool that each of us can use to foster our own development and that of others.

"One Song, Many Voices," the vision of the Eleventh Lens, is a metaphor for the possibility of work groups, organizations, and whole communities to realize the positive potential inherent in their diversity. We must remember, as any choir director will tell you, that achieving perfect harmony does not come easily. Sheet music and instruments, while essential, are insufficient. Also required are practice, commitment, informed and courageous direction, a fundamental belief in the possibility of success, and valuing achieving it. *The 10 Lenses* gives us the equivalent of the sheet music and the piano; whether and how we use it is up to us.

David A. Thomas
Naylor Fitzhugh Professor of Business Administration
Harvard Business School, August 2001

Appendix

Table 1

Evaluations Provided at the Mid-Winter Conference of the Society of Psychologists in Management (SPIM)

Please rate the presentation on a scale from 1 to 5, with 1 as low and 5 as high (superlative).

Presentation: *One Song, Many Voices*
Presenter: Mark Williams, CEO and President
of the Diversity Channel

	Mean	Median
The presenter was well prepared.	4.94	5
The concepts were well explained.	4.79	5
The presenter was responsive to questions.	4.91	5
This presentation met the learning objectives.	4.73	5

The Gallup Organization survey of a random sample of 1,001 used a stratified probability design and was designed to represent the adult population living in households with telephones within the continental United States. The interviewing was conducted during January and the first week of February 2001. The survey employed a calling design that required interviewers to make up to five dialing attempts to reach a respondent within each selected household. The margin of error for a percentage estimate derived from the total sample at the 95 percent level of confidence can be estimated to be ±3. For smaller samples, the error would be larger.

Other surveys are being planned, in particular, within groups that consist of larger minority populations and therefore lend themselves to greater analysis. Surveys will be conducted at each Lenses seminar. The data will be summarized and reported. At the present, some of the results from the national survey can be reported for reference purposes.

Here are observations from that data:

- Multiculturalism received the highest rating from the 1,001 national sample; Seclusion received the lowest mean rating. The ratings, by means, were as follows:

Table 2

Lenses Ranked According to the Mean (Average) Score for each Lens (n = 1,001)

Lens	Mean
Multiculturalism	21.09
Eleventh Lens	20.49
Colorblind	20.34
Transcendent	18.44
Meritocratist	17.99
Assimilationist	16.46
Integrationist	16.09
Victim/Caretaker	13.23
Culturalcentrist	10.97
Elitist	10.87
Seclusionist	9.36

- Some of the lenses were more common than others. When a respondent "strongly agreed" with every statement attributed to a lens, the total score on that lens was 25 (five statements times a weight of 5 = strongly agree). We can consider that a rating of 5 on every statement tells us how an individual perceives the world. In the survey of 1,001, the following frequencies of 25 were found:

Table 3

Rankings of the Lenses According to the Number Who Provided Each Lens the Highest Rating (5) and Estimates of the Percent of People in the Population Who Use Each Lens

Lens	Number	Percent
Colorblind	230	23
Multiculturalist	179	17.5
Eleventh Lens	130	13
Transcendent	42	4.1
Meritocratist	41	4.0
Assimilationist	18	2.0
Integrationist	10	1.0
Victim/Caretaker	4	.4
Elitist	3	.3
Culturalcentrist	2	.2
Seclusionist	1	.1

- Some respondents provided 25 on two or more lenses. The reader is cautioned to remember that these results are self-ratings, and "social desirability" may have been an influence in the self-ratings. At any rate, it seems that our U.S. culture is oriented toward Colorblind and Multiculturalism and moving away from Seclusionist and Culturalcentrist.

- Lenses can be grouped into families. Because some of the lenses seemed to be related, a factor analysis was computed. Factor analysis aids in the discovery of the underlying continuities in data, and in this case, the resulting groupings lend understanding to the Lenses. The three factors and the Lenses related to them are as follows:

  I. The Transforming Lenses
      A. Eleventh Lens
      B. Multiculturalist
      C. Colorblind
      D. Transcendent
      E. Integrationist
  II. The Distancing Lenses
      A. Elitist
      B. Culturalcentrist
      C. Seclusionist
      D. Victim/Caretaker
  III. The Individual Responsibility Lenses
      A. Meritocratist
      B. Assimilationist

- Men provided higher ratings to the Meritocratist and Seclusionist Lenses.

- Older persons tend to be more aligned with the Assimilationist and Transcendent Lenses.

- The Elitist and Seclusionist Lenses are negatively correlated with income. The higher the scores on the Elitist and Seclusionist Lenses, the lower was the reported income.

- Those who provide higher ratings to the Multiculturalist Lens are likely to have more education. The Assimilationist, Colorblind, Culturalcentrist, Elitist, Seclusionist, and Victim/Caretaker Lenses correlate negatively with education.

Bibliography

"The 1964 Civil Rights Act to the Present." 2000. Online Source: The Columbia Electronic Encyclopedia, 6th ed. www.encyclopedia.com/articles/06408The1964CivilRightsActtothePresent.html. New York: Columbia University Press, 2000.

Anderson, Peggy, ed. 1992. *Great Quotes by Great Women*. Illinois: Celebrating Excellence Publishing.

Appiah, K. Anthony, and Amy Guttman. 1996. *Color Conscious: The Political Morality of Race*. Princeton: Princeton University Press.

Arthur, John. 1996. *Color, Class, Identity: The New Politics of Race*. New York: Westview Press.

Asante, Molefi Kete. 1993. *Malcolm X as Cultural Hero and Other Afrocentric Essays*. Trenton: Africa World Press.

Ban Breathnach, Sarah. 1995. *Simple Abundance*. New York: Warner Books.

Beck, Sanderson. "Emerson's Transcendentalism." Online Source: www.san.beck.org.

Bender, David, and Bruno Leone. 1996. *Interracial America*. San Diego: Greenhaven Press.

Berliner, Michael S., and Gary Hull. 1998. *Diversity and Multiculturalism: The New Racism*. The Ayn Rand Institute Web Pages: www.multiculturalism.aynrand.org/diversity.html.

Blum, Edward, and Marc Levin. "Kudos to HISD Board for Moving Beyond Tribalism." *The Houston Chronicle*. (January 4, 2000).

Brimelow, Peter. 1996. *Alien Nation*. New York: HarperPerennial.

Brooks, Roy L. 1996. *Integration or Separation?: A Strategy for Racial Equality*. Cambridge: Harvard University Press.

Buchanan, Andrew. "Chicago: Diverse But Segregated." The Associated Press (March 16, 2001).

Buchanan, Patrick. "On the Issues." *USA Today* (Feb. 21, 2000).

Center for Healing Racism Page. Houston, Texas (March 7, 2001): www.centerhealingracism.org.

Chin, Andrew. "Elaine Chao: Poster Child for the 'Model Minority' Myth." *Model Minority: A Guide to Asian American Empowerment*. (January 11, 2001): www.modelminority.com/politics/chao.htm.

Chopra, Deepak. 1994. *The Seven Spiritual Laws of Success*. California: New World Library.

Clark, Kenneth B. 1985. *King, Malcolm, Baldwin: 3 Interviews*. Middletown: Wesleyan University Press.

Clegg, Roger. "Beyond Quotas." *Policy Review* no. 89 (May–June 1998). www.policyreview.org/may98/quotas.html.

Clinton, Bill. Interview. *Dialogue on Race*. WETA-TV, PBS. Washington, D.C. (July 8, 1998).

"The United States: A Nation of Diversity and Promise." Online Source: Electronic Journal of the U.S. Information Agency, vol. 4, no. 2 (June 1999).

Cohen, Richard. "Diversity: It's Not all Phony." *The Washington Post*, (August 3, 2000): A29.

Collier, Peter, and David Horowitz. 1991. *Second Thoughts About Race in America*. New York: Madison Books.

Cordasco, Francesco. 1990. *Dictionary of American Immigration History*. London: The Scarecrow Press.

Cose, Ellis. 1997. *Color-Blind: Seeing Beyond Race In A Race-Obsessed World*. New York: Harper Collins.

Cowan, Paul. 1979. *The Tribes of America*. New York: Doubleday.

Crenshaw, Kimberle. 1995. *Critical Race Theory*. New York: The New Press.

Dalton, Harlon L. 1995. *Racial Healing*. New York: Doubleday.

Delgado, Richard. 1996. *The Coming Race War?* New York: New York University Press.

Du Bois, W.E.B. 1995. *The Souls of Black Folk*. New York: Signet.

Dyson, E. "Reflections on the Parliament of the World's Religions (POWR). Aug. 25–Sep. 5, 1993." *Earthkeeping News*. vol. 3, no. 2 (November/December, 1993): www.nacce.org/1993/powr.html.

Foner, Eric. 1991. *The Reader's Companion to American History*. New York: Houghton Mifflin.

Fromm, Erich. 1955. *The Sane Society*. New York: Rinehart.

Gibran, Kahlil. 1951. *The Prophet*. New York: Alfred. A. Knopf.

Glazer, Nathan. 1997. *We Are All Multiculturalists Now*. Cambridge: Harvard University Press.

Henry III, William A. 1994. *In Defense of Elitism*. New York: Anchor.

Hing, Bill Ong. 1997. *To Be An American: Cultural Pluralism and the Rhetoric of Assimilation*. New York: New York University Press.

King, Colbert I. "Bush Caters to the Bigotry of Bob Jones." *Washington Post* (February 28, 2000): A15.

King, Jr., Martin Luther. "I Have a Dream" Speech. In The Martin Luther King, Jr. Companion. New York: St. Martin's Press, 1993.

Kivel, Paul. 1996. *Uprooting Racism: How White People Can Work for Racial Justice*. Philadelphia: New Society Publishers.

Lamy, Philip. 1996. *Millenium Rage*. New York: Plenum Press.

Landau, Elaine. 1994. *The White Power Movement*. Connecticut: The Millbrook Press.

Lapham, Susan J., Patricia Montgomery, and Debra Niner. 1993. "We the American...Foreign Born." Washington, D.C.: U.S. Department of Commerce, Bureau of the Census.

Lerner, Michael, and Cornel West. 1995. *Jews and Blacks: Let The Healing Begin*. New York: G.P. Putnam's Sons.

Lincoln, C. Eric. 1996. *Coming Through the Fire: Surviving Race And Place in America*. Durham, N.C.: Duke University Press.

Lollock, Lisa. "The Foreign-Born Population in the United States." *Current Population Reports*. Washington, D.C.: U.S. Department of Commerce, Bureau of the Census, 2000. www.census.gov/prod/www/abs/for-born.html.

Marable, Manning. 1995. *Beyond Black and White*. New York: Verso.

McCulloch, Richard. 1994. *The Racial Compact*. Florida:Towncourt Enterprises.

Melville, Herman. 1957. *Redburn*. New York: Doubleday.

Mitford, Nancy. 1986. *Noblesse Oblige*. New York: Atheneum.

Naylor, Larry L. 1997. *Cultural Diversity in the United States*. London: Bergin & Garvey.

Njeri, Itabari. 1997. *The Last Plantation: Color, Conflict, and Identity*. New York: Houghton Mifflin.

Page, Clarence. 1996. *Showing My Color: Impolite Essays on Race and Identity*. New York: HarperCollins.

Pessen, Edward. "Mobility, Social and Economic." Online Source: My History is America's History, National Endowment of the Humanities (2001): www.myhistory.org/history_files/articles/mobility.html.

Rand, Ayn. 1964. *The Virtue of Selfishness*. New York: New American Library.

Redfield, James. "Celestine Insights." Online Source. (April 2001): www.celestinevisions.com.

Reed, Ishmael. 1997. *Multi-America: Essays on Cultural Wars and Cultural Peace*. New York: Viking.

Ridgeway, James. 1995. *Blood in the Face*. New York: Thunder's Mouth Press.

Roosevelt, Theodore. "The Duties of American Citizenship." (January 26, 1883): www.tamu.edu/scom/pres/archive.html.

Schlesinger Jr., Arthur M. 1991. *The Disuniting of America*. New York: W.W. Norton & Company.

Shipman Pat. 1994. *The Evolution of Racism*. New York: Simon & Schuster.

Sleeper, Jim. 1997. *Liberal Racism*. New York: Viking.

————— "Toward an end of blackness: an argument for the surrender of race consciousness." *Harper's Magazine*, vol. 294, no. 1764 (May 1997).

————— Interview. "Letting Go of Race." *Atlantic Unbound*. August 21, 1997. www.theatlantic.com/unbound/bookauth/sleepint.htm.

Smith, Paul Chaat, and Robert Allen Warrior. *Like a Hurricane: The Indian Movement from Alcatraz to Wounded Knee*. New York: The New Press. 1996, p. 128.

Steele, Shelby. 1990. *The Content of Our Character: A New Vision Of Race In America*. New York: St. Martin's Press.

Steinberg, Stephen. 1981. *The Ethnic Myth: Race, Ethnicity, and Class in America*. Boston: Beacon Press.

Takaki, Ronald. "A Different Mirror: To See The United States as a Multiracial Society." *US Society and Values*. USIA Electronic Journal, vol. 2, no. 3 (August 1997).

Taylor, Charles. 1994. *Multiculturalism*. Princeton: Princeton University Press.

Terkel, Studs. 1992. *Race: How Blacks & Whites Think & Feel About the American Obsession*. New York: The New Press.

Thernstrom, Stephan, and Abigail Thernstrom. 1997. *America In Black And White: One Nation, Indivisible*. New York: Simon & Schuster.

Trillin, Calvin. "The Dynasticks." *Time Magazine*. (January 29, 2001): 20.

United for a Fair Economy. Online Source: "Wealth Inequality Charts." (2000): www.ufenet.org.

Warner, Carolyn. 1992. *The Last Word: A Treasury of Women's Quotations*. New Jersey: Prentice Hall.

Washington, Booker T. "The Atlanta Exposition Address." In *Up from Slavery: An Autobiography*. 1901. New York: Doubleday; Reprint, New York: Carol Publishing Group, 1989.

Weiss, Rick. "Life's Blueprint Is Less Than an Inch." *Washington Post*. (February 11, 2001): A1.

White, Jack E. "Are Blacks Biased Against Braininess?" *Time Magazine*. (August 7, 2000).

Wilber, Ken. 1996. *A Brief History of Everything*. Boston: Shambala.

Wilkinson, III, J. Harvie. 1997. *One Nation Indivisible: How Ethnic Separatism Threatens America*. New York: Addison-Wesley.

Williamson, Marianne. 1997. *The Healing of America*. New York: Simon & Schuster.

Winfrey, Oprah. "Inner Revolution." (January 2000): www.zukav.com/index.htm.

Wortham, Anne. 1981. *The Other Side of Racism: A Philosophical Study of Black Race Consciousness*. Columbus, Ohio: Ohio State University Press.

Wynter, Leon. "The Jordan Effect: What's race got to do with it?" Salon.com. January 29, 1999.

X, Malcolm. 1965. *The Autobiography of Malcolm X*. New York: Grove Press.

Young, Jr., Whitney M. 1969. *Beyond Racism: Building an Open Society*. New York: McGraw-Hill.

Zukav, Gary. 1989. *The Seat of the Soul*. New York: Simon & Schuster.

Quotes:
Eleanor Roosevelt: www.bemorecreative.com/one/13.htm.
Gandhi, Mahatma: www.quoteaholic.com/quotes/unity.html.

About the Author

Mark A. Williams

A well-known consultant and educator as well as composer/producer, radio and webcast talk show host, Mark A. Williams uses The Ten Lenses to help businesses and communities create inclusive environments in which people live and work together more productively. He is the chief executive officer, chairman, and founder of The Diversity Channel, a next-generation diversity education company that uses engaging new media along with in-person training and consultation to enable Fortune 1000 clients to respond sensitively and strategically to issues related to diversity.

Over the past twenty years, corporate audiences have been inspired and motivated by the insight, sensitivity, humor, and dynamic style of Mr. Williams in his educational workshops and interactive seminars. He has provided education, coaching, and consulting to senior executives at such organizations as Exxon Chemicals, Sara Lee, AT&T, the United States Department of Defense, the Federal Aviation Administration, EDS Corporation, the Agency for International Development, the Central Intelligence Agency, the Peace Corps, Harvard Medical School, UNISYS, and Marriott International.

Deeply committed to the worldwide mission of building harmony across our many differences, Mr. Williams established the One Song, Many Voices Foundation, an organization that promotes tolerance and cultural appreciation around the globe. Allies and supporters of the Foundation's work include the Friends of the United Nations, General Motors Acceptance Corporation, the American Association for Retired Persons, and The Gallup Organization. In 1998, Mr. Williams received the Global Tolerance award from the Friends of the United Nations for his anthem, "One Song, Many Voices," which has been named the official anthem for the United Nation's International Day for Tolerance celebrated annually on November 16.

Mr. Williams holds a bachelor's degree in political science and a master's degree in organizational psychology from American University in Washington, D.C. He is a faculty member of the NTL Institute, which serves Fortune 500 companies. He lives in Bethesda, Maryland, with his wife and two sons.

Index

How to Take the Lenses Survey

If you would like to take the full Gallup Lenses survey and begin a more in-depth educational process related to your lens preferences, please visit our web site at www.thediversitychannel.com.